CITIZENSHIP AND

Politics and Culture

A Theory, Culture & Society series

Politics and Culture analyses the complex relationships between political institutions, civil society and contemporary states. Individual books will draw on the major theoretical paradigms in sociology, politics and philosophy within which citizenship, rights and justice can be understood. The series will focus attention on the importance of culture and the implications of globalization and postmodernism for the study of politics and society. It will relate these advanced theoretical issues to conventional approaches of welfare, participation and democracy.

SERIES EDITOR: Bryan S. Turner, *Deakin University*

Also in this series

CITIZENSHIP AND SOCIAL RIGHTS

The Interdependence of Self and Society

Fred Twine

SAGE Publications

London • Thousand Oaks • New Delhi

SAGE Publications Ltd
6 Bonhill Street
London EC2A 4PU

SAGE Publications Inc
2455 Teller Road
Thousand Oaks, California 91320

SAGE Publications India Pvt Ltd
32, M-Block Market
Greater Kailash – I
New Delhi 110 048

British Library Cataloguing in Publication data

A catalogue record for this book is available from the
British Library.

ISBN 0 8039 8613 0

ISBN 0 8039 8614 9 (pbk)

Library of Congress catalog card number 94–067329

Typeset by Photoprint, Torquay, S. Devon
Printed in Great Britain by Biddles Ltd, Guildford, Surrey

CONTENTS

Acknowledgements   viii

Introduction   1

PART ONE   SOCIAL INTERDEPENDENCE: A BASIS FOR
SOCIAL RIGHTS   7

1   Self and Society: the Development of the 'Social
    Self'   9
2   Labour Markets and Interdependence: the Kinds of
    People We Are Able to Be   15
3   Lifecourse Interdependence: the Social Connections
    and Networks of Life   28

PART TWO   ENVIRONMENTAL INTERDEPENDENCE   47

4   The Sustainability of the Means to Life   51
5   GNP and the Mis-measure of Progress   65
6   Externalities: Environmental and Social Costs   69

PART THREE   A POLITICS OF REDISTRIBUTION, SUFFICIENCY
AND PARTICIPATION   76

7   Redistribution and Sufficiency   77
8   Political Participation: Beyond and Below the Nation
    State   85

PART FOUR   EXPLORING SOCIAL POLICY AND SOCIAL
RIGHTS   93

9   Social Exclusion and Social Rights   95
10   The Social Rights of Citizenship   102
11   Sources of Income and Forms of Taxation   113
12   Welfare State Regimes   145

PART FIVE   TOWARDS EUROPEAN SOCIAL RIGHTS   151

13 Social Citizenship in Europe: the European Social
    Charter   153
14 A Basic Income: an Embodiment of Social Rights? 163

PART SIX   CITIZENSHIP: UNDERSTANDING AND PERCEPTION 170

15 The Sociological Imagination   171
16 Having and Being   176

References   181

Index   188

With love to my wife Christine,
my daughter Joanna and my son Richard.

ACKNOWLEDGEMENTS

I must first acknowledge some debts from my more distant past. To my parents for their support to an upwardly mobile son who then moved away. To my lunchtime discussions with Alec Pendle when we were both draughtsmen with British Railways, which first set me on this path. To the McColgan family and the Ceeney family who tolerated my 'giving forth' on numerous occasions. To Mike Jackson my friend and discussant over the two years we studied at the Co-operative College. To Adrian Sinfield for his moral and intellectual inspiration over many years.

Thanks for rekindling my current interest in citizenship are due to members of the Church of Scotland Working Party on the Distribution of Wealth, Income and Benefits. And for its continued development I thank those who gave a friendly reception to my first substantive paper on citizenship presented to the 2nd International Conference on the Future of Adult Life in Holland. And especially to Bryan Turner who encouraged me to develop my ideas into a book.

In the course of writing I was particularly fortunate to have Ruth Lister as the reader for Sage. I thank her for her detailed and perceptive comments that did much to clarify my thought and improve my argument, especially on gender issues.

To my wife Christine, to whose companionship and loving support through the difficult times in which the book was written I owe more than she probably realises.

In expressing my 'self' through writing this book I hope they will all recognise something of their 'self' in what I have written. I hope they enjoy it.

The views expressed in the book are those of the author, who accepts responsibility for the interpretation of data and for the views expressed.

Fred Twine
University of Aberdeen

INTRODUCTION

This volume is aimed at all those whose interest has been aroused by current debates over citizenship. It is hoped its interdisciplinary perspective will be attractive to both public and undergraduate audiences, particularly those interested in social policy, sociology and politics. Its concern is to develop a distinctive argument for social rights built upon notions of interdependence. It lays out a quite different perspective for understanding the relationships between individuals and society from the largely individualistic and sometimes asocial views of the New Right. Much of the discourse challenges the presumptions of New Right[1] thinking and its dominant market view of the world. Though this is a common thread throughout the text, priority is given to developing a coherent alternative social perspective of human beings and their social interdependence.

A discussion of the interdependence of 'self' and society is found in Chapter 1, providing an alternative perspective to the individualism of the New Right. It is argued that the latter is a limited notion of freedom that focuses only on the capacity of individuals to choose without also considering the social conditions under which that capacity may be exercised. We are social individuals who require a society in which to develop our essential human, that is, social, capacities.

The notion of 'social interdependence' implies, first, that human beings can only be properly understood by appreciating that, although they have the freedom *potentially* to make themselves, they do not do so in circumstances of their own choosing, but in conditions inherited from the past. Human beings are distinctively made by society, even as they are engaged in the making and remaking of their society. Human beings are essentially social creatures. What they are and what they might be depends both on themselves and upon the societies in which they grow up and make their choices. Choices, however, are always made within some framework of constraint. Yet, human beings acting collectively, especially through democratic institutions, can, in principle, change and mould the frameworks of constraints within which they make their choices. For, example, in the twentieth century the inventions of the welfare state have significantly changed the framework of constraints and thus affected the choices that citizens have been able to make. By redistributing resources, choices are also redistributed and new possibilities opened up.

Second, 'social interdependence' also recognises that members of complex industrial societies through the complex divisions of labour, both in the workplace and in the home, are involved in complex networks of interdependence. The behaviour and choices of any one individual have repercussions for many other individuals. The choices that people make as consumers affect the choices of other consumers and a range of producers. We can no longer, if we ever could, consider individuals as being involved in discrete and isolated market choices. All market exchanges involve externalities that are not registered in the market prices of the exchanges between willing buyers and sellers. Many market exchanges take place because they do *not* involve all the costs of the transaction. For some these externalities bring social benefits whilst for others they bring social costs. The ignoring of the social costs of social change has given an exaggerated view of social progress.

Third, 'social interdependence' exists over the lifecourse between members of families and between generations. At different points in the lifecourse of individuals and families some members will be dependent upon others whilst others take care of them, only to find that they in turn will be dependent. We are all at some time in our lifecourse children and most become old folk. Due to their poor or privileged position in the labour market some members of society need help or give help to others. This is especially true of the care of children and old folk. It is also true of gender relationships where many women, because they are the bearers of children, are simultaneously dependent on their husbands, whilst their children are dependent upon them. Their husbands are at the same time dependent on their wives for provisioning for their return to the labour market. Furthermore, because women reproduce their society in its species form the wider society is dependent on them and their families for the reproduction and continuity of society. Therefore, society has an interest in seeing that each new generation is not handicapped by the social circumstances into which they are born.

Fourth, it is characteristic of industrial societies that nearly all of us are dependent on selling our, or our spouses', labour power as a means to life. Where that sale is poorly rewarded, or sale is not possible through widespread unemployment, or due to unpaid work in the home, society has an obligation to provide a level of living sufficiently high for the personal development of its societal members. This obligation arises from our social interdependence. For members of society to experience social exclusion due to inadequate material resources such that their personal development is stunted must be considered a major threat to their sense of 'self'. The commodification of labour power means there is a basic tendency in market-dominated societies for human beings to be treated as 'things'. Yet, because we make society even as we are made by society we continually resist being treated as 'things'. That, partly, is the reason for the development of social rights to a minimum wage or unemployment compensation. We know little of the circumstances under which many of the products we buy are produced by our fellow citizens. The low price we enjoy as consumers may be due to the low pay and dangerous working conditions of those who produce the goods. There is a 'social interdependence' between us. Our benefit is their cost. Because the social relationship between the consumer and producer is limited to a simple cash nexus it tends to extinguish from the exchange all moral obligations between those involved. Human lives are essentially moral or they are nothing. Therefore, in these contexts of 'social interdependence', arguments for social rights to well-being take on a new salience. These issues are explored in Part One.

The second part of the book is concerned with another kind of interdependence, that between human beings and their physical environment. Over the past two or three hundred years, as industrialisation gathered pace, human beings tended to treat their natural environment as an endless resource that they could exploit without limit. It was assumed that the consumption of raw materials and the disposal of waste products could go on indefinitely. The question of the sustainability of this project has been increasingly questioned during the past twenty years. The recent recognition that there might be limits to growth, or at least the need to rein back in environmental exploitation, has led some people to question the assumption that human wants are limitless. The problematic nature of these underlying assumptions of economic theory, along with economists' disregard for the externalities of economic activity, are leading to a growing questioning of many of the assumptions of economic models of human welfare. Increasingly, gross national product (GNP) as a measure of national well-being is questioned as discussion turns to notions of 'sustainable development' rather than 'economic growth'. Economic growth has been relied on by all political parties as a means of improving everyone's level of living over time. Increasingly during the post-war period, economic growth has taken the pressure off any politics of redistribution. It promised that everyone could be better off without anyone being worse off. The promise was held out to developing nations that they too could enjoy tomorrow what the developed nations enjoyed today. That project is now in question. As economic growth is questioned as the route to improved well-being, issues of distribution and redistribution become more central to political debate and social rights to resources for human development become the focus of priority.

Part Two seeks to highlight a paradox. In Part One it is argued that we need to develop social rights to provide the material base for the development of the 'social self', whereas in Part Two it is argued that there are growing environmental and therefore material limits to such projects. The resolution of this paradox is sought in Part Three through the redistribution of current and future available resources within and between nations. This requires a more informed and participatory form of democratic politics and a change in value orientations, particularly in developed nations, away from 'having' towards 'being'. As we begin to recognise the limits to material growth as the driving force of industrial societies, and seek to establish social rights to well-being, people are slowly turning, or we might say returning, to questions of social participation. As the limits of economic theory as a basis for decisions becomes more problematic in the face of environmental externalities, and as externalities come to be seen as more pervasive in industrial societies than economists recognise, so political rights of democratic participation become more central. However, because many of these problems are both global *and* local in nature we must seek political participation beyond and below the nation state. Supra-national agreements are necessary so as to co-ordinate action between nations, yet at the same time, because only smaller communities have direct knowledge *and* direct interest in environmental impacts on their well-being, more decision-making powers must be devolved. Political participation is also central to the development of the 'self'. The opportunity to express one's 'self' in debate leads to the further development of the 'self'. In expressing your own views you test them against the views of others, which express their sense of 'self'. There is a confrontation of ideas, values and projects. Each, despite him or herself, learns to appreciate some aspect of the other's ideas, values and projects; to appreciate some aspects of his or her opponent's 'self'. Each is thus dependent on the other for the development of his or her 'self'. These matters are the concern of Part Three.

Having spent much time laying out the perspectives that inform the arguments for social rights, Part Four focuses on the nature of welfare state regimes that might provide a basis for social rights to well-being. Policies that involve de-commodifying social relationships are considered as the basis for social rights. This is done through discussion of some of the traditional limitations of means-testing, as well as work-based benefits. This is followed by an examination of Esping-Anderson's use of the concept of de-commodification as a way of measuring social rights. However, because social rights to well-being have to be financed to some considerable degree through the sharing mechanism of taxation, detailed consideration is also given to whether we may identify any citizenship principles of taxation for funding social rights. Peters' typology of tax regimes is then outlined. When this typology is compared with Esping-Anderson's typology of welfare state regimes we find a remarkable correlation between the grouping of nations. This suggests that particular tax regimes accompany particular welfare state regimes. Visible high personal tax regimes go along with greater de-commodification. This may provide some guidance as to the future tax and welfare direction that we should go in if we wish to develop social rights to well-being.

In Part Five, paths to social rights are considered in the context of the European Community and the Social Charter. Is it possible to identify the possibilities for a European route to the development of social rights? Or do the complex differences in welfare state traditions of member nations present major barriers to such a development? Within this section particular attention is given to the limitations of basing social rights on paid work to the neglect of the part-time and unpaid work undertaken by women. Because women lose out in the labour market they also lose out in the benefit system. A social right should be right of citizenship, not of labour market participation. De-commodification must be accompanied by defamilalisation. These twin issues are subsequently addressed through considering whether the development of a Basic Income would be an appropriate strategy for resolving these and many of the other issues raised throughout the book.

In Part Six, our focus turns to consideration of the changes in understanding and perception that are required if all human beings are to maintain a sustainable world in which their human development remains possible. Here it is boldly suggested that we should all develop a 'sociological imagination' through which we might be more sensitive to the social nature of human existence. Whilst arguing for the benefits of historical and anthropological sensitivities, the sociological imagination is, perhaps, most important to the development of a critical sensitivity. A sensitivity to the fact that our human worlds and our 'self' are socially created and that therefore, in principle, they can be re-created. That re-creation, however, due to environmental limits to material well-being, needs to be more in terms of values of 'being' than 'having'.

Arising from our social interdependence, democratic citizenship should be directed to the social development of all. First, through provision of social rights and, second, through participation in the re-creation of society. This might provide a secular 'object of devotion', and one with which people from many religions and none might come to agree.

Note

1 Some readers may be less familiar with views of the New Right and the debates surrounding their ideas. They may like to sample among the following references. Works by the New Right: Friedman, 1962; Nozick, 1974; Friedman and Friedman, 1980; Gilder, 1982; Berger and Berger, 1983; Murray, 1984; Mead, 1986; Berger, 1987; Butler and Kondratis, 1987; Novak, 1987. Discussion of, or debates with, the New Right: Bell, 1976; Mishra, 1984; Levitas, 1986; Block, 1987; Jordan, 1987; Loney, 1987; Gamble, 1988; Flynn, 1989; Jordan, 1989; Esping-Anderson, 1990; Handler and Hasenfield, 1990; Andrews, 1991; Coote, 1992; Pierson, 1991; Vogel and Moran, 1991; Plant, 1992; Roche, 1992.

PART ONE
SOCIAL INTERDEPENDENCE: A BASIS FOR SOCIAL RIGHTS

The opening three chapters introduce the reader to a range of perspectives and arguments that inform later discussion of citizenship and social rights. These chapters are intended to provide an understanding of the essential social nature of human life. They view human beings as 'socially interdependent' and connected over the lifecourse through complex social networks. Some of these social networks are relatively open to our understanding and direct experience whilst others are less visible and poorly perceived. The more dominant intellectual traditions of industrialised nations are imbued with forms of 'individualism' which, in trying to understand human life, tend to abstract people from their social contexts. They lack what C. Wright Mills (1970) called a 'sociological imagination'. The sociological imagination seeks to understand the biographies of individuals by placing them within the history of the epochs in which they live. What kinds of biographies could people live in different epochs, what kinds of people were they able to be? In living out their biographies, people engage with their society and its institutions. They make choices within the circumstances they encounter, and choices that sometimes change those circumstances. They, and their choices, are not wholly determined by circumstances nor are they, and their choices, free from constraints. People make themselves, but not in circumstances of their own choosing. It is this dynamic of 'self' and 'society', this notion of the 'social self', that is so often lacking in contemporary thought. The 'social self' is societally dependent. Humans are essentially social beings who require social relationships for their development. However, many social relationships are crucially structured by the distribution of material resources in society. Access to material resources affects the choices people are able to make and the kinds of people they are able to be. The choices that people make in turn affect the choices that other people can make. In many ways choices are interdependent. We are not always aware how the choices we make affect the choices others are able to make. It is argued that these networks of 'social interdependence' provide the essential moral basis for social rights. That is the task of the first part of the book.

1

SELF AND SOCIETY: THE DEVELOPMENT OF THE 'SOCIAL SELF'

Citizenship is fundamentally concerned with social relationships between people, and relationships between people and the institutional arrangements of complex industrial societies. Thus, exploring citizenship requires an examination of both people and the institutions they have created. In Mills' (1970) terms, we are concerned with what kinds of persons we are able to be and the kinds of persons we might be. What kinds of opportunities and constraints confront people in terms of current institutional arrangements? Understanding the conception of citizenship developed in this volume requires an elaboration of a particular conception of the 'self' and the manner in which institutional arrangements may provide opportunities for, or place constraints upon, self-development. How may we best understand the nature of a person, a human being? A useful starting point is an examination of what is popularly referred to as 'human nature'. Common everyday phrases such as, 'you can't change human nature' imply that human nature is a fixed, unchanging characteristic of human beings. This is to suggest that human nature is a biological rather than a social phenomenon. Though it is true that human beings are biological and have genetic attributes, they are also essentially social creatures who have and need a social milieu in which to develop their recognisable human qualities. As humans are essentially social beings, their nature must be understood in social terms, and therefore what is 'human nature' will vary in time and place as evidenced in the actions and beliefs of human beings. Furthermore, the nature of human beings is developmental, that is, it changes and develops over time in response to economic, political and social contexts. Not only that, the actions and beliefs of human beings affect the development of these contexts which in turn affect human beings. The process is dialectical. That is, human beings make themselves and their social institutions, but not in conditions of their own choosing. There is always a historical inheritance into which we are born and grow up. For example, different age cohorts in Britain have grown up with different institutional frameworks of economic prosperity and welfare state provisions. To be sick or unemployed in the 1920s was very different from being sick or unemployed in the 1960s. The choices for action were different. The different opportunity structures that humans create affect the kinds of people they are able to be. Therefore, we should more correctly talk not of 'human nature' but of the 'social nature of human beings'. The kinds of people we could be or can be are affected by such institutional arrangements and provisions or the lack of them. At the time Marshall (1950) was writing his seminal essay on citizenship, the Keynes–Beveridge welfare state had only recently been established. It was identified by Marshall as a key element in his notion of citizenship because of the new opportunities resulting from its provision of social rights to minimum levels of well-being for the sick, unemployed and retired.

British Conservatism in the 1980s drew on certain American ideologies of the asocial individual in the market, which in Margaret Thatcher's famous phrase, declared 'there is no such thing as society, only individuals and their families'. This 'individualism abstracted from social context' has characterised much New Right thinking. The argument here, from the intellectual traditions of sociology, is that human beings are essentially social individuals for whom society is the key context for their development as persons. However, like New Right thinkers, there is a central concern with freedom and choice in this conceptualisation of citizenship. Choice is always constrained by circumstances, but circumstances are not fixed but are open, in principle, to change through human agency. Thus, there is always the relatively open question: in what circumstances do human beings exercise their choices? As circumstances affect choices so they also affect the self-development of people. In discussing citizenship and social rights we are fundamentally concerned with the social conditions for the development of the 'social self'. The 'social self' cannot develop outside society, and the human self in developing within society also changes that society. This is the 'interdependence of self and society'.

The interdependence of self and society

As Parry observes, 'It is not possible to abstract from ourselves all our natural and social bonds, allegiances and commitments and still understand ourselves. . . . [We are concerned with] 'a concept of the self as linked by a "narrative" which connects up the events of one's life and places them within a specific historical context' (1991: 180–1). Recognition that the development of the 'social self' is influenced by the communities within which it develops tended to be absent from the Thatcher perspective of Britain in the 1980s. Yet, as MacIntyre says, 'an essential element in the story of one's life is the community into which one is born, or is brought up. . . . these give a person's life "its own moral particularity" . . . the story of my life is always embedded in the story of those communities from which I derive my identity' (1981: 205, quoted in Parry, 1991: 182). What we are or are able to become depends to an important extent on the wider community in which we live. 'Any sharp distinction between public and private life must be rejected to the extent that the wider community, and its idea of a particular common good, also shapes individual character' (Parry, 1991: 182). Each is dependent on the other for the development of his or her 'self'. In an important sense the 'social self' is constructed from a network of social relationships, past and present. It is neither fully autonomous nor fully determined. The 'social self' chooses but, at any one time, choices are constrained. The developmental nature of the 'social self' is found in this dynamic of 'choice and constraint'. This dynamic is crucially mediated by the social distribution of available material resources. For human beings, freedom as 'self-development' comes from social membership and participation. Without inclusion in a society the essentially 'social self' cannot develop. Social rights are thus concerned with establishing the material and cultural conditions for social inclusion and participation such that the 'social self' may develop. Forms of social exclusion therefore pose major threats to the development of the 'social self' (Townsend, 1979; Warr, 1985; Fryer and Ulah, 1987). Indeed, forms of social exclusion are likely to damage the 'social self', to spoil self-identity, as is often intended through measures to punish people: imprisonment, exile, transportation, sending to Coventry, or stigmatisation through means-tested service provision. Consequently, social inclusion and participation in terms of access to the material conditions for well-being in society becomes an important social pre-condition for freedom (Townsend, 1979).

If people are excluded from such access, the development of their 'social self' will be impaired. As Gould has argued, 'individual freedom is to be understood not only as a capacity for free choice but as an activity of self-development . . . access to the material conditions of well-being is a necessary condition for self-development' (1988: 25). By self-development we refer to the 'freedom to develop oneself through one's own actions, or as the process of realizing one's own projects through activity in the course of which one forms one's character and develops capacities . . . a process of the development of the person over time' (Gould, 1988: 40). Development of the 'self' is a life-long process, it does not come to a sudden end at, say, the age of 21. Freedom to develop the 'social self' must therefore be understood in terms of development over a person's lifecourse. As Gould argues,

> this notion of freedom, . . . has a biographical or historical dimension in that it concerns the individual's self-transformation through the course of his or her life, and also has a social dimension in that social relations and common purposes provide a fundamental context for such self-development . . . in order to effect such choices concretely a wide range of actual options need to be available to people. . . . It is through making . . . choices in their actions in particular situations over the course of time that people come to be who they are and develop their qualities and character. (1988: 41, 46)

Opportunities or rights to self-development?

It is a limited notion of freedom that focuses only on the capacity to choose without also considering the conditions under which that capacity may be exercised. Thus, if opportunities to exercise choice are unequal, then, for some people, so will be freedom to develop qualities and character. Their 'social self', the kinds of people they are able to be, will be limited. Where this notion of freedom departs fundamentally from that of the New Right is in the view that 'unequal conditions result in unequal power of choice and in a democracy this threatens political rights and choice. [There is a] continual tension between equal capacity to choose and unequal conditions to exercise that capacity, and make it a reality' (Gould, 1988: 63). Therefore to equalise freedom to choose requires action to equalise the material and social conditions for the exercise of choice over the lifecourse.

Redistributing resources also redistributes freedom and choice. This is necessary and expected in a political democracy, otherwise gross inequalities in the development of the 'social self' will threaten social order. This requires that social policy be understood and developed from a lifecourse perspective (see Chapter 3). Social rights over the lifecourse are thus a key element of citizenship because they provide the material and social conditions for choice and help to equalise the self-development of all citizens.

The manner in which the development of the 'social self' arises from social interdependence powerfully underpins Gould's work, and is discussed in more detail below. She observes we are not simply concerned with

> internal self-transformation in a subjective sense but also objective changes in a world in which the agents act to effect their purposes. . . . Such individuals are not isolated, but rather are social individuals. That is, they express who they are, and become who they want to be, in large part through their relations with others. Moreover, many of their actions are such that they are essentially social; that is, they are *joint actions that could not be carried out by individuals alone.* (1988: 48–9, my italics)

Social relations are not only a condition for self-development but are themselves developed through the collective choices of people. Through participation in debate and in collective decision-making the 'self' is both educated and developed. Thus, the nature and content of political rights affect collective projects for individual self-development. In late twentieth-century democracies, political rights mediate the development of civil and social rights. Thus, considerations of citizenship must work with a complex concept of freedom as self-development, as development of the 'social self'; this conception . . . involves not only freedom of choice but access to material and social conditions, freedom from domination and the conception of the realization of projects, the cultivation of capacities, and the formation of character over time' (Gould, 1988: 58). Thus, Marshall's (1950) three elements of citizenship – namely, civil, political and social rights – can best be seen as directed to the development of the 'social self'; or, in Mill's (1970) terms, to the 'kinds of people we might be'.

In relation, however, to circumstances where access to material conditions is constrained by problems of sustainable economic development (Brundtland Report, 1987; Daly, 1990), we shall also need to consider Fromm's (1979) distinction between 'having' and 'being' as modes of personal development. These questions are considered later. Indeed, our focus upon the development of the 'social self' enables us to emphasise the social relationships of resource distribution rather than the maximisation of resource consumption. What are the minimum or optimal needs for self-development (Doyal and Gough, 1991)? Questions of resource *distribution*, which are social or 'public issues' may, in the future, become more important in industrialised societies than *absolute* levels of consumption. Recent research indicates that reducing income inequalities in industrialised countries has more impact on reducing health inequalities than general increases in income that leave inequalities untouched (Blaxter, 1990; Wilkinson, 1986b; Quick and Wilkinson, 1991). It is the *relative* income positions that are important. They embody positive and negative social identities and degrees of difference in social status, and thus affect social relationships and the sense of 'social self'. Income inequalities affect not only choices and possibilities for self-development but also self-identity. As observed earlier, insofar as income inequalities in a society lead to social exclusion the development of the 'social self' is impaired. Societal messages of low worth and stigmatisation damage self-identity and affect health behaviour, in addition to the higher health risks encountered by those on lower incomes. Intriguingly, the research emphasises that the correlation between income inequalities and health inequalities extends over the lower 60–70 per cent of the income range. These studies add an important new income dimension to the work showing 'class gradients' in health experience (Townsend and Davidson, 1988; Whitehead, 1988). The primary distribution of income derives from the division of labour and differences in participation and reward in the labour market. The resulting social class and gender differences in income crucially affect life-chances for the development of the 'self'.

2

LABOUR MARKETS AND INTERDEPENDENCE: THE KINDS OF PEOPLE WE ARE ABLE TO BE

This chapter suggests that the social relationships that surround the need to sell your labour power as a means to life are central to arguments for social rights. It is argued not only that labour markets commodify social relationships and thereby limit them, but also that income and employment insecurity threaten the kinds of people we are able to be. The inequalities and insecurities of both class and gender relationships in the labour market have to be addressed through social rights so as to provide a secure resource base for the social relationships necessary for human development.

Commodification: the selling of labour power as the means to life

Relations of production, therefore, present major problems for the development of social rights. To understand the crucial nature of this point we must refer back to the 'great transformation' (Polanyi, 1957) that brought about capitalist industrial society. It is in a concern to understand the social consequences of these societal changes that we find the origins of sociology as an academic discipline. The importance of sociological understanding is argued in Chapter 15. Giddens (1982a) roots sociology in the diverse reactions to the 'two great revolutions' that have transformed human society in the past 250 years: the 'Industrial Revolution' and the 'French Revolution'. Our immediate concern here is with the consequences of the Industrial Revolution, though we shall return to the French Revolution later.

For most of their history, human beings have lived in small communities, thinly scattered throughout the world, existing by hunting animals and gathering plants. People made their own clothes, often constructed their own dwellings and made their own furniture. The majority of the population catered directly for most of their own needs, and where they did not they drew upon the services of others in their local community. With the Industrial Revolution of late eighteenth-century Britain, whole communities were subject to dramatic social upheaval. Enclosure of Common land was intensified, people lost their traditional rights to graze animals on commons and in woodlands, and the right to collect firewood. Many lost their homes and the small plots of land on which they grew food. As their means of subsistence, their means of life, were lost they became landless labourers. As landless labourers they needed to obtain paid employment, and this they were more likely to find in the emerging and growing urban industrial towns. Furthermore, as the nineteenth century opened, domestic forms of production such as handloom-weaving were undermined as the newly developed machines were installed in new factories close to sources of water power. This emerging factory production together with the migration of landless labourers seeking paid employment fuelled the growth of urbanisation. Factory production increasingly replaced domestic household production and separated home and work as spheres of distinct gender activity.

In his important book *The Great Transformation*, Polanyi highlights the crucial development affecting human relationships that was brought about by the development of a market economy as part of the Industrial Revolution. What is distinctive, he says, 'is the notion of the self-regulating market' (1957: Chapter 6). Emphasis on its 'self-regulating' character is important. 'A market economy is an economic system controlled, regulated and directed by markets alone; order in the production and distribution of goods is entrusted to this self-regulating mechanism. . . . An economy of this kind derives from the expectation that human beings behave in such a way as to achieve maximum monetary gain' (Polanyi, 1957: 68). It is the 'transformation of the natural and human substance of society into commodities' (1957: 42), to be bought and sold, that is the 'great transformation'. For competitive markets to operate all factors of production, not only machines and raw materials, but also human labour, have to be given a price. Therefore, markets have to treat the labour power of human beings as something to be bought and sold. However, the labour power of human beings cannot be detached from the human beings who carry that labour power. Thus, human beings come to be treated as commodities. It is this central social relationship of 'commodification' which Esping-Anderson (1990) argues has to be addressed in any discussion of social rights. We come to this later.

Though it will be examined later in the context of the environment, concern here is not with the market mechanism as such, but with the human consequences of treating labour power as a commodity. Human beings are significantly different from most other market commodities, in that labour power, that is, human beings, are not specifically produced for sale – at least not usually; we would call that slavery. As Polanyi states, however, 'It is with the help of the commodity concept that the mechanism of the market is geared to the various elements of industrial life. A commodity is an object produced for sale in the market. Everything is produced for sale, as then and then only will it be subject to the supply and demand mechanism interacting with price' (1957: 72). He observes that 'to allow the market mechanism to be the *sole* director of the fate of human beings and their environment – would result in the demolition of society, for the alleged commodity "labour power" cannot be shoved about, used indiscriminately, or even left unused, without affecting the human individual who happens to be the bearer of this peculiar commodity: labour power' (1957: 73; my italics). Yet labour market processes do tend to treat human beings as though they are commodities. The tendency is for their labour power to be bought as cheaply as possible and for it to be discarded when it is more economically efficient to replace it by new technology or cheaper workers. As a factor of production, labour power, and its human carrier, is subject to similar market forces to other factors of production.

What is distinctive about complex industrial societies is the way in which our material life-chances and social relationships are crucially affected by our *need* to sell our labour power as a means to life. We are constrained to behave *as though* we are commodities, and to treat others in the same way. This places considerable power in the hands of the buyers of labour power. Our day-to-day social relationships are overshadowed by these commodity relationships which constrain our choices. The unequal distribution of resources through labour markets further constrains choices and social relationships. This is only a tendency, however, for human beings, unlike machines, can think and act, and they resist being treated as commodities. This resistance is only partially successful. There is a constant tension in labour markets between treating employees as commodities and as human beings. This tension manifests itself through civil rights in conflicts over the 'effort bargain' and a 'fair day's pay for a fair day's work', and through political rights in democratic demands for social rights.

Selling your 'self'

Most people when they take on a job have only a vague sense of what they will have to do for the money they get. It is only once the job is underway that the nitty-gritty of the 'effort bargain' begins to emerge and develop as the worker is told what to do. What, in the *widest sense*, do you actually have to do for the money you get? As human beings are carriers of the labour power that is bought and sold they may be required to sell more of themselves than they really want to. The need to obtain or hold on to a job, especially where family responsibilities are involved, may place the seller under considerable pressure. We give little consideration to such questions yet they crucially affect 'the kinds of people we are able to be' (Mills, 1970) and our relationships with one another. The reader is asked to consider: what is it about you as a person that is not for sale? In order to get a job or keep a job do you have to sell more than your labour power? What is it about yourself that you had to sell or were pressured to sell? Was it turning a 'blind eye' to the manufacture or sale of shoddy or dangerous goods? Was it lying to customers? Was it asking other workers to risk their health and safety? Was is it blind obedience to the orders of those in authority even though you knew the sad consequences for others? Most of us come under pressures of this kind, from time to time, in the course of our work. When an employer buys our labour power they may wish to buy a lot more, thus dependence upon selling our labour as means to life may mean selling part of our life, that is, part of our 'self'. We may sell our self-identity as a carrier of a belief in fairness or justice. We may sell the very possibilities for our own human development because all we can get is a boring routine task that makes no call on our intelligence and does not engage our human abilities. In order to obtain the means to life many people sell that very life. The means to life becomes an end in itself and the person leads a stunted existence. In such circumstances fundamental dilemmas of *moral* choice arise. How much of yourself, as a human being with values and beliefs, do you sell when you sell your labour power? In response, it may be asserted that compromises are an inevitable part of the everyday choices in the real world of work, but we all know when we have crossed our own personal line; it does not feel right, we feel uneasy in ourselves. We feel 'we should not have to do that'; we feel, however indirectly, coerced. Coerced choices are not freely made; we feel caught between a 'rock and a hard place'. We become other than the person we really wish to be. The self is undermined.

The same may be true of the choices of the employer as they try to stay afloat in competitive markets. Because labour power is one of the costs of production, competitive market processes pressure employers to cut costs. However, cutting the costs of labour power means adversely affecting the human beings that are the carriers of that labour power. This involves social relationships between real live human beings, not materials and machinery. Again, social rights may protect labour power from being treated as 'a thing'. However, protecting workers from being treated as 'things' within work may lead, through loss of competitive position for the employer, to the worker being treated as a 'thing' in another fashion: being cast aside through unemployment. The commodification of social relationships through the need to buy and sell labour power threatens our essential human qualities and social relationships. Therefore, de-commodifying relationships and providing social rights to the means of life also helps to protect the integrity of the 'self' and the honesty of our social relationships with each other.

When people are unemployed (or sick or retired), however, this tension between treating them as commodities or as human beings takes its starkest form, for without the ability to sell their labour power their means of life itself is threatened. Welfare states are concerned to provide some means of life that is not dependent upon a person selling his or her labour power as a commodity in the labour market. However, because human beings are more than biological entities, social rights must provide sufficiently for human social development. There are major questions concerning the level of the means of life that is to be provided as a social right (Gould, 1988; Doyal and Gough, 1991). For the moment we can state the primary goal of social rights should be to ensure that the means of life provided is sufficient to maintain social inclusion and self-development in the society of which the person is a member (Townsend, 1979). Countering social exclusion is central to the concept of social rights. As Marshall observed, the social element of citizenship means 'the whole range, from the right to a modicum of economic welfare and security to the right to share to the full in the social heritage and to live the life of a civilised being according to the standards prevailing in society' (1950: 11). Thus, in our examination of social rights we must establish what level of welfare and security is to be provided through social rights such that a person is able to participate in the heritage and civilisation of his or her society, independently of the vagaries of the labour market. Therefore, social rights are to do with the de-commodification of social relationships and the maintenance of social integration (Esping-Anderson, 1990: Chapter 2). As will be argued later, this requires policies of redistribution and reduction of the inequalities that continually arise from the treatment of labour power and its human carriers as a commodity within the labour market.

Social rights and de-commodification

In complex industrial societies, 'There is a constant tension between the commodification and the de-commodification of social relationships' (Offe, 1982, in Giddens, 1982a: 86) – a tension between the labour market treatment and reward of people, and the social rights they establish through exercising their political rights. Through the exercise of political rights they may establish social rights that challenge the predominance in people's lives of labour market relationships. Sociologists have been concerned that the dominance of such economic relationships in people's lives leads to their being treated as less than human. If a commodity is any product or service that can be bought or sold, then a commodified relationship is one that a price can be put on, that is, it is marketable. De-commodification means removing social relationships from the marketplace, organising them by criteria other than the economic.

The commodification of labour power tends to reduce social relationships and social obligations to the cash exchange of the labour contract to the exclusion of the rich networks of social obligations and social relationships within which people are embedded as human beings. When, for whatever reason, a person is unable to sell his or her labour power the lack or limitations of social rights are likely to shrivel the human qualities of life towards those of mere physical and biological survival. Thus the varied developments of social security policies that provide income as of right when a person is outside the labour market, when unemployed, sick, retired, or looking after children or elderly relatives, are examples of varying degrees of de-commodification.

Individuals' human needs are, to some degree, recognised outside their ability to sell their labour power. The adequacy of, and rules of entitlement to, such provisions are, of course, debatable and will be the subject of later analysis and discussion. Similarly, human life may be sustained other than by income and through the direct provision of services by the state. The provision of largely free educational opportunities by all industrial nations or free hospital care by some are examples of de-commodified services. In such nations, access to education and health services is not restricted by an ability to pay based upon terms related to the selling of labour power. Such provisions crucially affect the kinds of people we are able to be, through changing the opportunity structures within which choices are made. Political choices to establish such provisions are examples of how people can make themselves by collectively remaking their society. People will live different biographies because they, or their parents, have affected the history of the epochs in which they live. Following the Liberal social reforms of 1906–11 and the Labour social reforms of 1945–51, the kinds of people we were able to be changed. Thus, we see that by the mid-twentieth century commodified relationships were modified in Britain and indeed in all industrial nations, and in most, but not all, as a consequence of establishing democratic political rights. There-fore, the later analytical task of Part Four will be to examine the quality, form, content and spread of social rights in various industrial nations, rather than their simple existence. However, as we shall see, access to such social rights is often based upon labour market participation, as, for example, in the European Social Charter (discussed in Part Five), and, through earnings-related benefits, may reflect the inequalities of the labour market. Women especially, but all low-paid workers, lose out when this is the case. The basis for a social right thus needs to relate not to a person's unequal and insecure relationship to the labour market but to his or her equal status as a citizen.

The uncertainty of labour markets

Alongside the social rights described above we also find similar provisions of income and services provided for selected groups either through the civil right of contract in the labour market (so-called fringe benefits) or through purchase of insurance in the market. It is perhaps more accurate to call this a 'civil opportunity' than a civil right (see below). Private education and private health care are examples, but these require the kind of resources not available to many people who rely totally on selling their labour power. Commodified relationships are essentially and necessarily single-stranded and insecure; they are obligations of cash that are only as secure as the demand for the person's labour power. Such demand may change overnight due to circumstances wholly outside the person's immediate control. A fundamental characteristic of competitive market economies is constant economic and social change: 'constantly revolutionising the instruments of production, and thereby the relations of production, and with them the whole relations of society. . . . uninterrupted disturbance of all social conditions, everlasting uncertainty' (Marx, 1967: 45). The 'capitalist labour contract' is essentially uncertain for it depends upon ever-changing market conditions. For many, over their lifecourse, it provides an insecure basis for the means to life. The everyday operation of markets as they affect human beings is one of benefits and costs. However, it is largely benefits that are signalled through market exchanges whereas costs are neglected. The social costs of social change are, to a considerable extent, left to lie where they fall (Kapp, 1963; Titmuss, 1968). It is this fragility and insecurity of labour market relations and the threats this brings to the means of life for citizens of industrial nations that underlies the need for social rights to income and resources. Inevitably, therefore, social rights must be distanced from relationships of the labour market and based upon principles of justice of a political and social kind; upon principles of citizenship. Occupational welfare is discussed in more detail later.

It is a little-noticed irony that environmental concern over resource depletion and pollution in the natural world is resulting in us needing to recognise the 'worth' of the natural world while at the same time we ignore the value of human resources and their waste. For a long time markets ignored the environment because it was treated as a free good; similarly, markets ignore human beings when they treat them as commodities. Environmental costs of productive activity are now increasingly recognised but the human costs of productive activity find little compensation, especially when 'benefits' are means-tested. This is most dramatically demonstrated in the case of unemployment. The constant 'revolutionising of the instruments of production' leads not only to new and cheaper products that benefit people as consumers, but also to loss of employment which is a cost to people as producers. Rewards in consumption may be linked to punishments in production, but often for different persons. The benefits of new and cheaper products may be of little comfort to the person who loses his or her job as result. These benefits and costs must be regarded as properties of the market system of production that structures choices for the buyers of labour power and results in episodic pressures to reduce production costs. This results in pressures to minimise labour costs or shed labour. These system pressures are largely outside the control of individual employers and present them with a set of rules that constrain their behaviour in certain directions.

However, from the outset of markets treating labour power as a commodity, the human carriers of that labour power have resisted the costs involved. Resistance has taken place within the labour market over the terms of contract of the 'effort bargain' in the civil 'rights' arena. Or outside of the labour market, where political rights have been exercised to establish a social right to either benefits or the provision of services, for example, public education and health. No isolated individual can withstand the effects of commodification of his or her labour power and the associated uncertainties of the labour market. Human beings, thus, come to act collectively to protect their means to life, at least in part, through public provision by the state. In a political democracy this means through collective political action.

Political rights: the emergence of political democracy

Here we turn to the other great revolution mentioned by Giddens: the French Revolution of 1789. Giddens observed, 'for the first time in history there took place the overall dissolution of a social order by a movement guided by purely secular ideals – universal liberty and equality. . . . this was altogether novel in human history; [these ideals] created a climate of political change that has proved one of the most dynamic forces of contemporary history' (1982a: 5). Forms of power started to move, often slowly (Moorhouse, 1973), from the divine right of kings to the present-day electors of democratic governments.

It is a central tenet of sociological understanding that our social worlds are 'socially constructed', that men (and women, though, to date, more problematically) make themselves but not in circumstances of their own choosing. 'Societies only exist in so far as they are created and re-created in our actions as human beings . . . we create society at the same time as we are created by it . . . we cannot treat human activities as though they were determined by causes in the same way as natural events' (Giddens, 1982a: 13–14). Economic relationships as forms of social relationship are socially created, the 'laws' of economics are not the same as the laws of gravity. 'If we regard social activity as a mechanical set of events, determined by natural laws, we both misunderstand the past and fail to grasp how sociological analysis can help influence our possible futures' (Giddens, 1982a: 15). The establishment of political rights, the coming of political democracy, has provided the means whereby the mass of people may shape their social worlds through collective action through public choice. Whole structures of opportunity can be provided (public education, health, income support) that *redistribute and democratise choice*. Because human beings are socially interdependent, choice cannot be properly understood in terms of the actions of isolated asocial individuals. The interdependence of actions and choices has to be understood. Thus *we* have come to make ourselves in ways undreamed of 250 years ago. The impact of social inventions, such as democratic politics and the welfare state, is often overshadowed in their importance by the inventions of technology because we do not yet fully appreciate the socially constructed nature of human beings and society. The long-term consequences of the French Revolution have meant that ordinary people have come, to a degree, to make their history and themselves through their election and dismissal of governments; they elect and remove decision-makers, at least in principle. There is a tension in the twentieth century, however, where all three elements of Marshall's (1950) concept of citizenship exist alongside each other.

Democracy and the 'capitalist labour contract'

As Giddens (1982b) observed in his discussion of citizenship, and Polanyi notes, 'a self-regulating market demands nothing less than the institutional separation of society into economic and political spheres' (1957: 71). We noted earlier the importance of the common need of most citizens to sell their labour power as the means to life. Therefore, the general debate concerning citizenship and its three elements (Marshall, 1950) must, to a large extent, revolve around the diverse consequences of the 'capitalist labour contract'. It will be noted, however, that this focus is limited by its neglect of relations of reproduction and the importance of the unpaid labour of women. These will be discussed later in Part Five. Giddens (1982b) argues that the 'capitalist labour contract' is, and has been, the 'basic concept involved in analysing the class structure of capitalism' during the past 250 years in which citizenship has developed. This involves two conditions of particular importance. 'First, the sphere of the "economic" – work life – became separated from that of the "political": participation in the state. Second, [this] undercut[s] the very freedoms upon which the state depended' (1982b: 173). The sphere of industry is specifically defined as being 'outside' politics.

In the twentieth century, where, significantly, all three elements of Marshall's citizenship – civil, political and social rights – exist alongside each other, it becomes necessary to delineate each element and its relationship to the others. In doing this some conclusions must be drawn as to the primacy of one element of citizenship over another. Of central importance here is the primacy of democratically established social rights over the civil right, or opportunity, of a labour contract as a means of life (Twine, 1992). In a political democracy, citizens will expect those they elect not to stand aside from forms of intervention in the economic sphere of the labour contract and the terms of the 'effort bargain'. Thus, social rights concern not only the means of life outside the market but also the means of life within the labour market through, for example, the setting of minimum wages and conditions of work. The evidence suggests that the capitalist labour contract cannot be left to determine the means to life even of those who *are* able to sell their labour power. There can be no substantive notion of citizenship without also affecting the terms of the labour contract; therefore, economics cannot be 'outside' of politics. This would otherwise require restricting the scope of democratic politics so as not to intervene in markets. And, in a democracy, who would do the restricting? It implies abdicating political power in favour of the economic power of employers of labour. That would give employers, especially transnational corporations, *de facto* political power. In reality, as markets have been socially created by human beings, there have always been degrees of intervention. 'Political economy' is the correct term for the study of economics, as the latter seeks to deny the social and political nature of economic life. Indeed, many observers (Thurow, 1983; Daly and Cobb, 1990) believe that continual state intervention is essential if markets are to work effectively in allocating resources whilst at the same time protecting citizens from the social costs of market operations. State intervention affects the means of life by redistributing market distributions and thereby redistributing opportunities and changing the material and social context within which choices are made. Through the exercise of political rights citizens may redistribute resources, change opportunity structures and thereby the circumstances within which they make themselves. The social inventions of the welfare state provide institutional examples of changed opportunity structures that affect choices as to the means of life in all industrialised nations.

Here we should pause to clarify the question of the role of state intervention in protecting the needy. Often today, and especially in the UK and USA, it is argued and asserted that state intervention to protect the needy should be minimised and if possible eliminated (Nozick, 1974; Gilder, 1982; Murray, 1984). The suggestion is that state intervention is, in some sense, abnormal. On the contrary, viewed historically, state intervention to protect the needy has been the norm, certainly in British society. This was so from the time of the Elizabethan Poor Law through to the Speenhamland System at the turn of the nineteenth century. It is attempts to withdraw from state intervention after 1834 which need to be explained.

> During the most active period of the Industrial Revolution from 1795– 1834, the creating of a labour market in England was prevented through the Speenhamland System. . . . subsidies in aid of wages were granted in

accordance with a scale dependent upon the price of bread, so that a minimum income should be assured to the poor irrespective of their earnings. (Polanyi, 1957: 77–8)

It was only at the beginning of the nineteenth century that government in Britain, elected in 1832 by about 5 per cent of adults, dramatically changed the form of support to the poor. This was through the introduction of the New Poor Law of 1834 which attempted to apply punitive sanctions to the poor and thus coerce them into the competitive labour market (Pinker, 1971). Support for the poor was not to exceed the payment available to the lowest labourer in the labour market. The attempt was made to force people needing relief into the workhouse by the ending of outdoor relief. The New Poor Law was an adjunct to the attempt to establish the economics of the market as the dominant form of social relationship. However, the New Poor Law was neither smoothly nor effectively applied throughout Britain. There was much local resistance. The social pain arising from destitution due to an inability to sell labour power was defined by the small group in power as the fault of the individual in not adapting (taking lower pay) to the changing labour market. The period from 1834 to 1906 in which attempts were made to turn labour power into a commodity must be considered as a most painful and unsuccessful experiment in transforming social relationships (Pinker, 1971). Such a realisation, and its attendant threat to social stability, was embodied in the increasing calls by the late nineteenth century for new, and more substantive, forms of state intervention to help the poor, found in the writings of T.H. Green (1986). Such demands are also partly reflected through the increasing spread of the male franchise in 1867 and 1984. This was to culminate in the pioneering social reforms of the 1906–11 Liberal governments, and the great reforms of the 1945–51 Labour governments.

At the heart of much discussion of citizenship is the question of the circumstances in which 'private trouble' comes to be seen as 'public issue' (see Chapter 15). Crucial to the outcome of such debates is whether we perceive human beings as sovereign individual choice-makers or whether we perceive them as socially interdependent choice-makers. This relates partly to our historical and comparative knowledge and understanding of human societies and their structures, and whether we can distance ourselves from two hundred years of pressure to commodify social relationships. Commodification and the labour contract have encouraged us to focus on single-stranded relationships of market exchange. The richness of human life tends to be reduced to the market price for labour power, the importance of the individual is shrivelled. We fail to see the society from which he or she comes, and the rich network of multi-stranded social relationships that are essential for human life. Human beings are above all social beings whose development arises from their interdependence with one another. These issues are explored in the next chapter.

3

LIFECOURSE INTERDEPENDENCE: THE SOCIAL CONNECTIONS AND NETWORKS OF LIFE

This chapter presents sociological and philosophical argument for the social rights of citizenship to be grounded in the notion of 'lifecourse interdependence'. It is necessary first to explain why a perspective of 'lifecourse interdependence' has been chosen and what it means. This requires consideration of the concepts of both the 'lifecourse' and 'interdependence'.

The term 'lifecourse' is used rather than the more common term 'life-cycle' as the latter implies fixed stages of a stable cycle. The 'lifecourse' recognises the flexible nature of people's biographies and the ways these are lived out in conditions of continual economic and social change. Individual biographies may contain many 'life events', such as leaving the parental home, setting up a home, obtaining and following a job, getting married, having children, job change and retirement. For some there will be divorce, unemployment, remarriage, injury and sickness, and early retirement. Different age cohorts will experience these events within differing social and economic structures of constraint and opportunity. Furthermore, due to these constraints and opportunities we may feel 'dependent' in relation to one situation whilst we feel 'independent' in respect to another. This is not simply a matter of our own volition. The lifecourses of some people are more constrained, whilst others have greater opportunities. However, because constraints and opportunities are not simply matters of volition but also depend on the structures of society, we must understand them not simply in individual terms but as socially constructed.

In the 1980s much political and social policy debate in Britain and the USA was preoccupied with maintaining something called the 'independence' of people in society. A simple dichotomy was normally used whereby taken-for-granted notions of 'independence' and 'dependence' were contrasted. However, it is highly debatable as to which of us might, in a general sense, be regarded as 'dependent' or 'independent' in complex industrial societies (Bould et al., 1989; Lister, 1992b). Some circumspection is required in the use and meaning of these terms otherwise they simply become elements in an ideological debate. The notion of 'independence' can be used as a variation of 'individualism' that tries to perceive people as independent of society; a form of freedom from society or more specifically freedom from the state. This dichotomy also fits well with the ideological assumptions of choice by advocates of competitive markets. There is a reluctance to accept our 'interdependence' with one another because to do so would present us with moral obligations to compensate those who bear the costs of our progress. This would detract from the notion of progress and be expensive in compensation to people for the costs they bear. However, we are often not conscious of our interdependence because it is not overt and visible, or due to a partial perspective it *appears* to us that we are either 'independent' or 'dependent'. Viewed, however, from the wider perspective of human development over the lifecourse we are all essentially socially interdependent. Once we move to consider the lifecourses of the many people who make up society it becomes clear that it is much more appropriate to talk of the 'interdependence' of lifecourses rather than focus upon moments in a particular lifecourse when a person may appear to be 'independent' (Bould et al., 1989). Most basically, the material and human reproduction of society involves relations and processes of interdependence. Apparent relations of dependence and independence are, from a lifecourse perspective, but one-sided and incomplete perceptions of the relationships. Furthermore, dependence can be a dangerous form of labelling; an unemployed man may be dependent upon the DSS but his family is dependent upon him, and to be employed he is dependent upon selling his labour power, and that in turn depends upon a whole number of society-wide interdependencies.

As Titmuss observed, much of this dependency is man-made. It arises from the interactions of the choices people make.

> In industrialised countries there are many causes of dependency; they may be 'natural' dependencies as in childhood, extreme old age and child-bearing. They may be caused by physical and psychological ill-health and incapacity; in part, these are culturally determined dependencies. Or they may be wholly or predominantly determined by social and cultural factors. These it may be said, are the 'man-made' dependencies. . . . They include unemployment and underemployment, protective and preventative legislation, compulsory retirement from work and delayed entry into the labour market . . . the dominating operative factor has been the increasing *division of labour* in society . . .

as man becomes more individual and more specialised he becomes more socially dependent [*that is, socially interdependent*]. This is of primary importance in understanding the development of systems of welfare . . . recognition of the 'man-made' causes of dependency is reflected in social policies. It has also influenced the growth of our other categories of welfare. (1958: 47; my italics)

Sociologically we are made by society even as we contribute to its making. In this process human action and choice are constrained by institutional arrangements rather than determined by them, but our actions in choosing in turn affect the structuring and distribution of choice. As social creatures human beings derive their essential characteristics from their complex social networks within society. A lifecourse perspective demonstrates our social interdependence. Three examples of 'lifecourse interdependence' are examined: the family, work and retirement.

Family: childhood, women and the reproduction of society

In industrialised nations children no longer work from the earliest possible age. Childhood has been socially created as an extended period of 'dependency', the costs of which are shared by parents (especially women) and the state (for example, through child benefit, education and health care). The extended period of dependency arises from, first, the need for human beings to undergo a period of primary socialisation, and, second, our need in complex industrial societies to have a literate, numerate and educated workforce. Reproduction of society, its continuity, is both biological (the physical human being) and social (the kind of human being). We have come to perceive people below the age of, say 16, as dependants. Children are dependent upon their parents and the wider society, yet society is also dependent upon children for its reproduction. There is a social interdependence between the individual and society that extends over the lifecourse of individuals and on into future generations. At any one time only a small proportion of the population are rearing children. For that time we are dependent upon them to reproduce society. In due course as those children enter adult life they join the workforce and start raising the next generation of children, meanwhile their parents continue to pay taxes towards the costs of other people's children. These are 'lifecourse reciprocities' which recognise social interdependence and the manner in which the costs of reproducing society fall unevenly upon persons and at particular points in their lifecourse. However, the full costs of raising children, especially the social costs that fall on women, are seldom recognised (Wynn, 1970; Land, 1989; Lister, 1989, 1993). Within the family there are also networks of social interdependence. Women are often dependent upon men to bring in the family income, but men are dependent upon women for bearing and raising their jointly produced children. Women also service the domestic needs of men in terms of food, clean clothes, the general ambience of the household and domestic accounting. And, of course, reproduction requires both women and men. All this has become commonplace in the sociological literature of the past ten years (Pahl, 1988).

Important questions for citizenship arise from the historical separation of home and work – the emergence of private and public spheres of social activity (Lister, 1993) – and the implications this has had for the roles of women and men in society. The key historical developments relate to the emergence of men as the main breadwinners as a consequence of factory production replacing domestic production in which the whole household took part. Men had to sell their labour power to meet the needs of the whole family and in this they were also given public social recognition and status as the key economic providers and power-holders. Such status overshadowed even the key role of women as child-bearers because men provided (at least in theory) the material basis for family existence. The private domestic unpaid production of women received little recognition outside the home as it was outside the market system of exchange, and therefore given no monetary value by the wider society. Furthermore, as most married women had no title to property until the Matrimonial Property Acts of the late nineteenth century, they had no independent source of economic power. Their property became that of their husbands. At that time property was important for accessing political rights. And, in Britain, it was not until the extension of the franchise in 1928 that women obtained political rights similar to those of men. Thus the citizenship rights of women have come much more slowly than those of men. Even today, social rights to welfare for women remain circumscribed by their restricted labour market participation, upon which such rights are often based. Furthermore, as a basis for social rights, their unpaid labour goes largely unrecognised. To a large extent women remain an appendage of their husbands for social security purposes, though this is slowly changing. Women today may more easily attain an income independent of their husbands through participation in the labour market, but this is limited by gendered job and career opportunities that often result in low-paid and part-time employment. To the extent that social rights are based upon a labour market status, that is, they are both gendered and class-based, then women will lose out. Furthermore, a social right of citizenship must recognise the contribution to society of the unpaid labour of women.

Surprisingly, a key interdependence in the family is often over-looked. Relations of love are relations of interdependence and to be substantive must be reciprocal. Our concern here is not what specifically attracts one human being to another, but what may be called the 'social relations of love'. This is to claim not that all familial relationships are those of 'love', for they often involve coercion, power, violence, but that within the family we *seek* and expect 'love'. Love must be regarded as a special and highly prized relationship that we all hope to experience and cultivate. It is a richly multi-stranded relationship by no means confined to the family, a point to which we return later. Love is a social relationship with special qualities, though it has qualities that we hope to extend and experience more generally. But what are the components of the social relationship 'love'? We may identify the following components: trust, reciprocity, altruism, commitment, sacrifice, tolerance, understanding, concern, solidarity, interdependence. These qualities overlap and reinforce each other in a rich matrix of social ties. Social relationships of love are crucial to the development and maintenance of the 'self', as only in such close relationships can certain elements develop. Such self-fulfilment and development may come from love, that we often seek some of its components in our relationships with the wider society. These involve social relationships of recognition and inclusion that are essential to self-development. Though love usually, but not exclusively, requires face-to-face interaction, some of its components are often extended to strangers and to relationships with the wider community. The development of social rights can be an embodiment and extension of components of love to our fellow citizens. Such love is evidenced in a whole range of public service and voluntary activity and contributions to organisations such as Oxfam, Amnesty International, and through our membership of the National Health Service and, dare we suggest, in our contributions to taxation and National Insurance. All forms of mutuality and solidarity embody aspects of love. Market exchanges downplay the altruistic nature of human relationships and human capacity for sharing. Consider the difficulties of applying some of the above elements of love to market relationships.

Work: commodification, unemployment and the material reproduction of society

As argued in Chapter 2, during the past two or three hundred years we have become dependent on selling our labour power; on being employed. We have created economic systems that treat our labour power as a commodity to be bought and sold. In pre-industrial societies a family lived off the land, eking out an existence that was to a large extent independent of other people. That level of living was limited by what the individual or more accurately the household unit might produce. At best this was 'household interdependence' rather than individual independence. To raise their level of living beyond subsistence they needed to trade with others. Emerging capitalism promised a rising standard of living that required more specialised production based upon technology and an increasing 'division of labour'; and a related division between home and work. An increasing 'division of labour' creates economic, that is, 'social interdependence' that becomes greater the more scientific and technologically specialised our systems of production become.

Interdependence is also embodied in the ways people relate to each other as both producers and consumers. We produce things other people want and consume things other people produce. This operates in two ways. You must sell what you produce and someone must buy what you produce. Being a consumer involves a single-stranded relationship in which you buy a product or a service at the asking price. We know little if anything of the circumstances, often taking place across the globe, under which the product has been produced. Were reasonable wages paid to the producers? What were their working conditions? What were the hidden costs of production in terms of industrial injury or pollution? The cheapness of our bargain may have been paid for by other people or we may pay more than we thought if there is long-term pollution of our environment. Externalities are excluded from market exchanges for, until recently, they were thought to be unimportant (Perrings, 1987; also see Chapter 6 below).

Employment is often seen as the keystone of independence in industrial society, yet very many are low-paid, unemployed or, for a variety of reasons, unable to work. Capitalist market systems have proved to be a very effective means of organising the production of goods resulting from the increasing division of labour, but poor distributors of the wealth and the social costs of production. At the same time processes of production have become less dependent upon people and more dependent upon technology. The productivity of the technologically based division of labour continually displaces people from the system of production. People are forced into unemployment, often for long periods of time. The very division of labour and the market production of goods that enables a rise in the general standard of living also has 'social costs' for certain sections of the population. Major problems arise for people and their families (and the human reproduction of society) if they become unemployed (or if their work is low-paid compared to their family responsibilities). They become dependent upon charity or publicly provided assistance. Thus, unemployment causes 'dependency', yet most people do not choose to be unemployed but are required to be unemployed in the interests of society, for example, due to policies to control inflation, to continual technological modernisation or the ebb and flow of markets. They are bearing the costs of other people's progress as the economy changes (Titmuss, 1968). However, the social costs of unemployment are not evenly spread across society but fall disproportionately upon the most vulnerable groups: the unskilled, the disabled, the older worker, ethnic minorities (Sinfield, 1981; Warr, 1985; Fryer and Ulah, 1987; White, 1991). Furthermore, the distribution of unemployment across a person's lifecourse is unpredictable. Some people suffer little or no unemployment whilst others experience long and repeated spells. More generally, as Sinfield and Fraser (1985) have detailed, there are major costs of unemployment that fall upon society as a whole in the form of lost production and tax revenues, and the cost of benefit payments. Finally, women's lifecourse labour market participation is further disrupted by childbirth and child-rearing, involving, in most cases, dependence upon their husbands.

There are thus clear 'lifecourse interdependencies' through the human and economic reproduction of society. Unemployment, low pay and unpaid caring work all crucially affect ability to build up pension entitlement over the lifecourse and, as will be shown later, this has class and gender implications for income levels in old age (Arbor and Ginn, 1991; Davies and Ward, 1992; Johnson and Falkingham, 1992).

A social right to compensation for unemployment, for bearing the costs of other people's progress, is essential to citizenship and for maintaining people's ability to participate in the 'social heritage of their . . . society' (Marshall, 1950). Yet, present levels of unemployment benefit in Britain leave most families of the unemployed in poverty (Oppenheim, 1993). In Britain, 69 per cent of households where the head of household or spouse was unemployed were in poverty in 1989–90.

Retirement: lifecourse interdependence and elderly people

Due to the centrality of employment to industrial market society the introduction of 'retirement' from employment has constructed potential dependency in old age. Indeed, retirement and early retirement of older workers have been used to reduce the unemployment of younger workers during periods of depression (Phillipson, 1982). Furthermore, health in old age reflects the quality of life and standard of living experienced over the lifecourse as a child, parent and worker. In Britain the lifecourse links between social class, poverty and poor health have been clearly documented (Wilkinson, 1986a; Townsend and Davidson, 1988; Whitehead, 1988; Quick and Wilkinson, 1991; Blackburn, 1991). The distinct relationship between unemployment and poor health has been shown by Warr (1985). Quality of life in old age strongly reflects the different costs of 'lifecourse interdependencies', of child-rearing and employment, and these vary by social class and gender (Walker, 1986; Groves, 1992; Twine, 1992). In the twentieth century, industrial nations have recognised to a limited degree 'lifecourse interdependence' through the development of state and occupational pension schemes. Britain has built on a basic flat-rate state pension a dual system of state and private earnings-related pension provision. These involve very different levels of recognition of 'lifecourse interdependency' by social class and by gender. Both involve elements of lifecourse transfer as well as transfers between social groups via contributions paid during periods of the lifecourse when people are employed. The resources people have and the quality of life people experience in retirement are often a crystallisation of complex lifecourse interdependencies. A discussion of pension provisions provides opportunity for a preliminary examination of a number of general issues affecting social rights to welfare. These issues are explored by way of a case study.

A case study: civil opportunity or social right to welfare in old age?

It is useful to consider the lifecourse and British pension provisions from the combined theoretical perspectives of citizenship (Marshall, 1950) and the social division of welfare (Titmuss, 1958). We start from an examination of two of Marshall's three elements of citizenship: civil and social rights as applied to pension schemes. According to Marshall, the civil element of citizenship 'is composed of the rights necessary for individual freedom – liberty of the person, freedom of speech, thought and faith, the right to own property and to conclude valid contracts, and the right to justice' (1950: 10). It is argued that Marshall confuses 'opportunities' with 'rights'. These need to be clearly distinguished. In the same way that there is no right to property, so there is no right to employment. There are, however, opportunities to own property or to be employed. Indeed, if you cannot find a job your chances of owning property, other than through inheritance, are small. For the 3 million persons officially unemployed in the UK in 1993, with job vacancies of well under 300,000, a 'contract of employment' is better understood not as a 'right' but as an 'opportunity'. To highlight this distinction in the following discussion of pensions and to make contrasts with social rights, the term 'civil opportunity' rather than 'civil right', is used to refer to contracts of employment. The 'civil opportunity' to conclude a 'contract of employment' in the labour market that may embody access to an occupational pension is of central importance as this in turn taps the fiscal welfare that governments provide through tax reliefs. These issues are discussed later, especially in Chapter 11. With respect to social rights of citizenship, Marshall refers to 'the whole range from the right to a modicum of economic welfare and security to the right to share to the full in the social heritage and to live the life of a civilised being according to the standards prevailing in society' (1950: 11). Social rights are thus a central element required for social inclusion and participation; a means of maintaining social integration in society. By endowing individuals with social rights, society is recognising them and including them, whereas lack of social rights may lead, through poverty, to social exclusion (Townsend, 1979; Walker and Walker, 1987). However, Marshall never spelt out the form and content of social rights necessary for social inclusion. Doyal and Gough (1991) have made a powerful attempt to do this. Concern here is with Marshall's failure to specify the relative level of economic welfare and security in old age to be embodied in social rights. Furthermore, his equation of social rights with state-provided social welfare led him to neglect the 'civil opportunity' route to welfare via occupational and fiscal programmes. The divisiveness of these routes was well captured in Titmuss's (1958) influential essay on 'the social division of welfare', and in the more recent work of Sinfield (1978), Field (1987) and Mann (1992).

In highlighting three major categories of welfare in post-war British society – social (state) welfare, fiscal welfare, and occupational welfare – Titmuss argued that 'this division is not based on any fundamental difference in the functions of the three systems or their declared aims. It . . . in the main, is related to the division of labour in complex, individuated societies' (1958: 45–6). A major factor in the development of all three categories of welfare has been the growth in 'states of dependency' that 'arise for the vast majority of the population whenever they are not in a position to "earn life" for themselves and their families; they are then dependent people' (1958: 47). The recognition earlier that unemployment and under-employment and compulsory retirement from work are man-made dependencies arising from the increasing division of labour in society also means recognising that 'as man becomes more indi-vidual and more specialised he becomes more socially dependent [socially interdependent]' (1958: 47). In the British context, it is argued that the social rights route to the original 1978 state earnings-related pension was better able to deal with lifecourse 'states of dependency' than the 'civil opportunity' route to occupa-tional pensions. This, despite the substantial tax subsidies received by the latter. Far from leading to social integration, this civil opportunity route to welfare is likely to exacerbate social divisions by embodying for some the 'man-made dependencies' of differing lifecourse employment and unemployment experiences, whilst for others it enables them to tap generous tax reliefs to boost their pensions. Despite the *promise* of a higher pension, an 'opportunity' is likely to prove less secure than a 'right' as a route to welfare in old age.

Pension systems, both public and private, embody beliefs and assumptions as to the appropriateness of relations between govern-ment, society and the individual. In Britain the pension structure has two main elements: a flat-rate basic state pension (BSP), supplemented by an earnings-related top-up either through the state earnings-related pension scheme (SERPS) or an earnings-related occupational pension scheme (OPS). In recent years either the SERP or an OPS may have been replaced by a personal pension (PP). In addition some 16 per cent of pensioners draw means-tested Income Support to bring their income up to the minimum level of the means-tested element of the social security system.

The SERPS is a 'Pay As You Go' scheme whereby the earnings-related contributions of those who are currently working go to pay the earnings-related pension of those now retired. This is thus a form of 'intergenerational reciprocity' (see Bould et al., 1989: 11, on the USA). Most importantly, membership of the scheme is affected neither by job moves nor by who employs a person. It is citizen-based rather than employer-based. Furthermore, the *origi-nal* 1978 scheme had a number of novel features: final pension was based on 25 per cent of the revalued average 'best twenty-years' earnings', rather than final year salary as with most OPSs. This particularly benefited manual workers by recognising their lower lifecourse pay and its decline near to retirement. It also recognised that manual workers are more likely over their lifecourse to change employer, experience unemployment, be ill and receive industrial injuries. All these lifecourse events limit lifetime earnings capacity. The distinctive lifecourse experience of women was recognised by the crediting of contributions at a basic rate when they were out of the labour market caring for dependent children or relatives. Once in payment the SERP was inflation-proofed. Widows obtained the full pension of their deceased spouse. However, for fear that the level of contributions of those working would become unacceptable (since challenged by Hills, 1993), key changes were made to reduce the cost of the scheme by the year 2053–4 from £35.3 billion to £16.3 billion. Now, for those retiring after 2001 the pension will be based on only 20 per cent of revalued average lifetime earnings. Non-earning years due to caring for dependent children or relatives will be left out of the calculation, providing that there has been at least twenty years' earnings. Non-earning years due to unemployment will continue to be left out of the calculation 'but the best twenty years rule could have been of assistance to people who had experienced unemployment' (J. Brown, 1990). Widows will inherit only half their husband's pension instead of the whole. This is likely to increase the numbers after 2001 who will still be dependent upon means-tested Income Support to top up their income. People may, however, contract out of the SERPS and pay reduced National Insurance contributions if they are in an approved OPS that must pay a guaranteed minimum pension, or since 1988 have taken out a PP.

In contrast, OPSs are crucially based upon joining an employer-provided scheme. Changing employer, however, usually means leaving that OPS, though the element of pension earned can be frozen until retirement or accrued contributions transferred to another scheme. However, the employee loses the accumulating benefit of long-term membership. Most OPSs are 'funded schemes' in which a person's earnings-related contributions go into a fund which is then invested to produce an annuity on retirement from which a pension related to final salary is then paid. There is a 'pension formula' whereby, if forty years' contributions are paid, final pension is usually based upon half final salary and may include a lump sum at retirement. This is thus an individual contract whose pension level reflects inequalities in individual lifecourse employment experience. A substantial state subsidy is provided through tax reliefs on employer and employee contributions, and on any profits from investing these contributions. The value of the tax relief to the employee will be higher the higher their marginal rate of tax. Once in payment most OPSs are not guaranteed against inflation, though some are. Since 1978 the government has inflation-proofed the guaranteed minimum pension element of OPSs. Continuity of employment with a firm is crucial to obtaining the maximum pension promised. However, according to Ginn and Arbor (1991), some 52 per cent of men and 66 per cent of women who were in OPSs in 1987 had lost some of their pension rights.

Since 1988, through substantial financial incentives, amounting to £9.3 thousand million by 1993 (Arbor and Ginn, 1991: 180), the government has encouraged people to opt out of the SERPS and OPSs and take out a PP. Whilst overcoming the transferability problems of OPSs, PPs do not resolve contribution losses arising from inequalities in lifecourse employment or caring activity (National Audit Office, 1990). Unlike OPSs, where pension is based upon a 'pension formula', PPs are 'money purchase' schemes. These have no guaranteed level of final pension as this depends on the stock market value of investments at time of retirement. Employers do not contribute to PPs. At the time of writing (May 1994) however, there is a growing controversy over the adequacy of advice given by pension advisers to many millions of people who transferred from well-established OPSs and the SERPS. In the spring of 1994 the Norwich Union insurance company sent all its pensions sales staff for retraining after independent investigation found the standards of its pension advice misleading. (More details of the British pension system can be found in Brown, J., 1990; Arbor and Ginn, 1991; Johnson and Falkingham, 1992.)

From the viewpoint of Titmuss, both state retirement pensions (BSP and SERPS) involve direct cash payment made in discharging collective responsibilities for the socially constructed dependency of retirement at age 60/65. As this is largely a payment from the Exchequer, it is treated as a 'public expenditure'. Over the lifecourse there is an interdependence between pensioners and those in work paying taxes and national insurance contributions. However, tax reliefs that subsidise the purchase of similar benefits through occupational and private pensions are not treated as public expenditure. Treasury conventions concerning public expenditure thus crucially influence ability over the lifecourse to establish adequate income for retirement. Though ideologically it is claimed that those in private schemes are making 'independent' provision for themselves and their families, and those on state pensions are 'dependent' on the state, the reality is more complex. Though the 'first is a cash transaction [and] the second is an accounting convenience [, in] their primary objectives and their effects on individual purchasing power there are no differences in these two ways by which collective provision is made for dependencies' (Titmuss, 1958: 48). They are both transfer payments. However, these two pension systems embody quite different principles concerning tax and public expenditure relationships between governments, society and the individual. As a consequence, when governments seek to control 'public expenditure' they look only at state pensions and ignore the expanding 'public expenditure' through tax reliefs on occupational and personal pension schemes. Routes to welfare in old age are thus crucially mediated through the exercise of political rights and political conventions as to what is regarded as public expenditure (Wilkinson, 1986a). But, it should be noted, both public and private pensions involve an interdependence with other taxpayers.

During the 1980s British governments sought to reduce public expenditure on state pensions in two ways. First, in 1980 the link between the BSP and movements in average earnings was broken; since then the BSP has kept pace only with inflation. Thus, over time, the gap between its value and average earnings has widened. Second, as detailed above, major changes have been introduced to reduce the value of the SERPS after 2001. At the same time, however, 'public expenditure' through tax reliefs on occupational pension contributions and profits from pension investments grew substantially between 1985 and 1993. This revenue forgone by the Exchequer will continue to grow into the 1990s, through governmental encouragement to contract out of the SERPS and join either OPSs or take out the newly introduced PPs. Yet, 'if as a society we genuinely cannot afford an adequate SERPS that mainly benefits the bottom half of income earners, how can it be fair to continue to afford tax reliefs on occupational pensions that benefit mainly the top half of income earners?' (Twine, 1988: 29).

With state pensions the relationship between the government, society and the individual is expressed through Marshall's social rights of citizenship, whereas with occupational pensions the relationship is expressed through what has been called 'civil opportunity'. Civil opportunity and social rights can thus be identified as alternative routes for providing income in old age, though each have their own rules concerning access, benefit level, tax treatment and public expenditure. Nevertheless, as both schemes assume labour market participation as the basis for building up pension entitlement, this undermines their basis as a social right of citizenship. This was less true, however, of the original 1978 SERPS because it recognised breaks or changes in paid employment and provided some compensation for different lifecourse experiences of dependency and caring. This was of particular significance for women whose lifecourse experience of paid work differs greatly from that of men, in terms of continuity, type of employer and level of pay (Glendinning and Millar, 1992).

Central to debate about citizenship must be a recognition of interdependence and a consequent concern for those members of society who bear the costs of social changes that are thought to be in the interests of society as whole. Significantly, pensions that are provided through the civil opportunity of a labour contract cannot incorporate social costs of social change. Indeed, the reverse is true: members of such schemes who bear the cost of unemployment will also bear the added cost of losing membership of their OPS and having their subsequent pension reduced. Because membership of an OPS is wholly labour market dependent it provides an insecure and thus inadequate basis for income in old age. It will be constantly threatened by lifecourse events outside the control of the individual but which may be in the interests of the wider society, for example continual industrial and occupational change. Thus, despite tax reliefs, for many individuals (but not all) civil opportunity as a route to adequate income in old age is an insecure basis for the social integration of the elderly into society. In contrast, this was less true of the original 1978 SERPS, where change in employment did not directly threaten membership of the SERPS, nor, because of the 'best twenty years of earnings' rule, was it likely to reduce the eventual pension. Individuals remained in the same scheme no matter how often their job changed and they were credited with a basic contribution. What is more, the scheme provided some compensation for other elements of 'socially constructed dependency' for women by incorporating provisions that allowed for the caring and nurturing life course events that affect their labour market participation, and which society still expects of them. These de-commodifying aspects of SERPS were substantially weakened by the changes of 1988.

We have identified aspects of a person's pre-retirement lifecourse that have different consequences for retirement income depending on whether his or her pension stems from a civil opportunity OPS or a social right original SERPS. The different rules of these schemes treat key lifecourse transitions and dependencies differently. The civil opportunity route to welfare is deficient for manual workers, and particularly for women with their different pattern of labour market participation. Other commentators (Land, 1989; Lister, 1989, 1993) have noted the difficulty of ensuring equal treatment for women and men in Marshall's concept of citizenship, and within the

Keynes–Beveridge welfare state. At present a majority of those who are in poverty in old age are women. As both the SERPS and OPSs are work-based, women lose out. Strengthening social rights to an adequate retirement income for people as citizens is essential if women are to obtain equal treatment in old age.

Though the quantity and quality of labour market participation will vary over an individual's lifecourse, retirement generally has a fixed point in the chronology of his or her life. However, the welfare prospects for the retirement years are largely set by the interaction of the three elements of citizenship prior to retirement. Thus, different cohorts of people reaching retirement age will have had different historical experiences of the content of citizenship, with key variations by class, gender and race: for example, in the UK, changes in pension policy occurring in 1948, 1978 and 1988; social changes related to smaller families arising from improved contraception; higher divorce rates, associated, in part, with greater ease of divorce; the increased labour market participation of women; and periods of high and low unemployment (Kiernan and Wicks, 1990). A lifecourse perspective on interdependence thus enables us to make important connections between the worlds of reproduction, work and retirement; what C. Wright Mills (1970) called the interplay of biography and history.

Pension reform: recognising the social rights of the low-paid and the unpaid

As long as civil opportunity takes precedence over social rights, those absent from or harshly treated by labour markets slip into poverty at various points in their pre-retirement lifecourse and, in consequence, in old age. This is particularly true for women (Walker, 1986; Groves, 1992), despite some attempts to provide equal opportunities for women in OPSs since 1978. If the right to an adequate pension in old age is to be provided for all citizens regardless of labour market participation, it requires a major rethink of our approach to the issue. This has recently been undertaken by Falkingham and Johnson (1993a, 1993b) in their proposals for a Unified Funded Pension Scheme (UFPS) for Britain.

> It is designed to: provide a minimum pension of one-third of average male earnings for all people over 65; encourage additional savings for retirement; ensure all pensions at least keep their value in relation to the retail price index; treat men and women equally; give credit for earlier non-waged work caring for children or other dependants; allow a fair

division of pension entitlements between partners upon divorce or permanent separation. (1993b: 8)

Their proposal would replace the 'current complex mix of state, occupational and personal pensions' (1993b: 9). This is particularly important for the low-paid, and for those doing unpaid work caring, mainly women. In the UFPS,

> a person whose contributions are so low that their personal retirement fund (PRF) falls below the level required to provide a minimum pension of one-third of average male earnings will receive an annual capital top-up into their PRF in the form of a loan from the government. . . . If in subsequent years [earnings rise sufficiently] then the loan will be repaid . . . otherwise it becomes an unconditional grant at age 65. This provision ensures that people accumulate a pension entitlement when they are doing socially valuable but unpaid work such as child-rearing (1993b: 8).[1]

Recognition of the contribution to society embodied in the unpaid work that arises from the social interdependencies discussed above is central to a social right of citizenship, and is discussed further in Part Five in the context of welfare state regimes and a Basic Income.

We can see the lifecourse interdependencies of child-care and -rearing, labour market participation and unemployment, and how pension income is currently dependent on these events. The interdependencies of the lifecourse as a whole, rather than snap-shots of moments of 'dependency', should be our focus for under-standing how needs arise and for arguing for their compensation as a social right. As pensions are an important social invention there are important aspects of the pre-retirement lifecourse in which people may intervene to effect their post-retirement years. This brings us to some preliminary observations on Marshall's third element of citizenship: political rights. A more extensive discussion is undertaken in Part Three.

The interdependence of social and political rights

For their development social rights require the mediating exercise of political rights, although we should not overlook that govern-ments also set the framework of rules within which civil opportunity operates, for example tax reliefs and pension law. Political rights refers to 'the right to participate in the exercise of political power, as a member of a body invested with political authority or as an elector of the members of such a body. The corresponding institutions are parliament and councils of local government' (Marshall, 1950: 11).

The exercise of political rights provides the crucial democratic arena within which a majority view may be established concerning acceptable degrees of inequality in society (Mack and Lansley, 1985). Present concern is with the potential that the exercise of political rights has to recognise lifecourse interdependencies when deciding the balance between civil opportunity and social rights as alternative routes to pensions in old age. The exercise of the civil opportunity to bargain collectively may provide the promise (though not the reality) of a good pension for sections of the labour force. This can bypass the need to exercise democratic political rights required to develop a social right to an adequate pension for all citizens. Here we may usefully draw on Marshall's comments on the historical development of the three components of citizenship:

> In the latter part of the 19th century there was a growing interest in equality as a principle of social justice and an appreciation of the fact that the formal recognition of an equal capacity for rights was not enough . . . there grew a conception of equal social worth, not merely of equal natural rights. . . . Citizenship requires a bond, a direct sense of community membership based on loyalty to a civilisation that is a common possession. [However,] even at the end of the 19th century, the mass of working people did not wield effective political power. The political rights of citizenship, unlike the civil rights [civil opportunities], were full of potential danger to the capitalist system, . . . [Yet] the foundations of the market economy and the contractual system seemed strong enough to stand against any probable assault. In fact, there were some grounds for expecting that the working classes, as they became educated, would accept the basic principles of the system and be content to rely for their protection and progress on the civil rights [civil opportunities] of citizenship, which contained no obvious menace to competitive capitalism. Such a view was encouraged by the fact that one of the main achievements of political power in the late 19th century was the recognition of the right of collective bargaining. This meant that social progress was being sought by strengthening civil rights [civil opportunities], not by creating social rights; by contract in the open market, not through a minimum wage and social security. (1950: 40–2)

By substituting the term 'civil opportunities' for 'civil rights' in the above quotation, its meaning and *implication* becomes much clearer.

Despite welfare state inventions, 'civil opportunity' has to a significant degree institutionalised inequalities of labour market bargaining power as a significant element in determining the pensions of people in old age. Pensions have become a common feature of trade union collective bargaining. Unions have become trapped within capitalism, and are now unwilling to support the more universalistic social rights route to welfare for all. They seem locked into this particularistic civil opportunity route that was established *before* a full adult franchise established democratic political rights. Hidden public expenditures on tax reliefs provide a major incentive for this choice (Wilkinson, 1986a). Yet the reality of an occupational pension is often much less than the promise (Ginn and Arbor, 1991). The civil opportunity route makes promises it cannot deliver to large numbers of people in OPSs. Despite enormous tax subsidies, this promise is undermined by the reality of lifecourse employment and unemployment experiences and diverts our attention from the long-term problem of poverty in old age.

Interdependence across time and space

The above discussion has highlighted certain aspects of interdependence between the generations but these extend beyond the issue of pensions. Concern for the future of our children and their children also raises questions of interdependence. Though children yet unborn cannot reciprocate directly to the present generation, the knowledge that future generations are provided for informs savings behaviour and patterns of inheritance. That is usually at a family level and may bring status and social recognition to those who pass on such inheritance even though they may be dead at the time. There are, however, forms of collective inheritance that can be best met by a concern for the future of all children and all the nations of the globe. This may be seen in the stewardship of the environment. Stewardship implies that the present generation should not do just as they please with the environment but that they have an obligation to future generations to 'steward' resources. They are not its owners but rather its custodians. They are guardians and protectors of the resources as with an adoptive parent who does not own the child but guards and protects it. As the rewards of parenthood are never fully known, so the rewards of stewardship are also an investment whose returns are never fully known to present generations. As with the love of parents for their children, so with stewardship there is trust placed in the hands of the present generation.

Albert Weale has argued that,

> the notion of citizenship itself implies duties to future generations, at least insofar as those future generations comprise the political community of the future. . . . The idea is that the resources available to different generations are not the property of any particular generation, and hence cannot be used disproportionately to benefit any particular generation. Another way of putting this point is to say that it is the political community as such which is the locus of ownership of these resources, and hence the members of one generation cannot lay claim to exclusive use and consumption. (1991: 160–1)

Environmental and economic interdependence

Weale extends his argument by posing a further question: 'it is significant that the notion of citizenship has provided grounds for duties that go beyond the borders of present time. . . . can they go beyond the borders of present place?' (1991: 161).

Since the Second World War market processes and operations have been transformed. In the 1990s markets operate on a global scale, with transnational corporations being key actors with limited respect for the political boundaries of nation states. We now exist within networks of global interdependence that pose quite new questions of citizenship that go beyond those identified by Marshall writing in 1950. Weale asks, 'is the notion of citizenship so tied to an exclusivist communitarian style of thought that it is intrinsically indifferent to duties beyond borders?' (1991: 157). He argues that

> the duties of citizenship go beyond place by appealing to the interdependence of states in respect of their relations and freedom of action with respect to one another. . . . Two sorts of interdependence are worth noting. The first of these is physical interdependence. Modern production methods have released the bound Prometheus. The transformation of the world of nature follows as a consequence. All the major environmental problems – acid rain, ozone depletion, global warming, the transport of hazardous waste, deforestation – have an international character. . . . the actions of one national actor have implications for the rest, . . . There is also economic interdependence. When price signals move around the world almost instantaneously, as they do, with modern electronic stock markets, then it becomes extremely difficult for governments to insulate their economies from the effects of distant events. . . . The minimum content of the democratic conception of citizenship, . . . the state acting in the name of citizens . . . means that, in a context of interdependence, the state necessarily acts beyond its borders. Thus, in facing the problems of environmental degradation or economic interdependence [, the state acts on behalf of its citizens, and citizens should therefore seek to] ascertain their responsibilities beyond their own borders. (1991: 161–3)

We turn now to more detailed discussion of questions of environmental and economic interdependence in Part Two.

Note

1 A full account of their proposals is to be found in Falkingham and Johnson, 1993a.

PART TWO
ENVIRONMENTAL
INTERDEPENDENCE

At first sight it may seem odd to include a consideration of environmental interdependence and sustainable development in a discussion of citizenship and social rights. Part One focused on the importance of developing social rights as the material base for human development. How are such social rights to be provided if there are environmental limits to the exploitation of material resources? This question requires we confront some fundamentally new dimensions of citizenship, of both a structural and a personal kind.

All Western industrialised nations promise through the structures of economic growth to improve the personal material well-being of their citizens, and this is in line with the assumption of neo-classical economics that human wants are unlimited. The means and ends of these two basic assumptions of the modernised world are now in question. How has this questioning come about?

The publication in 1972 of *The Limits to Growth* (Meadows et al.), though largely dismissed at the time, sent an initial shock through the academic and political élites of many industrialised nations. It questioned in a dramatic fashion the presumptions of the Industrial Revolution and the whole process of modernisation: that humans could transform and exploit the natural world without end. The prospect that continued economic growth would deliver to the poor tomorrow the material level of well-being of today's rich was put in question. The belief that developing nations could with confidence follow the path of developed nations to greater prosperity through high-energy industrialisation was placed in doubt. The economists' assumptions that human wants were unlimited and could be pursued with impunity through markets were given limits. Economic growth, the desired means of nearly all political parties in all nations, was itself questioned as a sustainable project.

If economic growth was no longer or less available to deliver

increased material well-being to the poor, then policies for redistribution of available resources would move to the centre of the
political agenda. This would require a change in values, goals and
increased levels of political participation in decision-making beyond
and below the level of the nation state (discussed in Part Three).
Though the media in many cases interpreted the conclusions of the
Limits to Growth study as predicting 'global catastrophe', the book
was in the event giving a warning, as we see now, ahead of its time.
It concluded,

> (i) If the present growth trends in world population, industrialisation,
> pollution, food production, and resource depletion continue unchanged,
> the limits to growth on this planet will be reached sometime within the
> next 100 years. The most probable result will be a sudden and uncontroll-
> able decline in both population and industrial capacity. (ii) It is possible
> to alter these trends and to establish a condition of ecological and
> economic stability that is sustainable far into the future. The state of
> global equilibrium could be designed so that the basic material needs of
> each person on earth are satisfied and each person has an equal
> opportunity to realise his or her human potential. (iii) If the world's
> people decide to strive for this second outcome rather than the first, *the
> sooner they begin working to attain it*, the greater will be their chances of
> success. (Meadows et al., 1972: 24; my italics)

That early warning was largely dismissed as scare-mongering and as
unscientific. At that time the issue was, apparently, quite simple.
According to Perrings,

> The models [such as those of Meadows et al.] showed that in a finite
> world where, by implicit assumption, the elasticity of substitution in
> global production was either very low or zero, the exponential growth of
> any one subsystem inevitably ran it up against the limits imposed by the
> availability of basic resources. On the other side, it was argued [by most
> economists] that in a finite world where, by explicit assumption, the
> elasticity of substitution in global production was very high, the rising
> scarcity of natural resources subject to exponentially increasing rates of
> exploitation by any one subsystem would induce substitution into less
> scarce resources – with no necessary check on the rate of growth of the
> subsystem concerned. (1987: 47)

Economists believed that price signals would give sufficient early
warning of any crisis of resource depletion and this would lead to
technological innovation in good time to avert any crisis. Thus, in
arguing that provided sufficient resources were devoted to the tasks
of substitutability of resources and pollution control, economists
defined away general questions of environmental limits to growth
(Perrings, 1987: 49).

It took some fifteen years, however, until the publication of *Our
Common Future* (Brundtland Report, 1987) for environmental

issues to begin to be taken seriously by nation states. This report of the United Nations World Commission on Environment and Development discussed many of the issues raised by *Limits to Growth*. Similarly, the publication in 1989 of *Blueprint for a Green Economy* (Pearce et al.) in the UK saw environmental questions being taken much more seriously and was a significant attempt to integrate economics with the environment. Previously, strange though it may seem, economics largely ignored the environment because, to a large extent, it was outside of markets and prices. In 1992, Meadows et al. published *Beyond the Limits*, in which they took stock of developments in the twenty years since their original report. If something like their scenario for sustainability is accepted, then it has profound consequences for debates over social rights and the mechanisms through which we distribute available resources within *and* between nations. And even if matters are not quite so urgent as they suggest, questions of social distribution and redistribution become more important as prospects for solving issues of resource allocation through growth and markets become more problematic. In particular, redistribution between nations becomes essential if world population growth is to be reduced, and in turn the pressure on world resources is to be eased. The distribution of resources within and between nations must become more equal if sustainable development is to be achieved. As markets largely ignore questions of distribution, questions of redistribution are predominantly political.

Though debate continues as to the *urgency* of resource depletion and levels of pollution, there is now a growing recognition that there is a problem, especially of pollution. Whilst some (Pearce et al., 1989) attempt to incorporate prices for the environment into their conceptual schema, others doubt that the practical problems of pricing can be overcome (Perrings, 1987), whilst still others see the response to the problems in terms of conservation, sufficiency and equity (Daly and Cobb, 1990). It is this latter, and perhaps longer-term, approach that underpins the argument for the development of social rights of citizenship as a response to growing resource constraints. This should be accompanied, at the same time, by reductions in the overall level of material consumption, mainly by the rich in developed nations. Thus, prong one of the approach is to develop social rights to the resources required for human development, whilst the second prong, as will be argued later, is to encourage the richer nations to reduce their material consumption by moving from 'having' to 'being' modes of behaviour. If jam tomorrow becomes more problematic, it becomes more important to examine the quality and distribution of jam today. Otherwise, conflicts over the distribution of increasingly scarce resources are likely to lead to increased social conflict. Redistribution of what we have now is important to maximising what we, or our children, may have in the future. As the Brundtland Report stated, 'Living standards that go beyond the basic minimum are sustainable only if consumption standards *everywhere* have regard for *long-term* sustainability. Yet many of us live beyond the world's ecological means, for instance in our patterns of energy use' (1987: 44; my italics). Furthermore, as the Brundtland Report observes, 'The environment does not exist as a sphere separate from human actions, ambitions and needs, . . . The "environment" is where we all live; and "development" is what we all do in attempting to improve our lot within that abode. The two are inseparable' (1987: xi).

Earlier chapters stressed the social interdependence of life. The notion of interdependence is further developed in Chapter 4, regarding interrelationships between people, economic resources, environment and development. Discussion of the issues involved in the debate over sustainability commences with a summary of the arguments contained in *Beyond the Limits* (Meadows et al., 1992) and then considers the concept of sustainability and some limitations of contemporary measures of economic well-being.

4

THE SUSTAINABILITY OF THE MEANS TO LIFE

As the behaviour of human beings and their institutional structures tends to change relatively slowly, we start with a more pessimistic definition of the problem of sustainability. Writing in 1992, Meadows et al. concluded that

> The human world is beyond its limits. The present way of doing things is unsustainable. The future, to be viable at all, must be one of drawing back, easing down, healing. Poverty cannot be ended by indefinite material growth; it will have to be addressed while the material human economy contracts. Like everyone else, we didn't really want to come to these conclusions. (1992: xv)

How did they reach these conclusions? They focused on the interconnections between changes in stocks and flows, and feedbacks and thresholds, in seeing the economy and the environment as one system. From this holistic perspective they examined global change and planetary limits to those kinds of changes continuing into the future. In examining global change they focused on population growth and economic growth, and relationships between the two. 'The human population and economy depend upon constant flows of air, water, food, raw materials, and fossil fuels from the earth. The limits to growth are limits to the ability of the planetary *sources* to provide these streams of materials and energy, and limits to the planetary *sinks* to absorb the pollution and waste' (Meadows et al., 1992: 8). Though many crucial sources are declining and many sinks overflowing, the current rates of throughput are more than is necessary to support a decent standard of living for all the world's people. However, the necessary choices to reduce the burden on the planet whilst improving efficiency in the use of material resources are either not being made, or not being made strongly enough to make the significant difference required. There is not sufficient urgency of concern. Through the use of computer models Meadows et al. provided simulations of different scenarios of the future. The core of their model was exponential growth (that is, doubling and redoubling) in population, use of resources and pollution and waste. Their first scenario concluded that if we go on much as we have done in the post-war years concerning population and economic growth, there will be social and economic collapse. However, acknowledging humanity's ability to look ahead, the authors built into their model various hypotheses about human cleverness, concentrating on technology and markets, and asked, 'What would happen if the world society began to allocate its resources seriously to the technologies of pollution control, land preservation, human health, materials recycling, and resource-use efficiency?' (1992: 9). Though this scenario improved prospects for a sustainable future, Meadows et al. concluded, 'because technology-market responses are themselves delayed and imperfect', this will not be enough. Something more is required; wisdom must supplement cleverness. For them wisdom involves two definitions of 'enough'; 'one having to do with material consumption, the other related to desired family size' (1992: 9). Their computer simulation then produces a world population stabilising at about 8 thousand million in 2030, in which all 'people achieve a level of material welfare roughly equivalent to that of *present-day Europe*. And, given reasonable assumptions about future market efficiency and technical advance, the material and energy throughputs needed by that model world can be maintained by the planet indefinitely' (1992: 9–10; my italics).

It is a sustainable future. This would seem to imply, however, that if all the projected 8 thousand million people are to attain the level of material welfare *currently* enjoyed by the average European, then many in the USA, Europe and Japan will need to reduce, and others level off, their current level of material welfare. These issues are not directly confronted in the discussion by Meadows et al., but are only obliquely inferrable from references such as: 'In fact we think it will be a revolution as profound as the Agricultural and Industrial Revolutions' (1992: 10). Indeed it would! Daly and Cobb (1990), however, in a work substantially influenced by the kind of analysis undertaken by Meadows et al., do provide a more detailed exposition of the changes they think are required. These are discussed later.

By 1992, Meadows et al. were able to rewrite their three conclusions of 1972 as follows:

(i) Human use of many essential resources and generation of many kinds of pollutants have already surpassed rates that are physically sustainable. Without significant reduction in material and energy flows, there will be in the coming decades an uncontrolled decline in per capita food output, energy use, and industrial production. (ii) *This decline is not inevitable.*

To avoid it two changes are necessary. The first is a comprehensive revision of policies and practices that perpetuate growth in material consumption and in population. The second is a rapid, drastic increase in the efficiency with which materials and energy is used. (iii) A sustainable society is still technically and economically possible. It could be much more desirable than a society that tries to solve its problems by constant expansion. The transition to a sustainable society requires a careful balance between long-term and short-run goals and an emphasis on *sufficiency, equity, and quality of life rather than on quantity of output*. It requires more than productivity and more than technology; it also requires maturity, compassion, and wisdom. (1992: xvi; my italics)

The issues of sufficiency, equity and quality of life are increasingly important considerations when we are discussing social rights, and are discussed later, particularly in Chapters 7, 14 and 16. Fundamentally, sustainable development requires the redistribution of resources within and between nations with a view to providing a social right to the material basis for human development.

What is sustainable development?

Following the Brundtland Report (1987), the contemporary debate over the environment and economic well-being has increasingly revolved around the concept of 'sustainable development'. The Report defined sustainable development as 'development that meets the needs of the present without compromising the ability of future generations to meet their needs' (1987: 43). At the heart of sustainable development lie two questions: first, the total amount of sustainable resources available to each generation, and, second, the pattern of distribution of those resources to each generation. However, because the manner in which resources are distributed affects their sustainability, we must pay much more attention to issues of primary distribution and, by implication, redistribution. As the Report observed,

Living standards that go beyond the basic minimum are sustainable only if consumption standards *everywhere* have regard for *long-term* sustainability. Yet many of us live beyond the world's ecological means, for instance in our patterns of energy use. Perceived needs are socially and culturally determined, and sustainable development requires the *promotion of values that encourage consumption standards that are within the bounds of the ecologically possible and to which all can reasonably aspire.* (Brundtland Report, 1987: 44; my italics)

How are such values and behaviour to be encouraged? They present particular difficulties, for dominant economic theory leaves questions of distribution to market mechanisms. Few economists show concern for the actual levels of living or resource consumption at either the top or bottom of the distribution. The response of some economists, having been confronted with the issue of sustainability that most previously dismissed as an issue, has been to attempt to incorporate resource constraints and pollution into the price mechanisms of the market. Resource constraints are incorporated by a process of 'discounting' and pollution through a range of tax measures. This was broadly the approach of Pearce et al. (1989). This took the view that the concept of sustainable development has implications for the way economic progress is measured, the pricing of goods and services and for general economic policy. Unlike Meadows et al. (1972, 1992) and the Brundtland Report (1987), however, few economists, exceptions being Daly (1990) and Perrings (1987), consider there may be a problem of continuing current trajectories of economic growth, or that present levels of material consumption are more than the earth's resources can sustain. Such recognition would require recasting the dominant economic paradigm to give priority to greater equity in the distribution of resources, and at the same time placing upper limits on levels of material consumption. It is doubtful whether the dominant economic paradigm can be adapted to consider such questions (Daly and Cobb, 1990; Perrings, 1987). As highlighted by Kuhn (1962), the initial response of scientists when their dominant paradigm is challenged is to develop auxiliary hypotheses so as to include the new information within the existing paradigm. This is broadly what Pearce et al. (1989) have attempted to do. At the same time they have had to acknowledge certain of the arguments found in Meadows et al. (1972) and developed more fully since, by Daly and Cobb (1990) and by the Brundtland Report (1987).

Pearce et al. (1989) provide us with a good example of how economists with a concern for the environment approach the issue of sustainable development. Importantly, they go beyond the traditional measure of standard of living in terms of real income per capita. 'There is now an emphasis on the "quality of life", on the health of the population, on educational standards and general social well-being. Sustainable development involves *devising* a social and economic system that ensures that these goals are sustained' (1989: 1; my italics). This implies that such a social and economic system does not yet exist. They summarise the means of achieving sustainable development in terms of three characteristics: valuing the environment, concern for future generations and equity within and between generations. Many economists have not been concerned with the 'value of natural, built and cultural environments, [now] environmental quality is seen as an increasingly important factor contributing to the achievement of . . . rising real incomes . . . and the "quality of life" ' (Pearce et al., 1989: 2). This is perhaps the beginning of a paradigm shift in economic thinking. Traditionally, economists have been preoccupied with the use of resources by today's generation and have tended to take for granted or left to politicians questions of equity of income and resource distribution within and between nations. The development of environmental economics is an example of reorientation in economic thought which holds it fundamental that there is an *interdependence* between the economy and the environment. 'There is an interdependence, both because the way we manage the economy impacts on the environment, *and* because environmental quality impacts on the performance of the economy' (Pearce et al., 1989: 4). It is the latter interaction which is less familiar to economists. The risks, highlighted by Meadows et al. (1972), of separating economy and environment became more apparent in the 1980s through, for example, manufacturers' production of chlorofluorocarbons (CFCs) that affect the ozone layer, resulting in global warming which in turn affects economic performance. Holistic systems analysis recognised this interdependence before conventional economics. It is now recognised more widely, but not yet internalised by all economists. However, Pearce et al. state that 'This *two-way interaction* is absolutely fundamental to sustainable development thinking' (1989: 4).

The problem as seen by environmental economists is that the services provided by the environment do not feature as an element of the price at which willing buyers and sellers exchange in the market. 'The central problem is that many of these services are provided "free". They have zero price simply because no market exists in which their true values can be revealed through the acts of buying and selling' (Pearce et al., 1989: 5). Put simply, because it has zero price, demand will exceed supply and the environment is used up without regard for its real value. The economists' solution is to give the environment a price so as reduce or control its use. However, markets are conventionally seen as balancing as price varies to balance supply and demand, and although prices for the use of the environment may be more easily incorporated *conceptually* in economic models, it is much more difficult in *practice* to insert a price for the environment into the exchanges between real live human beings. Such environmental cost insertion requires government action, for example in the form of a carbon tax. This would raise the costs of production and make goods more expensive. Thus, cost insertion by governments into market exchanges will make the good less competitive with those produced elsewhere.

This will act as a pressure on national governments to minimise such cost insertions to maintain competitiveness and economic growth, unless competitor nations also apply similar carbon taxes. The issues clearly become political, requiring not only understanding and agreement between nations but also the understanding and agreement of electors within each nation. Proper costing of the environment may lead to a fall in correctly measured GNP, and this would require careful explanation. It would be easy for political parties within nation states to compete with each other as to the minimal level of the required carbon tax to attract electoral support.

When real economic growth falls, how are such costs shared within the nation? The historical picture is that the poor suffer more than the rich, through unemployment and increases in the cost of living. What is sometimes neglected by economists is that the price people are prepared or able to pay for a product is affected by their total income. As prices rise, the income of the poor comes under greater pressure than that of the rich. The rich are more able to afford higher prices, whereas the poor consume less or have to go without. This is one of the difficulties with 'making the user pay' for the costs of pollution without also considering the ability of the poor to pay. As Quiney notes, 'Even if the price of basics such as electricity and gas or food is increased significantly, there are no good substitutes, nor can people easily cut down their consumption' (1990: 15).

The increasing importance of redistributing resources

However it is done, incorporating additional costs of the environment into exchanges where previously they were excluded will cause living standards to fall, at least in the short term. The question then is how that fall in living standards is distributed and what the political repercussions might be. Questions of distribution become more politically sensitive. That is why, if environmental costs are to be incorporated, governments and political parties must have new political agendas which depart from simple measures of political success in terms of conventionally measured growth in GNP. A politics of human development in the widest sense of 'quality of life' must increasingly replace the politics of economic growth. In this context unfettered market systems of production and exchange come increasingly into question if there is to be increased equity in sharing of that quality of life. Where resources are constrained, unless all citizens have a social right to the resources necessary for their human development, governments may not be able to sustain support. The situation becomes analogous to that of wartime Britain when greater equity in the distribution of food, clothing and other basic items was regarded as essential to maintain social peace when resources were problematic. These items were rationed to ensure basic needs were met. Whereas the 'common enemy' was easily identified during the war, it will be more difficult to convince people, especially the poor, of the common threat arising from resource depletion and environmental pollution. Pollard (1992), however, has noted that the living conditions of unskilled and semi-skilled workers improved during the war. Where expectation of rising living standards cannot maintain social peace, a more equitable distribution of the available resources is required, and is seen by the population as fairer in the circumstances. Social rights to the resources required for human development may provide an acceptable social goal in these circumstances.

Present versus future consumption: the question of 'substitutability'

There is a tendency for electorates and politicians to prefer current consumption. This preference, which reflects assumptions of un-limited wants and unlimited resources, must now be questioned. Time preferences for the environment, whether it is preferable to consume environmental resources now rather than later, depend upon whether it is judged preferable to consume now and *react* later to the future costs of that consumption, or whether to forgo present consumption patterns in *anticipation* of the future costs of that consumption. Where current consumption of the environment leads to irreversible damage, clearly losses cannot be compensated for in the future.

> The potential for irreversibility is thus sufficient for us to be highly sceptical of reactive policy: it should be undertaken only if we can be sure that damage can be reversed and at a cost that can be afforded by the future. What the future can afford depends on what we leave them by way of inherited wealth, natural and manmade. (Pearce et al., 1989: 9)

This raises the important issue of 'substitutability', in two senses. First, the extent to which natural capital can be substituted for by man-made capital as a form of wealth, and, second, whether there are unique elements of the environment whose chemical nature makes them essential complements to productive processes and for which there are no substitutes. As Georgescu-Roegen has pointed out, 'Every chemical element has at least one property that characterises it completely and hence renders it indispensable for some technical recipes' (1979: 1035, quoted in Perrings, 1987: 61). The second sense of substitutability involves assumptions or predictions about the ability of technology to always find or create human-made substitutes for elements of nature; the belief that the rising price of increasingly scarce natural resources will lead to incentives to technological innovation to produce alternatives. 'Because of its strange assumptions of perfect substitutability of matter the [early] models of the liberal economists assume the economy may expand without limit at the expense of its environment, and dispose costlessly of unlimited quantities of waste material within its environment' (Perrings, 1987: 5). As soon as such an assumption is given a time dimension its ludicrous nature is apparent. It is a science fiction world in which key minerals or materials available in nature are inevitably substituted for in the future when they run out of their usable form. The axiomatic nature of the early economic models deludes their believers into thinking that they have omnipotence over the physical reality and physical properties of the environment. It denies that once certain resources are used they cannot be used again. Because of technological innovation some substitutability will be possible, but such innovations will themselves use resources and consume energy. This leads to the question of whether the accumulation of man-made capital to be passed on to future generations will compensate them for the loss of natural capital that they will inherit.

Further problems related to time preferences for consumption concern the issues of 'uncertainty' and 'surprise'. These arise from the pervasive nature of the environmental impacts of economic activity. In the view of Pearce et al.,

> This pervasiveness arises from the simple fact that all economic activity uses up materials and resources and requires energy, and these, in turn, must end up somewhere – in dumps, dissipated in the atmosphere, disposed of to the oceans or whatever. This pervasiveness . . . contributes to the uncertainty about how environmental impacts will manifest themselves. (1989: 10)

However, because such impacts are poorly understood, they may, as Meadows et al. (1992) and Perrings (1987: 48) observe contain unexpected 'surprises' that may be extremely costly or impossible to respond to. The long-term effects of Chernobyl provide an example as to the uncertainty of the long-run costs of pollution of the environment, as does the effect of CFCs on the ozone layer. And as Pearce et al. acknowledge, 'There is high potential for "surprises" in climatic change' (1989: 14). Moreover, 'there are really no rules for choosing which policy to undertake in the face of uncertainty. A risk-averse strategy favours anticipatory and not reactive environmental policy' (1989: 10). Again, such decisions concerning pollution control, in the absence of price signals in the market, are essentially political in nature. Furthermore, because these environmental impacts are global in nature they will require political action beyond the level of the nation state.

> No one country acting alone can do much to prevent or contain these impacts: only coalitions of governments world-wide can do this. Yet the costs of such coalitions are high in terms of changes to consumption and investment pattern. . . . International cooperation to contain greenhouse effects to an 'acceptable level' is vital and urgent. The urgency arises because of the nature of the risks if the worst outcome occurs; because the longer the delay the more the world is 'committed' to increased warming and hence increased danger; because future adjustment is likely to be expensive; and because the only form of containment is through international cooperation which will be complex and difficult to secure. Global pollution problems underline the need for anticipatory policy. (Pearce et al., 1989: 12, 18)

The problematic nature of 'optimal pollution'

Even where environmental costs can be incorporated into market exchanges, two important questions remain. First, will the price put on the environment be enough to *sufficiently* protect it, and second, once the income and job opportunities derived from proper use of the environment have been maximised, what then will protect the environment? Market pricing still leaves a situation where at some point in time the price of conserving the environment compared to using it becomes *too* high for certain people. This means that market solutions can buy time but in the long run may not be sufficient in themselves to protect the environment. Furthermore,

> Economic theory talks in terms of optimal pollution, and the aim is to minimise the costs of meeting that level. In the static theoretical world, any technical progress in methods of production which makes them less pollutive would result in increases in industrial output at the same level of pollution, *not as reductions in pollution level*. (Quiney, 1990: 18; my italics)

This has dangers as in the real world we do not know what an 'optimal level of pollution' is, because we do not have a concept of a limit to the *scale* of economic activity at the global level (Daly, 1990). Therefore, along with the proposals of Pearce and his colleagues we also need to start now to change people's life goals in a less materialistic direction. New understanding and perception will need to lead a value change before the time bought by market pricing of the environment runs out and we press against the limits to the scale of growth. That requires challenging the very dynamics

that underpin markets as systems of resource distribution. Fundamentally, markets must continually grow and expand. Once
resource constraints prevent this, technology may allow growth but
only so long as it is able to substitute for nature. This, too, will have
its limits. Thus we must start now the debate over new ways to
conserve and distribute resources, lest we are caught by 'surprise' as
we come up against limits to the scale of resource use. The
watchwords thus become conservation, sufficiency and redistribution. This becomes doubly important when we recognise that
projected growth in world population, about which Pearce et al.
(1989) says nothing new, will add significantly to pressures on the
environment.

Redistribution to the poor to reduce population growth

Daly argues that, 'Sustainable development ultimately implies a
stationary population. . . . Sustainability is compatible with a large
population living at a low level of per capita resource use, or with a
small population living at high levels of resource use per capita'
(1990: 37). Indeed, it is precisely poor populations which are
growing fastest that presently place great strain on their local
environment, just to keep alive. In global terms, however, the
higher consumption of rich nations may place the greatest strain on
the environment in terms of pollution. Perhaps most profound is
debate over the energy that goes into transforming natural capital
into man-made capital. The wealth of the industrialised nations
depends upon enormous consumption of energy both directly by
industry and directly and indirectly by consumers. This requires a
scale of energy use and a scale of waste production that many
believe is not sustainable, and not transferable to developing
nations. Redistribution of world resources to the poor was recognised by the Brundtland Report as essential if their birth rates were
to decrease. If the environment can sustain further economic
growth it must be directed more to the world's poor. Market
relations between rich and poor nations have, however, steadily
decreased the economic growth of poor countries as world commodity prices have halved in the past ten years or so. At the same
time debt repayment from poor to rich nations has taken some one-
third of their GNP. Market relations between rich and poor nations
are draining the natural resources of the poor nations to meet the
consumption needs of the rich. Meanwhile, the poverty of the poor
nations causes them to over-exploit their natural resources not so
much to feed themselves as to supply the rich nations. These sales in

turn provide them with income to repay their debts. This requires redistribution from rich to poor. The rich must pay more for the goods they consume so that the poor may live. Of course, we might just leave them to die; that would be more economically efficient and consistent with treating human beings like any other commodity! However, the world-wide nature of interdependence places a moral obligation on us to try to take citizenship beyond the nation state.

A systems approach to sustainability

As economics focuses upon the pricing of privately owned resources within market exchanges it encounters major practical difficulties where markets for goods do not exist, as in the case of the environment. Economics tends to presume there is a market for everything or that, at least conceptually, markets can be hypothesised. However, following Bowers (1990), Quiney observes that 'the problem is one of *missing* markets, rather than one of assigning property rights or of pricing known costs. This means that there is no opportunity for, or possibility of, an economic bargain over the environment because the market does not exist' (1990: 13; my italics). It may therefore be fruitful to consider another approach to environmental issues. Compared to economics, systems theory offers a more holistic approach to environmental questions. Meadows et al. argue,

> From a systems point of view a sustainable society is one that has in place informational, social, and institutional mechanisms to keep in check the positive feedback loops that cause exponential population and capital growth. That means that birth rates roughly equal death rates, and investment rates roughly equal depreciation rates, unless technical change and social decisions justify a considered and controlled change in the levels of population and capital. In order to be socially sustainable the combination of population, capital, and technology in the society would have to be configured so that the material living standard is adequate and secure for everyone. In order to be physically sustainable the society's material and energy throughputs would have to meet economist Herman Daly's three conditions: (i) its rates of use of renewable resources do not exceed their rates of regeneration, (ii) its use of non-renewable resources do not exceed the rate at which sustainable substitutes are developed, (iii) its rates of pollution emission do not exceed the assimilative capacity of the environment. (1992: 209)

Where there are doubts about the operability of environmental pricing and its effectiveness in reducing resource depletion and pollution, physical limits to the scale of resource use and pollution may be more effective in achieving sustainability.

Herman Daly's approach to sustainability

Important contributions to the debate over sustainability have been made by World Bank economist Herman Daly. As his definition of sustainable development goes beyond conventional economic models it seems clearer and preferable to that of Pearce and his colleagues. Daly has highlighted three conceptual issues that he believes are critical for clear thinking about economic development and the environment.

> The first issue is whether the basic conceptual starting point of economic analysis should be the circular flow of exchange value, as it presently is, or the one-way entropic throughput of energy-matter. The latter concept is virtually absent from economics today, yet without it, it is impossible to relate the economy to the environment. . . . Economists are interested in scarcity, and during the formative years of economic theory the environment was considered an infinite source of raw materials and an infinite sink for waste materials. . . . Only scarcity entered into exchange. (1990: 25, 27)

The economy takes from the environment what are often finite resources with no account of whether they are renewable, then at the end of the production or consumption process it produces waste that is released into the environment. Whilst economists focus on the changing exchange value of a combination of man-made and natural resources that are broadly seen as substitutable, the systems approach focuses on the finite character and non-substitutability of natural resources. The theoretical abstraction involved in economics tends to treat economic exchange as an enclosed system, ignoring the social and environmental interdependencies involved. This, as will be argued later, is a form of sub-system rationality. To adapt Daly's phrase, the economy is treated by most economists as a 'self-contained perpetual motion machine' (1990: 15) where resource inputs and waste outputs are treated as infinite.

> The concept of optimal allocation among alternative *uses* of the total resource flow (throughput) must be clearly distinguished from the concept of an optimal *scale* of total resource flow relative to the environment. Under ideal conditions the market can find an optimal allocation in the sense of Pareto. *But the market cannot find an optimal scale any more than it can find an optimal distribution. The latter requires the addition of ethical criteria; the former requires the further addition of ecological criteria.* . . . Once throughput is recognised as a fundamental and indispensable concept, then the question of its optimal scale within a finite economic system naturally arises, along with the recognition that the question is different from that of optimal allocation. *Once we face the question of limiting scale, we recognise the collective or social nature of the task and the futility of leaving it up to individualism of the market,*

which can only deal with allocation. The independence of allocation from distribution is widely recognised; the independence of allocation from scale is not widely recognised, but it is easily understood. In theory whether we double the population and the per capita use rate, or cut them in half, the market will still grind out a Pareto optimal allocation for every scale. Yet the scale of the economy is not a matter of indifference. . . . In trying to reduce scale issues to matters of allocation (just get the price right), economics has greatly obscured the relation between the economy and the environment. While an optimal allocation can result from the individualistic marketplace, the attainment of an optimal scale will require collective action by the community. (1990: 25–6; my italics)

It is the uncontrolled *scale* of economic activity that is endangering the environment and leads to arguments for its social control. Thus, far from leaving such decisions to the marketplace, we shall need to improve democratic understanding, procedures and participation such that we make collective choices as to the appropriate scale of economic activity. This seems likely to be a particularly difficult political question in the coming decades. During the past two hundred years, and especially since the growth of the adult franchise, electorates have expected and parties have promised to continually improve material living standards through economic growth with little regard for the scale of economic activity and its impact on the environment. Conveniently, economic growth promised more for everybody without having to address the politically sensitive issue of inequality. 'The growth ideology is extremely attractive politically because it offers a solution to poverty without requiring the moral disciplines of sharing and population control (Daly, 1990: 26). It poses no questions to the rich and their use of resources, whereas issues of scale do raise questions of what the rich spend their money on in terms of resource use. They can command markets to supply to them those goods that use up scarce resources which should be conserved and shared out in relation to need. If the cake ceases to grow, however, the only way to address the improvement of the poor is through redistribution. Thus, if sustainability is to be pursued, this presents both electors and parties with quite new choices. They will have to consider not only redistribution within nations but, even more crucial and contentious, redistribution between nations (Brundtland Report, 1987). Political and economic thinking must develop at the same time a global perspective and a more local perspective. The need to go beyond and below the nation state is argued in Part Three.

Daly's third issue relates to how sustainable development is to be attained. He suggests that

much confusion could be avoided if we could agree to use the word 'growth' to refer only to the quantitative scale of the physical dimension of the economy. Qualitative improvement could be labelled 'development'. Then we could speak of a steady-state economy as one that develops without growing. . . . Limits to growth do not imply limits to development. . . . What is being sustained is a level, not a rate of growth, of physical resource use. What is being developed is the qualitative capacity to convert that constant level of physical resource use (throughput) into improved services for satisfying human wants. (1990: 27, 33)

Daly rightly notes that these three interrelated issues threaten the absolute priority of growth in economic policy. If national success may no longer be measured by increase in GNP, new measures of 'human development' must replace 'economic growth' as measures of national success (Doyal and Gough, 1991; Nussbaum and Sen, 1993). Daly's conclusions here seem close to those of Pearce et al. (1989). The focus of measurement changes from growth to the 'quality of life'. Once political goals focus more strongly on the 'quality of life' of citizens, elected governments will need to take social rights more seriously, and that means taking redistribution of resources more seriously.

5

GNP AND THE MIS-MEASURE OF PROGRESS

The current widespread use of gross national product or GNP as the measure of welfare, and growth in GNP as a measure of improvement in welfare, is increasingly recognised as misleading. The basic problem has been well summarised by Pearce et al.:

> If GNP increases that is economic growth. GNP is constructed, however, in a way that tends to divorce it from one of its underlying purposes, to indicate, broadly at least, the standard of living of the population. If pollution damages health, and health care expenditures rise, that is an increase in GNP – a rise in the 'standard of living' – not a decrease. If we use up natural resources then that is capital depreciation, just as if we have machines we count their depreciation as a cost to the nation. Yet depreciation on man-made capital is a cost while depreciation of environmental capital is not recorded at all. . . . It is not really credible any longer to use the national accounts that measure GNP to indicate the quality of life. (1989: 23)

As the debate has turned from economic growth towards sustainable development, so we find commentators from different perspectives agreeing we need new measures of the 'quality of life' (Lederer, 1980; Miles, 1985; Doyal and Gough, 1991: Chapter 8; Sen, 1987; Nussbaum and Sen, 1993). The United Nations Development Programme (UNDP) in 1990, for example, produced a 'new human development index (HDI), which combined life expectancy, educational attainment and income indicators to give a composite measure of human development' in each nation (UNDP, 1992). L.R. Brown has observed, 'Developed a half century ago, GNP accounts helped establish a common means among countries of measuring changes in economic output over time. For some time this seemed to work reasonably well, but serious weaknesses are now surfacing . . . [It] can provide a misleading sense of national economic health (1990: 8). Yet, as measurement is central to economics, and rational calculation is seen as a defining feature of industrial societies, unless the way progress and improvement are measured is appropriate, then we will not know where we are going.

There is a tendency for governments, for example, to exaggerate their national wealth by treating receipts from liquidating natural assets as income. During the 1980s the British government 'sold the family silver' through the one-off generation of income from the privatisation sales of accumulated public capital. Once income from privatisation sales dries up it must be replaced by a regular flow of income from another source. Daly cites two reasons why tradition-ally, in the USA, natural capital has been left out of National Accounts:

> (1) The scale of the economy relative to the environment used to be negligible, and consequently natural capital regeneration was either automatic or perceived as unimportant because it was not a limiting factor. However, between 1950 and 1986 the *scale* of the world population doubled (from 2.5 to 5.0 thousand million), while the *scale* of gross world product and fossil fuel production each quadrupled.
>
> (2) Neo-classical economic theory has taught that manmade capital is a near perfect *substitute* for natural resource, and consequently, for the stock of natural capital that yields the flow of these natural resources. . . . Contrary to neo-classical assumptions, natural and manmade capital are more *complements* than substitutes, with natural capital increasingly replacing manmade as the limiting factor in development. . . . Strong sustainability would require maintaining both manmade and natural capital intact separately, on the assumption they are not really substitutes but complements in most production functions. (1990: 34; my italics)

It is possible, as Daly suggests, for traditional measures of GNP to be improved by adjusting National Accounts. 'First, subtract an estimate of the value of natural capital depreciation. Second, subtract an estimate of defensive or regrettably necessary expendi-ture made to protect ourselves against the unwanted side effects of other production' (1990: 35). That still leaves, however, a funda-mental drawback of GNP as a measure of well-being. 'It includes only those goods and services which are sold on the market' (Lecomber, 1975: 15). Thus it incorporates a very narrow definition of value, and leaves a lot of good things out of the measure of 'standard of living'. In measuring the 'quality of life', we have to remind ourselves that it is not only things that are bought and sold in the market that have value. This requires a substantial review of measures of economic well-being and the development of other indicators of the quality of life, and in Fromm's (1979) terms consideration of questions of 'being' rather than 'having'. The UNDP's Human Development Index is a move in that direction, as is the pioneer work of Doyal and Gough (1991). Fromm's ideas are explored in Part Six.

Wants, needs and sufficiency: changing values and aspirations

Brown, Flavin and Postel have identified several important assumptions that underlay the call for an environmentally stable society.

> First, is that if the world is to achieve sustainability, it will need to do so within the *next 40 years*. Second, though new technologies will develop, . . . the future we sketch here is based only on existing technologies and foreseeable improvements in them. Third, is that the world economy of 2030 will not be powered by coal, oil and natural gas. Societies are likely to opt for diverse solar-based systems. Fourth, is assumptions about population size. A stable or slowly declining population of 8 billion by 2030. Lastly, by 2030 the world will have achieved a more equitable and secure economy. (1990: 174–5; my italics)

A similar time-scale has been identified by Meadows et al. (1992). However, although it certainly seems reasonable to assume time is limited, these estimates may be too pessimistic. On the other hand, the significant changes in societal values and goals envisaged will not come overnight. Commentators emphasise a number of important points. They refer to

> changes in the social, economic and moral character of human societies. During the transition to sustainability, *political leaders and citizens alike will be forced to re-evaluate their goals and aspirations, to redefine their measures of success, and to adjust work and leisure to a new set of principles that have at their core the welfare of future generations.* (Brown et al., 1990: 187; my italics)

In similar vein, Daly comments that if sustainability is to be achieved, 'the "needs of the present" requires some *distinction between basic needs and extravagant wants*. . . . Sustainable development is about *sufficiency* as well as efficiency' (1990: 35; my italics). Redirecting economic activity away from wants to needs presents major problems for neo-classical economic theory and the operation of market economies. This has been extensively examined by Doyal and Gough (1991).

The Brundtland Report observed that, 'The earth is one but the world is not. We all depend on one biosphere for sustaining our live. Yet each community, each country, strives for survival and prosperity with little regard for its impact on others' (1987: 27). The interdependence of 'sub-system rationalities' is much neglected, as are conflicts between sub-systems. There are a large number of national sub-systems whose rationality in pursuit of their interests conflicts with the rationality of the total world system. Similarly, within each nation commercial undertakings may be considered sub-systems.

An individual firm may manufacture a product to sell at a particular price, and there may be willing buyers at that price. An exchange takes place. But, due to the nature of our interdependent world, every exchange between two parties, the willing seller and willing buyer, involves other people and they often bear costs that are ignored in the exchange between buyer and seller.

6

EXTERNALITIES: ENVIRONMENTAL AND SOCIAL COSTS

Economic theory long denied the importance of external costs because they threaten the axiomatic assumption that prices contain all the information required to make a decision. 'Once we begin to conceptualise the behaviour of economy-environment systems over time, unprotected by the assumption that the price system contains all the information we need to know, we find not the comfortable order of stable or relatively stable equilibria but a seemingly chaotic drive to change' (Perrings, 1987: 7–9; Daly and Cobb, 1990: Part One). Once it is acknowledged that the price at which exchanges between buyers and sellers takes place in the market excludes environmental costs, that price then contains a degree of arbitrariness. The question then arises whether externalities are a more pervasive phenomenon ignored by market exchanges. This can only be answered at the overall system level, yet the building block of economic theory is exchanges at the micro-level. As long as there are willing buyers and sellers at a particular price the individualistic focus of market exchange finds it convenient to assume externalities are not important. For many years that was the assumption concerning environmental costs. Economists now recognise their existence, but are there also social costs involved in market exchange which go unrecognised by economists' focus on micro-exchange? There are reasons to believe there are if we examine social systems as a whole, as we were required to do in the case of environmental costs. Then, the interdependencies of an environmental kind have their counterpart in interdependencies of a social kind. Evidence of 'progress' in terms of economic growth ignores the unemployment caused by constant technological change and changes in consumer preferences. So long as human labour power is treated as a commodity, then the economist's mode of thought is unconcerned with the depreciation of the market value of labour power manifested in either unemployment or in lower wages. Cheaper price of exchange results for willing buyers and sellers, but only by ignoring the humanity of the carriers of labour power, who bear the social costs of unemployment and low pay. It is ironic that economists are now more likely to recognise environmental externalities than they are social externalities. The former has arisen from a global or systems approach to environmental costs. Because focus on willing buyers and sellers is a micro- or sub-system approach it can ignore costs outside that micro-exchange, but the costs are nevertheless real and can be identified at the level of the total system. This was highlighted by Kapp in 1950 (see Kapp, 1969), but largely ignored at that time. More recently Perrings has observed, 'Although external effects are all-pervasive, it is by no means universally accepted that they constitute a significant "problem" for economic theory' (1987: 1). It is slowly becoming more widely acknowledged that 'environmental external effects represent fundamental flaws in the axiomatic structure of the dominant models of the economic system' (Perrings, 1987; see also Daly, 1990: 51–8).

Many exchanges take place in the market not because all costs are incorporated in the price but *because they are not*. They involve cost-transfer-maximising behaviour. Indeed, much apparent profit-maximising behaviour may in reality result from cost-transfers to third parties or society as a whole. The exclusion of social and environmental costs from such exchanges is a major cause of inequality in the distribution of resources both within and between nations.

The market exchanges of individuals are essentially limited in their rational calculus. If taken as a measure of economic value, they destroy many of us, through unemployment, in the same way that they threaten the environment. It is the very basic economic individualism of the values embodied in market exchange that limits the discipline's ability to deal with these problems. Economic individualism ignores third party effects. Recognition of the interdependence of economy and environment undermines economic individualism, as does recognition of our social interdependence. Thus, at a different level, arguments can be made concerning social costs of social change. As mentioned earlier, Richard Titmuss observed that, 'The social costs of economic advance tend to be pushed out of sight by the strength of the collective motive for an improvement in the material fabric of life' (1958: Chapter 6). It is important that we recognise that economic change brings both costs and benefits. We tend to welcome the benefits but neglect the costs, yet the meeting of need for one group may increase needs for other groups. It is suggested that it is characteristic of technological change in industrial society that it provides opportunities for shifting some portion of costs from the producer and consumer on to third parties or society as a whole. And that this is a *general and pervasive phenomena* of highly industrialised technological society. 'The concept of social costs may be criticised on the grounds that it covers a great variety of social losses and, therefore, lacks clear definition and precision' (Kapp, 1963: 20), or that 'social costs are the price we pay for economic growth – the short run inefficiency of an alleged long run efficiency' (1963: 17).

We have already noted, however, the question mark placed on conventional measurement of economic growth once we recognise environmental costs of economic growth. All this is really a call for improved evaluation of social costs, instead of accepting the illusion of quantification and precision implicit in much current economic discussion. As Kapp observed, 'to trace and identify the social costs of growth and long run efficiency is not only a necessary undertaking, but is clearly called for by the canons of economic rationality. . . . Nothing is more irrational than an incomplete system of cost accounting' (1963: 17).

Externalities are manifestations of social interdependence within complex industrial societies, and between them and less developed nations. Social costs require we recognise the far-reaching cumulative interdependencies of individuals, institutions and nations as *typical* phenomena of a complex global economic system (Kapp, 1963). Such social interdependence undermines the individualistic assumptions of economists' theory of rational human behaviour. Thus, 'if economic units with *unequal power* are able to shift part of their costs to others – and moreover are able to plan their sales and consumer demand through sales promotion strategies – market costs and prices must be regarded as more or less arbitrary and indeed unreliable measures of economic rationality' (Kapp, 1969: 335; my italics). Indeed, it may be more appropriate to describe much business and industrial activity not simply as 'profit-maximising', but as *'cost-transfer-maximising'* in that it involves attempts to transfer costs to third parties or society as a whole. We need to know the extent to which apparent profitability of an activity is really a function of the power and ability to transfer costs from a particular firm's business transactions to third parties, for example pollution of rivers, technologically produced unemployment. Thus, much economic growth and social change in industrial societies takes place only because there is little compensation for these social losses. Much economic and social change can be justified only by ignoring the social costs to less powerful members of society or of other nations. Economists' assumption of willing buyers and sellers presumes an equality of power between the agents, and that neither has the power to ignore consequences for third parties. Market exchanges are assumed to be coercion-free – they may not be.

Of course, not all externalities are intentional. In circumstances of interdependence the unintended consequences of purposive action may place major costs upon sections of the population even as others are benefiting, for example in the case of unemployment, which many people will experience for long and repeated spells over their lifecourse (Sinfield, 1981). These unintended consequences may be more easily identified within nation states than outside them. They may remain relatively invisible when they affect other nation states, especially developing countries. It is much more likely that citizens affected will give voice to their concerns to democratic national governments, and that they will respond for fear of electoral defeat. Unintended consequences that fall outside the nation state are more easily ignored and may not be capable of influence by the nation states affected. Social costs of market activities are a major example of unintended consequences that arise where willing buyers and sellers make an exchange that does not embody third-party costs and their effects. These neglected aspects of economic activity lead to increased inequalities in the total economic and ecological systems at national and international level. Indeed, this power to maximise cost-transfers may be an essential foundation of profit within a company or within a nation.

The existence of externalities poses difficult problems for the notion of profitability. *Profitability becomes a sub-system property*, at individual, company or nation state level; for example, the costs of unemployment transferred to the wider society whilst firms shedding labour make profit at the sub-system level. Though it may be argued that in the long term the profitability of individual firms will lead to economic growth that will reduce unemployment in the wider society.

Current preoccupation in the UK with citizens as consumers (Saunders, 1990) overlooks the fact that many consumers are also producers. How they are treated as producers influences the choices they may make as consumers. Consumerism is a blinkered perception of citizens that fails to consider them in the round and ignores the interdependence of production and consumption. What is seldom considered by the willing buyer is the nature of the processes and relationships that lay behind the manufacture of the goods at the price paid. The price may be lower than competitors for a whole range of reasons, for example the lower pay and unsafe working conditions of employees. The manufacturing process may depend on unsustainable use of resources or have resulted in toxic waste that had environmental costs for the local community, the whole nation or people in another country.

Because such costs occur on an everyday basis due to the interdependencies of complex industrial activity, a framework of law that lays down rules and regulations is essential. That is why today, much more than even fifty years ago, market economies must be managed by democratically elected governments. Market economies have always been managed to some degree and in varying ways and for varying purposes: there is no free market. For example, the post-war Bretton Woods agreement that created the World Bank, the IMF and GATT was an international system of management. And at national level the post-war use of Keynesian techniques was used by most governments. Until very recently, management of market economies has given relatively little regard to social costs. This despite the growth in interdependence of economic activities, and growing awareness of environmental interdependence.

Here it is important to note that economic activities are but one form of social activity and economic behaviour should not be artificially separated from the total activities of human beings. We are concerned with the real behaviour of people, in all its complexity, and not its confinement to abstract economic models. It is only by examining the actual behaviour of firms that we can hope to tease out how profit is obtained and which costs may be involved. This is a far more difficult task than assimilating behaviour to economic models through the making of sometimes odd assumptions (Thurow, 1983; Perrings, 1987). In consequence, research into economic behaviour needs to be increasingly interdisciplinary. The social sciences have become too separate, too isolated from each other. This is most true of economics, which through its econometric techniques talks largely to itself, hidden behind its mathematical formulae. Not all economists are happy with this situation: Lester Thurow (1983) has produced a powerful reflective study of their approaches, as have others such as Hirsch (1976).

Uncoupling the notion of progress from the pursuit of economic growth

Mishra (1984) has highlighted how social policy debates have tended to take for granted questions of production and have concentrated on issues of distribution. Until the 1970s economic growth tended to be taken for granted even if it was not as large as was hoped or was subject to unfortunate fluctuations. It was reasonable to assume there would be some economic growth each year. This meant that social policy development could be financed out of growth whilst at the same time real incomes might rise. Thus, each year economic growth enlarged the cake that was to be distributed; shares of the national cake could grow in absolute terms and some shares might increase as a proportion of the total cake without a decline in the actual size of any share. That was the promise of economic growth. Economic growth enabled difficult political problems of an increase in one person's share requiring a decrease in the share going to someone else to be avoided, or so it seemed. However, this was to assume, first, that the way in which economic growth was measured was a satisfactory measure of the improvement in national well-being, and, second, that there were no externalities or social costs left outside the calculation.

What is to replace the promise of economic growth? Without economic growth, as understood so far, issues of redistribution come to the forefront of political debate. Conflicts over distribution may increase. It may be argued that wealthier groups in industrial societies have so far been able to defend their wealth by holding open the prospect to the less wealthy that they may aspire to that level of living in the reasonably near future. If that promise cannot be met, the less wealthy can only improve their lot by redistribution downwards from the wealthy.

Perrings summarises the economists' solution to the problems of the interdependence of the economy and environment as follows:

> two judgements underpin the market solution [to environmental con-
> straints to economic growth]: that it is proper to discount the future
> effects of present activities at a positive rate, and that it is proper to seek
> that discount rate in the current transactions between private economic
> agents. This arises from a strong technological optimism among econ-
> omists; it is the assumption that in the long period substitutes exist for all
> exhaustible resources, and *the implicit assumption that individuals know
> not only what is best for them, but what is best for society as well*. (1987:
> 128–31; my italics)

This chapter has argued that in complex industrial societies where social and environmental interdependence leads to pervasive exter-nalities individual market decisions have important limits to their rationality for society as a whole. In the market, the good of the individual does not equal the good of society. Therefore, as was argued earlier, as human beings are social creatures the good of society must be sought through collective agreement as to what is the 'common good'. It is a social project not an individual one. It is a matter for social dialogue and debate. It is a matter of politics. Drawing upon the research of anthropologists Perrings observes,

Wherever common property has been collectively regulated, it has if anything led to the under-utilisation and not the exhaustion of environmental resources. Collective interest in the sustainability of production turns out to be a much more powerful incentive to conserve a given set of resources than private interest in the maximisation of the income derived from exploiting resources wherever they are located. (1987: 162)

Can we come to collective agreement over such regulation in complex industrial societies? What are the implications of this debate over economic growth and environmental and social externalities for the debate over citizenship and social rights? Discussion here picks up Meadows et al.'s conclusion that we require 'an emphasis on sufficiency, equity, and quality of life rather than on quantity of output. It requires more than productivity and more than technology; it also requires maturity, compassion, and wisdom' (1992: xvi), and that, in the widest sense, requires expression through political participation. Social progress is to be sought through political participation rather than economics, or, more specifically through a return to 'political economy'.

Part Two of this book has sought to highlight a paradox. In Part One it was argued that we need to develop social rights to provide the material base for the development of the 'social self', whereas, in this section, it has been argued that there are growing environmental and therefore material limits to such projects. The resolution of this paradox is to be sought in redistribution of current and future available resources within and between nations. This requires a more informed and participatory form of democratic politics and a change in value orientations, particularly in developed nations, away from 'having' towards 'being'. This entails better understanding and perception of human relationships, as is argued in Part Six. We turn now to consider some issues of redistribution, sufficiency and political participation.

PART THREE
A POLITICS OF REDISTRIBUTION, SUFFICIENCY AND PARTICIPATION

It was suggested in Part One that if social rights to sufficient resources for the human development of all citizens were to be provided, this would require a redistribution of resources. It was further suggested in Part Two that as we approach some of the environmental limits to economic growth as a route to material well-being, the redistribution of resources would come more to the centre of the political agenda. In both cases the quality of democratic participation and consent become more important, if redistribution for sufficiency is to be achieved. Furthermore, participation in decision-making enables people to express themselves, to test their ideas against those of other citizens, and this aids the development of the 'self'. The 'self' is both expressed and developed through participation in the exercise of power. For the moment, however, we focus on questions of redistribution and sufficiency involved in this new politics. Issues of political participation are discussed later.

7

REDISTRIBUTION AND SUFFICIENCY

Redistribution and sufficiency are two related policy issues. First, there are problems related to redistribution from the developed to the developing nations and, second, there is a need for a radical change in lifestyle concerning resource use within the industrialised nations. Both essentially require action within developed industrial countries to redistribute resources within and between nations. A key political debate is slowly emerging as concern for sustainable economic behaviour grows in both industrialised and developing nations (Brundtland Report, 1987). This debate involves difficult confrontations with existing assumptions concerning political and economic beliefs. Conventional economic analysis in terms of market choices that ignore the social costs of economic and environmental interdependence cannot fully address these issues. It is a political question. Can democratic political systems address the questions of redistribution whilst at the same time responding to the expectations of rising living standards within nation states? If conventional lifestyle aspirations in terms of ever-increasing material well-being cannot be met, it is the aspirations to the development of the inner self that must be addressed. People will need to be asked what is really fundamentally important to their lives, rather than leaving the market to offer and advertise more and more material consumption. Are such value changes politically realistic? It does not seem so, yet what may be the alternative? The potential long-term degradation of the planet and levels of living for many people that do not allow for their human development? And what of the future of our children? Can politicians brought up to seek political support largely by offering electorates material goods now turn the political agenda to fundamental questions of 'being' rather than 'having'? This seems highly problematic, yet discussion within communities may provide some surprising answers concerning 'sharing'.

The economists' assumption of wants being endless can no longer remain unquestioned, ever-expanding consumption is not possible, and has never been enough anyway. Thus current political offerings to citizens as consumers are largely misdirected. Consumerism and its attached world of advertising have, in many ways, turned means into ends. Citizens must be addressed with quite different values and with a perspective of human interdependence rather than individualism. It is individuality of the social self that becomes more important and the individualism of consumer choice of material goods that is reduced (Turner, 1986). The balance needs to change. So long as we did not come up against the limits of finite resources and environmental degradation, economic growth appeared to be the path to increased human well-being. That was really, however, only a means to an end, yet it has increasingly become an end in itself. As Alasdair MacIntyre (1981) has observed, we have lost a sense of 'telos'. Where is the purpose in life? What is it all about? It must be about providing sufficient material resources to all for their human development. We must concentrate on the development of the person but, at the same time, not ignoring that we all require sufficient access to material resources. A positive sense of self in Fromm's sense of 'being' is a realisable goal for all of us whereas there is a limit to the 'having' of resource-intensive products. How much more do we really need to buy; how important is a particular purchase? What do we actually get out of it? Is what we really want to be to be bought in the market or is it something else? As Mills (1970) asked, what kind of people have we become and what kind of people might we be?

The poor, the rich and sufficiency

The issues of sustainability discussed above call for a new kind of politics based less on the promise of ever-increasing material well-being and more on the quality of life and the relationships between people. The quality of relationships between people crucially revolves around the degree of inequality within and between nations. Not just in the sense of whether we feel we live in a 'just' society that 'fairly' distributes the resources, but whether the distribution of resources is objectively such that none are socially excluded. Townsend sought to define poverty objectively in terms of social exclusion. Calculations by Desai (1986) based upon the data collected by Townsend (1979) and Mack and Lansley (1985) suggested there was an income threshold in Britain below which people were socially excluded from participating in the commonly shared activities and resources of their society. That threshold was around 150 per cent of the then Supplementary Benefit level, implying that the minimum benefit levels were too low for poorer people to maintain their social participation in society.

The issue of sustainable development also means asking awkward questions about levels of living at the top of society. The Brundtland Report observed,

> Living standards that go beyond the basic minimum are sustainable only if consumption standards *everywhere* have regard for *long-term* sustainability. Yet many of us live beyond the world's ecological means, for instance in our patterns of energy use. Perceived needs are socially and culturally determined, and sustainable development requires the promotion of values that encourage consumption standards that are within the bounds of the ecologically possible and to which all can reasonably aspire. (1987: 44; my italics)

Resources are so unequally distributed that both the poor and the rich make, for quite different reasons, unsustainable demands on environmental resources. In attempting to maintain a level of social participation in society the poor have less regard for environmental quality, 'Poverty reduces people's capacity to use resources in a sustainable manner, it intensifies pressure on the environment' (Brundtland Report, 1987: 47). On the other hand, the rich can demand a range of goods beyond the average which they do not really 'need'. Where resources are finite the concept of 'wasteful use' becomes particularly important. Cars that have low miles per gallon in the use of finite petrol resources are a clear example of waste that the rich can afford but the wider, and poorer, community cannot. Thus the unequal distribution of income and wealth can lead to the wasteful use of resources, simply because in markets money commands resources or resource-intensive products. The rich are, per capita, the disproportionate consumers of the world's resources. Once it is accepted that those who are not rich cannot achieve the level of resource consumption of the rich without destroying the world – the consumption levels of all cannot grow indefinitely – then the disproportionate consumption of the rich is seen as immoral, not to say life-threatening to the poor. Rich people can afford to waste resources much more than poor people.

Behaviour to a large extent reflects levels of income and other resources. In market economies rich people can afford to demand relatively frivolous items whilst the poor, even in industrial nations, cannot demand even basic necessities such as housing or nutritious food. Most people in the industrialised nations have wardrobes full of little-used clothes, many of which they are unlikely ever to wear again due to changing fashion. Changing 'fashion' has long been a major marketing ploy that leads to more and more production of goods whose time-span of use is essentially and intentionally limited to fuel market growth. Fashion shoes have become a classic example; they do not even keep out water. Following from Brundtland, a concept of 'over-consumption' must be placed alongside that of 'poverty' and the relationships between the two understood both within and between nations. Once we conceptualise resource use in terms of both poverty *and* over-consumption, then we can consider democratically the concept of 'sufficiency'. Thus, it may be made easier for the poor of the world to obtain at least minimum levels of living if those of us who live beyond the world's ecological limits change our consumption patterns. A narrowing in the distribution of resources would help both the poor directly and all members of society indirectly by maintaining a sustainable world. However, it is recognised that the political slogan 'we offer you less' does not have the ring of the conventional slogan 'we offer you more'. Yet the truly realistic questions relate to less or more of what, and its *security*. Discussion of privilege has recently been introduced into the citizenship debate by Scott (1992; 1994).

Sufficiency and the redistribution of paid work

Strangely, we all seem to want to continue to work the same long hours no matter how much our material standard of living rises. This is undoubtedly related, in part, to the insecurity we feel concerning a level of material well-being that depends upon our being able to sell our labour power. We need the security of a reliable flow of income. We have to work to obtain the means to life, but what is the 'life we wish to lead'? This never-ending chase after increased material consumption does not seem to satisfy for many the development of the 'social self'. At the same time it threatens the sustainability of life itself on a finite planet.

If minimum but reasonably high levels of material well-being can be assured, then we may look for less material goals to pursue. It is a question of distinguishing means and ends. What are the ends of material acquisition? Is it just more and more material consumption or is it human development? Are there social limits to material consumption or are we continually looking for 'things' to buy and consume (Hirsch, 1976)? What do we really want from life? In many respects much of this argument is not new, though it takes place in this new environmental context. As Brown et al. reflect, 'Throughout the ages, philosophers and religious leaders have denounced materialism as a viable path to human fulfilment. Yet societies across the ideological spectrum have persisted in equating quality of life with increased consumption. Personal self-worth typically is measured by possessions, just as social progress is judged by GNP growth' (1990: 190). It is likely that future generations will regard these as childlike aspirations encouraged by the misplaced individualism of market capitalism. As Meadows et al. observe,

A sustainable society would be interested in qualitative development, not physical expansion. It would use material growth as a considered tool, not a perpetual mandate. It would be neither for nor against growth, rather it would begin to discriminate kinds of growth and purposes for growth. Before this society would decide on any specific growth proposal, it would ask what is the growth for, and who would benefit, and what it would cost, and how long it would last, and whether it could be accommodated by the sources and sinks of the planet. A sustainable society would apply its values and its best knowledge of the earth's limits to choose only those kinds of growth that would actually serve social goals and enhance sustainability. And when any physical growth had accomplished its purposes, it would be brought to a stop. (1992: 210)

It is the insecurity of the labour market that leads to the domination of the economic over the social in people's lives. As people are treated as commodities, as things, in the labour market, so they come to relate to the world around them in terms of things and their ownership. Their human capacities for development and for re-creating their social world remain undeveloped. The non-sustainability of ever-increasing material consumption may break that 'commodity' relationship, but only if those material resources that are sustainable and available are distributed in a more equitable fashion. In the industrialised nations this may mean working fewer hours and consuming less material goods, and instead using this increased de-commodified time for education and self-development. We still tend to under-estimate, for example, the manner in which experience of higher education transforms people's sense of their 'self'. Mature entrants to university often comment on this experience. They say they have become a different kind of being. This is a vital aspect of self-development.

The industrial nations, in part, consume more than their share of the world's material resources because they insist in continuing to work long hours as commodities. This is partly manifested in the situation in the UK whereby more than three million people are totally unemployed (ignoring the black economy), whilst some 25 million are working 38 to 40 hours per week. At the same time, about a quarter of male manual workers in employment work more than 48 hours per week (Department of Employment, 1992). There are gross inequalities in paid hours of work. We should recognise, however, that long hours often reflect low pay, and in the 1980s an increasing number of the newly created jobs in Europe were part-time, mainly occupied by women.

Greater equality of resource distribution may reduce competitive comparisons and feelings of relative deprivation. Above a certain level of income, people may tend to work fewer hours, the more equally resources are distributed. If many of us took less paid work, we could have more leisure time; that is, time that we control. It would mean a reduction in marketable time and marketable relationships. At the present time the unequal spread of unemployment might be interpreted as an unequal spread of leisure time, though benefits are too low for unemployment to be experienced as leisure. If work and unemployment, however, were more evenly shared, both those in and out of work might experience gains to their lives. That would also require a more equal redistribution of labour market reward itself, as suggested in the later discussion of a Basic Income.

Underlying this speculation is the question whether the full employment (40 hours a week for 48 weeks a year) of all people aged 16 to 60/65 is sustainable in industrial countries. With a growing world population, can the impact of this work activity and its related consumption of world resources continue? If it cannot, then redistribution of paid work, leisure and income, and, from a gender perspective, the redistribution of unpaid caring and domestic work, become issues of major public concern. This may require new definitions of 'full employment', perhaps measured over a person's lifecourse and involving fewer weekly hours of full-time paid employment (Gorz, 1982). This is not idle speculation for in the course of writing debate broke out in Germany over reducing working hours to 35 per week, and this was introduced in some industries. Similar proposals were part of the European election campaign in a number of nations in 1994.

A new politics of redistribution leading to social rights of sufficiency

Growing environmental concern seems to be placing new questions on the political agenda as it opens up new ways of thinking about the ways we live. Meadows et al. argue that, 'For both moral and practical reasons any sustainable society must provide material sufficiency and security for all. To get to sustainability from here, the remaining material growth possible – whatever space there is freed up by higher efficiencies and lifestyle moderations on the part of the rich – would logically be allocated to those whose need is most' (1992: 211). They identify three areas where completely new thinking is most urgently required. First,

> *Poverty*: 'Sharing' is a forbidden word in political discourse, probably because of the deep fear that real equity would mean not enough for everyone. 'Sufficiency' and 'solidarity' are concepts that can help structure new approaches to ending poverty. Everyone needs assurances that sufficiency is possible and that there is a high social commitment to ensure it. And everyone needs to understand that the world is tied together both ecologically and economically. (1992: 215)

The development of a range of social rights can provide assurance concerning sufficiency. Interestingly, the encouragement of lower levels of material consumption through, for example, the security of a Basic Income would contribute to sustainable development in the interests of all citizens. The arguments for a social right to a 'citizen's income' are discussed in Chapter 14.

Second, Meadows et al. argue for an economic system where work will develop the creative abilities of everyone. Work would become, more than at present, an expression of human development.

> *Unemployment*: Human beings need to work, to have the satisfaction of personal productivity, and to be accepted as responsible members of their society. That need should not be left unfulfilled, and it should not be filled by degrading or harmful work. At the same time, employment should not be a requirement for the ability to subsist. Considerable creativity is necessary here to create an economic system that uses and supports the contributions that all people are able and willing to make, that shares work and leisure equitably, and that does not abandon people who for reasons temporary or permanent cannot work. (1992: 215)

Finally, whilst emphasising sufficiency of material needs, the authors also highlight the neglected areas of human existence related to non-material needs, and provide one answer to the question: what kinds of people do we want to be?

> *Unmet non-material needs*: People do not need enormous cars; they need respect. They do not need closets full of clothes; they need to feel attractive and they need excitement and variety and beauty. People do not need electronic entertainment; they need something worthwhile to do with their lives. People need identity, community, challenge, acknowledgement, love, joy. To try to fill these needs with material things is to set up an unquenchable appetite for false solutions to real and never-satisfied problems. The resulting psychological emptiness is one of the major forces behind the desire for material growth. A society that can admit and articulate its non-material needs and find non-material ways to satisfy them would require much lower material and energy throughputs and would provide much higher levels of human fulfilment. (1992: 216)

How can we evolve a social system that tries to solve these problems? A shared understanding will need to develop and that is more likely to emerge from participation in debate. We may apply our critical reasoning to these problems and attempt to reconstruct our social world in more conscious directions. In all democratic societies, however, opportunities to participate are limited, as is knowledge and understanding. It is remarkable how few opportunities there are to experience the cut and thrust of debate within organisations that have democratic decision-making procedures. And few people, for example, have the skills to properly conduct democratic debate. Yet, such participation is itself educative and developmental. Debating issues does change people's minds, even if they do not acknowledge it at the time. In this sense, participation in democratic decision-making is essential to the development of the 'self'. If the changes suggested above are to gain support people will need to be given more opportunities to participate in decision-making. More institutional forms of participation must be created so that more people can be brought into debate over the kinds of people they want to be.

8

POLITICAL PARTICIPATION: BEYOND AND BELOW THE NATION STATE

It was argued much earlier that the exercise of political rights was crucial to the notion of democratic citizenship. In the twentieth century, both civil and social rights are mediated by the exercise of political rights. Therefore if all three elements of citizenship are to be effective in providing rights we shall require effective political institutions. Furthermore, as the non-material world is socially created, and therefore is continually re-created, many more people should be brought into participating in the processes of re-creation. Through participation in re-creating their social worlds, people not only express themselves in action and in debate, they also develop their 'self'. In expressing your own views in debate you test them against the views of others, which is an expression of their sense of 'self'. There is a confrontation of views, ideas and projects. Each, despite him- or herself, learns to appreciate some aspects of the other's ideas, views and projects. Each appreciates some aspects of the 'self' of his or her opponents through debate. Each is dependent on the other for the development of his or her 'self'. As they pursue their projects, people change their 'self' and adjust their projects. Those who have experienced positions of power and decision-making where such exchanges take place will know how their 'self' is expressed in such encounters. Their sense of 'self' is tested, confidence developed and powers of argument and intellect expressed. Such people develop an enhanced sense of their 'self' and its potential. Unfortunately, few have such experience. In contrast, those who do not engage in such exchange and debate have less opportunity to express and test their 'self', thus it is less likely to develop.

Brown et al. echo the belief in the creative potential of human beings to remake their world and develop their 'self'. 'In the end, individual values are what drive social change. Progress towards sustainability thus hinges on a collective deepening of our sense of responsibility to the earth and to future generations. Without a reevaluation of our personal aspirations and motivations, we will never achieve an environmentally sound global community' (1990: 175). Social responsibility is likely to evolve out of deliberating with others as to what human projects are possible. So, we are concerned to see more opportunities for deliberation above, and particularly below, the nation state. The view that political participation must be strengthened both 'below the nation state', and 'beyond the nation state' is growing (Brundtland Report, 1987; Gould, 1988; Pearce et al., 1989; Daly and Cobb, 1990). It was aptly summed up by contributors to the World Watch Report: 'It may be among the ironies of future political development that even as individual nations move to decentralise power and decision making within their own borders, they simultaneously establish a degree of co-operation and co-ordination at the international level that goes well beyond anything witnessed today' (Brown et al., 1990: 189).

Thus we are concerned with two processes: decentralising decision-making downwards and developing international co-operation beyond the nation state. These processes are developing in Europe through the ambiguous principle of 'subsidiarity' (Spicker, 1991). There is a search for the most appropriate level at which different kinds of decisions should be made, with an emphasis on it being the lowest level. We can see the process of decision-making beyond the nation state embodied within the drive towards European integration of economics, politics and social policy. This is a slow and erratic process, as shown in the discussion of social policy in Part Five. The contrasting process of decision-making below the nation state can be found in the emergence of the European 'committee of the regions', as well as in the established federalism of Germany and demands for regional autonomy in Spain or for devolution in Scotland.

It was observed earlier that the re-emergence of debate over citizenship in the UK was in part a response to the ideas of the New Right. There has been a parallel response to the experience of New Right governments in the UK. A debate has developed over the manner in which the UK is governed, a debate as to the nature of political rights in the country. This is discussed briefly, but serves to illustrate something of the crisis of citizenship that has developed in the UK, a fuller discussion of which can be found in Dearlove and Saunders (1991).

At the centre of concern is the unique British constitutional convention of 'parliamentary sovereignty'. Put simply, 'Parliament could make and unmake any law whatsoever; there was no higher legislative authority; and no court was in a position to declare properly passed Acts of Parliament invalid or unconstitutional'

(Dearlove and Saunders, 1991: 32). There is concern that this had developed into an 'elective dictatorship'. Though this term was originally coined by the Conservative Peer Lord Hailsham with reference to the Labour government of the 1970s, it highlights a continuing weakness of the British Constitution. This problem has a number of dimensions and may be summarised as follows:

1   Under a 'first past the post' electoral system it is possible in the UK for a party with considerably less than majority electoral support to obtain a large majority of seats in Parliament. This results if electoral support is split among three parties each with significant support. During the 1980s the Conservative Party formed strong governments with around 42 per cent of the popular vote.
2   Once elected, that large parliamentary majority means the party can force through almost any legislation it wishes by 'whipping' its backbench members. Parliamentary scrutiny and amendment of legislation are limited. The Cabinet effectively decides, though the Lords may delay.
3   Furthermore, the position of Prime Minister in Cabinet has become more presidential, yet without the checks on that power that exist in the USA.

As the UK has no written constitution, no Bill of Rights, no proportional representation in elections and no Freedom of Information Act, political power is highly centralised, yet can have less than majority support of the electorate.

Through the way in which the doctrine of 'parliamentary sovereignty' has evolved into an 'elective dictatorship', it is argued that all three of Marshall's elements of citizenship have been undermined. In the field of civil rights there has been an extension of police powers, the interception of communications, restrictions to freedom of assembly, controls on trade union membership, and the 'public interest' defence in revealing secret government decisions has been removed (Ewing and Gearty, 1990).

In the field of political rights, political power has been drawn away from democratically elected local government and either centralised in the ruling party at Westminster or placed in the hands of 'quangos' (quasi-autonomous non-governmental organisations) whose members are appointed by the government Minister concerned. It is argued that these are largely the placemen and placewomen of the Conservative Party. Thereby, control by the party at the centre is increased. Furthermore, the strong support for some form of devolution to Scotland has been ignored.

In the field of social rights, benefit levels have been made less generous and have become more means-tested. A market system has been introduced into the National Health Service that is undermining its service ethic as cost-efficiency slowly undermines medical need. Schools are given financial incentives to opt out of local democratic community control. Public services are increasingly required to contract out their work to private companies through competitive tendering. Tenders are largely won on a basis of a worsening contract of employment for staff. In these circumstances the debate over citizenship, largely taking place within academic circles, spills over into a debate and a demand for constitutional reform among sections of the general public. These demands for constitutional reform have coalesced in an organisation called Charter 88 (1990), its name derived from Charter 77 in former communist Czechoslovakia. They argue for twelve reforms:

1 A Bill of Rights.
2 A Freedom of Information Act.
3 An accountable government.
4 A fair electoral system.
5 A reformed House of Commons.
6 A democratic upper chamber to replace the House of Lords.
7 Reform of the judiciary.
8 Redress for all state abuse.
9 Independence of local government.
10 Scottish and Welsh assemblies.
11 Devolution of power.
12 A written constitution.

It will be seen that these proposals are intended to provide citizens with greater information about their society and its government, to increase their knowledge. Through proportional representation political institutions would become more representative and political debate would become more open in the manner in which people express their 'self'. Through independent local government and devolved assemblies political participation and decision-making below the nation state would be increased. More opportunities for participation in democratic debate and decision-making would be provided and more people would be able to play an active part in re-creating their social world. Both Liberal and Labour Party programmes are being influenced by this debate, and a change of government seems likely to transform the quality and structure of UK democracy dramatically.

The emerging new politics also has concern for sustainable development and political participation beyond the nation state. This is not easy for most of us who have grown up with the nation state as the focus for democratic decision-making. However, the difficult issue of nation states giving powers to supranational agencies is evolving most strongly within the European Community, whereby a range of policy issues is decided either by unanimous or by majority votes of the member states. What is lacking so far in this process is proper democratic participation in decision-making on these issues.

On the other hand nation states can make international agreements. As most commentators agree, including Pearce et al. (1989), international agreement is required to set either taxes or physical limits to pollution. The mechanism may be the United Nations or groupings of industrial nations such as the European Community. Or, for example, the meeting of governments in 1987 which 'adopted an Environmental Perspective to the Year 2000, that defined a broad framework to guide national action and international co-operation for environmentally sound development' (IUCN/UNEP/WWF, 1991: 1).

The obtaining of international agreements on pollution control and resources depletion, if they are to be successful, also requires the devolution downwards of decisions so that debate may take place at the local community level. This is not as contradictory as it may at first seem, but becomes more important as we replace the goals of economic growth with sustainable development. The difficult choices involved in sustainable development will require widespread understanding and democratic consent.

> Making the difficult choices involved in achieving sustainable development will depend on the widespread support and involvement of an informed public and of non-governmental organisations, the scientific community, and industry. Their rights, roles and participation in development planning, decision making, and project implementation should be expanded. (Brundtland Report, 1987: 21)

This will require major debates that involve as much participation as possible in framing the new rules and priorities for distribution. A political consensus or at least majority political support will be required to carry out the necessary social changes, if the basic needs of all people are to met in an equitable fashion. The Brundtland Report has set the tone for this debate.

> Poverty is not only an evil in itself, but sustainable development requires meeting the basic needs of all and extending to all the opportunity to fulfil their aspirations for a better life. A world in which poverty is endemic will always be prone to ecological and other catastrophes. Meeting essential needs requires not only a new era of economic growth for nations in which the majority are poor, but an assurance that these poor get their fair share of resources required to sustain that growth. Such equity would be aided by political systems that *secure effective*

citizen participation in decision making and by greater democracy in international decision making. Sustainable global development requires that those who are more affluent adopt life-styles within the planet's ecological means – in their use of energy for example. (1987: 8–9; my italics)

For industrialised nations this implies that growth should be directed towards the reduction of inequality within the nation state and, particularly, between nation states. In these circumstances what needs refining is not so much the mathematical models of economists but the processes for participation in the democratic political process. If a project for sustainable development is to be agreed, more people must be brought into deliberation on the issues. As control of human numbers and the distribution of their production and consumption are central to achieving sustainability, citizens must be brought more and more into decision-making if their values and aspirations are to adjust. In this respect participation has an important educative function in thrashing out shared understanding as to needs and priorities. Increasingly some of the most important choices have to be made collectively, whereby governments are elected to undertake chosen social projects, which underpin the ability of individuals to undertake their chosen life projects.

These demands for increased participation in democratic politics clearly increase the agency of government in our lives, and thus run counter to the views of the New Right. The notion of government overload became a central feature of New Right criticism of government in the UK in the 1980s (Mishra, 1984: Chapter 2). Their response was to argue for the removal of decisions from democratic government, which it was argued could not cope efficiently, and to transfer more and more decisions to the market, where more efficient decision-making would take place. This was part of the rationale of British governments for privatisation of public assets as well as reducing the powers of democratically elected local governments. Though privatisation removed criticism from government decisions to those of the market, the market has little *public* accountability. It is market exchanges between willing buyers and sellers that determine the outcome of events not democratic pressures. Those with less material resources tend to lose out. Meanwhile, the increased inequality arising from less democracy and more markets went unaddressed and was increased by restructuring the tax system away from direct to indirect taxation.

Social interdependence in a world of increasing externalities presents us with the choice of leaving social costs to lie where they fall through reliance on markets, or to attempt to compensate for them through democratic state action. Markets divide people through the pursuit of their individual interests, whereas political participation forces people, however imperfectly, to deliberate on the public interest. Due to networks of interdependence, more and more the choices of individuals affect the choices of others within the nation state and outside it. For example, market exchanges mobilise growing networks of interdependence stretching beyond national boundaries. Complex industrial societies based upon technological divisions of labour widen choice whilst at the same time extending networks of interdependence. Thus, increased freedom of choice invokes increased interdependence, and increased interdependence means that our choices have increased external effects. There is an increase in serendipity; an increase in unintended social costs to others in the networks of interdependence. In the past market exchanges may have involved none other than the two people who were party to the exchange; this is less and less the case. Today social costs are so widespread that ignoring them constitutes a major element of irrationality in all industrialised countries and in their external relationships. We are seeking new mechanisms to deal with these complex networks of interdependence that have grown out of the desire to extend individual choice through markets. This raises the Durkheimian dilemma of satisfying what are seen to be humanity's unlimited wants. This was the promise of economic growth in a world without environmental constraints. This is less of a dilemma, however, if wants are replaced by needs, and these are not seen wholly in material terms. If material consumption is only a means to an end, then human goals may be pursued through other means. That is the argument of Fromm (1979). If the needs of men and women for human development are less dependent upon the accumulation of material resources, and we accept the earlier proposition that human beings make themselves, then the manner in which they make themselves may become less dependent upon material resources. Less material lifestyles have not been encouraged by the marketisation of society, and it is likely to be difficult to convince publics that such lifestyles are desirable. More open political debate on these problems would be a start.

Once all three of Marshall's elements of citizenship exist together, then in political democracies it is the exercise of political rights that sets the rules, the parameters for civil and social rights. It is therefore essential to have a range of levels of rule-making institutions that provide opportunity for participation. The answer to the Durkheimian dilemma of social control in a context of supposed unlimited wants must be sought through systems of democratic participation and control that enable citizens to make their society in a sustainable fashion. The New Right's promise of freedom through ever-expanding individual choice through uncontrolled markets, in a context of interdependence, externalities and unsustainable economic growth, becomes a recipe for social breakdown through increasing inequality, and eventual environmental catastrophe. Perrings perceptively observes that,

> What marks off the quiescent environmental strategy is the role of the collectivity in translating the collective perception of intertemporal equity into rules of behaviour and their supporting institutions. . . . Underpinning the anti-growth ideas of most proponents of the stationary state is an egalitarianism that is fundamentally antithetical to the present-oriented individualism of the market solution. It demands that the collectivity restrain the narrow selfishness of the current members of society in the interests of members yet to come. (1987: 150)

Societies have to decide the balance between rampant market individualism that is destructive of society and the environment, and authoritarian collectivism that is destructive of individuality. Increased democratic participation in decisions on collective provision of social rights for all should enable us to steer a path between these two extremes. We are seeking a concept of citizenship that desires social integration through the development of social structures that provide a degree of sustainable economic and social equality that is widely accepted as morally legitimate. That moral legitimacy will lie in the extent to which in developing a common project it also allows for the development of the 'self' of all. One of the main investments we can make in our societies is to produce citizens who have the opportunity and confidence to debate their views with others. In the clash of ideas each will develop him- or herself at the same time as he or she develops each other. Increased political participation is necessary both for the development of society and for the development of the individual 'self'. There is further reflection on these issues in Part Six. For the moment we turn to an exploration of social rights.

PART FOUR
EXPLORING SOCIAL POLICY AND SOCIAL RIGHTS

It is noticeable how little public support for the welfare state has been eroded (Taylor-Gooby, 1991), despite the apparent influence enjoyed by New Right ideas in the 1980s. This is largely because state welfare provision is considered a core element of citizenship in Western societies, even if electors do not use the actual word 'citizenship'. At the same time, it is true that the 1980s saw significant changes in the form and generosity of welfare provisions with the growth of means-testing and 'workfare' type programmes (Hills, 1991a). This part, therefore, whilst making some arguments for state welfare provision, concentrates more on the *forms* of such provision, in particular social security, and the extent to which they meet the criteria of a social right of citizenship. Thus, we are concerned with 'the way in which welfare provision ought to be viewed' as part of a notion of citizenship. It will be argued that the concept of citizenship requires a social right to welfare, but not all welfare provisions meet the criteria of a social right. For, as King and Waldron have argued,

> Such provision should constitute more than a simple safety net; it refers to the universal provision of education, health, social security and welfare benefits (financed through a system of redistributive taxation), available as attributes of citizenship and not granted as a residual fund to help the least well off cope with excessive hardship as Hayek and Friedman would accept. (1988: 418)

As was argued in Part One, a fundamental basis for citizenship in modern industrial societies arises from our social interdependence. This interdependence brings both benefits and costs but these are unequally distributed. Of central importance among these benefits and costs are those that arise from labour market processes. Most fundamentally, 'welfare state institutions counter market process by providing citizens with a minimum income, a basic standard of social services (health and education) and respite against economic uncertainty' (King and Waldron, 1988: 420–1). As social change brings costs as well as benefits, an essential characteristic of much welfare state provision is that it provides *compensation* to those who bear the costs of other people's progress (Titmuss, 1968). This is primarily a recognition of the twentieth century, though sometimes a reluctant one. This was not the response, however, of society in the nineteenth century when the poor were often punished rather than compensated. Poverty was seen then as a personal trouble for which the individual was responsible rather than a public issue arising from the structure and organisation of society. The poor were subject to social exclusion lest they contaminate the rest of society. It is important to note the way in which the poor in Britain were treated in the past. Far from poverty being an occasion for action to provide resources to the poor to maintain their participation in society, it was an occasion for their deliberate exclusion. As Marshall noted, the 1834 Poor Law

> treated the claims of the poor, not as an integral part of the rights of citizenship, but as an alternative to them – as claims which could be met only if the claimants ceased to be citizens in any true sense of the word. For paupers forfeited the civil right of personal liberty, by internment in the workhouse, and they forfeited by law any political rights they might possess. (1950: 81)

The poor were excluded from citizenship. During the twentieth century, however, we have to a degree progressed through conditional inclusion to universalistic programmes, though there have also been periods of retrenchment in some nations (Baldwin, 1990; Esping-Anderson, 1990). As King and Waldron note,

> At the minimum, to associate welfare provision with citizenship is to make a proposal about how welfare *should* be handled in society. For example, . . . it is to endorse the replacement of the Poor Law approach to welfare with provision for need that is given universally, that is provided without supplication or stigma and that avoids as far as possible the invidious operation of official discretion. (1988: 422; my italics)

These issues are examined below.

9

SOCIAL EXCLUSION AND SOCIAL RIGHTS

It is argued that welfare provisions that involve means-testing, stigmatisation and discretion present key difficulties for the concept of citizenship and the development of social rights. The welfare states of most nations are a combination of 'means-tested' and 'as of right' benefits. The latter may be further divided between those that depend on a contribution record, such as unemployment benefit, and those that are tax-financed, as happens with Child Benefit in the UK. Only Child Benefit meets the citizenship criteria as it does not depend on labour market participation nor is it means-tested. However, we note that eligibility for means-tested Income Support for lone-parent families does not require the parent to seek work.

In the UK, differential treatment under the social security system revolves around the distinctive roles of 'means-tested' and 'as of right' benefits. Furthermore, these two types of benefit often interact to constrain choice for those having difficulty in maintaining economic activity in a competitive labour market. National Insurance benefits are payable 'as of right' in contingent situations of unemployment, sickness and retirement, *provided* the necessary contribution conditions have been met. Thus, most importantly, any other income or savings the applicant or applicants' spouse may have do *not* affect the level of benefit paid; they top it up. Other resources do not have to be diminished or consumed to establish need. Therefore, persons solely dependent on insurance benefit may have total spendable resources above the insurance benefit level.

Unlike the USA and continental Europe, the term 'compensation' is little used in the UK. However, where the means to life depend upon selling your labour power, National Insurance benefit should, more appropriately, be regarded as a *compensation* for a loss of workplace income. The concept of a social right to a compensation for an unwarranted social and economic loss is central to any notion of solidarity between citizens. More on this later.

By contrast, Income Support in the UK (introduced in 1988 to replace Supplementary Benefit) is payable on a 'means-tested' basis. This either tops up National Insurance benefit or totally replaces it where eligibility for insurance benefit has been exhausted or a person is barred from it by the rules and regulations of the scheme. The basic level of Income Support may be reduced to take account of elements of other income or savings the applicant or the applicant's spouse may have. Savings in excess of £8,000, for example, bar a person from Income Support, whilst savings between £3,500 and £8,000 are presumed to provide income that is then used to reduce the level of Income Support. Other resources, therefore, have to be drastically reduced before a person is eligible for Income Support. Thus, persons partly or solely dependent upon Income Support are more likely to have much lower spendable resources than those on National Insurance benefit. Prolonged lengths of time on either benefit results in a fall in living standards, but especially, and earlier, for those on Income Support. In certain circumstances, however, a person may be ineligible for both benefits, and thus receive no form of benefit, and have recourse to charity or begging (Sinfield, 1981).

The distinction between 'as of right' and 'means-tested' benefits, though not unambiguous (Abel-Smith and Titmuss, 1987: 227), is important both in terms of the ideological debate over welfare provision and its cost, and in terms of the different ways claimants are treated and helped to maintain their income *and* their social inclusion (Deacon and Bradshaw, 1983). The original Beveridge proposals of 1942 envisaged a system of benefits 'as of right' based upon insurance contributions from both employee and employer, plus a sizeable tax contribution from the Exchequer (Field, 1987). At the centre of Beveridge's proposals was the intention to end the means-tested dependency of the pre-war years.

> National Assistance [the forerunner of Supplementary Benefit and Income Support] is an essential *subsidiary* method in the whole Plan for Social Security, But the scope for assistance will be narrowed from the beginning . . . The scheme of social insurance is designed itself to guarantee the income needed for subsistence in all normal cases. (Beveridge Report, 1942: 12; my italics)

It was Beveridge's expectation and intention that, with full employment, dependence upon the means-tested 'safety net' would diminish as the National Insurance scheme became fully established. Due mainly to the initial level of benefit being set too low by the post-war Labour government, and the subsequent reluctance of governments to make the expected level of Exchequer contribution, this has not proved to be the case (Field, 1987). Whereas in 1948, about 1 in 33 persons were dependent upon National Assistance, by the early 1990s around 1 in 7 persons were dependent upon Income Support (Oppenheim, 1993). A major reason for this increase, primarily in the past twenty years, has been the growth in unemployment, and particularly long-term unemployment, and, to a lesser extent, the increase in single-parent households due mainly to the increase in divorce. At the same time it must be recognised that the real value of Income Support has increased, but not to the same extent as average earnings. The income of the poor is falling behind that of the working population.

Social exclusion and means-tested benefits

Means-tested benefits are considered inferior to 'as of right' benefits for a number of reasons. Applicants are required to go through a detailed examination not only of their financial means but also, due to the rules of eligibility, into many aspects of their private life and personal behaviour. Many find the continual requirement to prove themselves deserving of assistance intrusive, demeaning and stigmatising. A question hovers over all applicants: are they deserving? As S.M. Miller has sharply observed,

> Stigma threatens the person stigmatised, the programme, and the society which condones stigmatisation. The stigmatised person experiences the fact of being separated from the rest of society, of being treated as someone different, marginalised, as less than others, as not worthy of the everyday exchanges and transactions that make up the community. This experience often produces a 'spoilt identity', a self-image which is damaged and diminished impeding the autonomous actions of the individual. (1987: 13)

A means-tested benefit cannot provide a social right of citizenship because it threatens the integrity of the 'self'. This is because the processes attached to proving you are deserving of means-tested benefits are processes of social exclusion. The stigma attached to means-testing threatens not only the applicants' sense of 'self', but also their ability to function as normal human beings. Their moral character is in question. Furthermore, partly in consequence of these processes a significant number of people fail to claim means-tested benefits. There is a problem of take-up, although the average amount forgone tends not to be large (Deacon and Bradshaw, 1983). It was Titmuss (1968) who made the important observation that many so-called benefits are not benefits at all in the sense that they add to a person's well-being. They are in fact partial compensations for losses, for bearing the costs of other people's progress in societies where we are all socially interdependent. In such cases how can a compensation for loss be means-tested?

Throughout most of the post-war years there has been a steady drift on to means-tested benefits in Britain. This took a sharp upturn in the early 1970s with the introduction of Family Income Supplement (now Family Credit) to low-paid workers with dependent children, and a national system of rent rebates (now Housing Benefit). It was the multiplication of forms of means-tested assistance for low-paid workers and their steep 'tapers' which resulted in Britain in the severe disincentives of the 'poverty trap'.

First, an aside. It is commonly assumed that people are basically motivated to maximise their income and that lower taxes will increase motivation to work harder. However, policies tend to assume that different groups of workers respond in different ways. In Reports of the National Board for Prices and Incomes in the 1960s it was argued that higher-paid professional groups needed significant pay increases to maintain or improve their incentives to work and innovate. Yet, in other reports they argued with respect to the lower-paid workers that they should first improve their productivity before they would be considered worthy of a pay increase. Apparently, higher-income groups work harder if you give them the money first, whereas lower-income groups work harder if you promise to pay them more in the future. The rich need the spur of more riches, whereas, according to Gilder (1982), the poor need the spur of their poverty. Similarly, in the 1980s it was argued by the government that reducing high marginal rates of income tax on the highest paid would release their pent-up desires to innovate and be more productive. The assumption was that if you left people with more money from work they would work harder; that higher income is an incentive to higher productivity. Subsequent research has cast doubt on that claim, as people do not always have opportunities to work harder than they already are or once they get more money they may work less and choose to increase their leisure time (Brown and Jackson, 1990: Chapter 17). It is not clear that there is a simple link, in either case, between pay and productivity. Social assumptions and prejudices affect perception as much as evidence. Work and motivation are more complex than simply money; it involves loyalty and trust, status and control at work, concepts of fairness (such as a 'fair day's work for a fair day's pay') and a trade-off between work time and leisure time. What may be more important in affecting productivity levels is the ratio of capital investment in equipment and technology that is used in co-operation with labour power.

Returning to the 'poverty trap'. This provides a rather different perspective on income and incentives as they affect low-paid workers. The poverty trap involves the interaction between labour

Table 9.1 *An example of the impact of the 'poverty trap'*

Increase in earnings of:	100.0p
Less income tax	20.0p
Less National Insurance	5.0p
Leaves	**75.0p**
Loss of Family Credit (70% of 75.0p)	52.5p
Leaves	**22.5p**
Loss of Housing Benefit (65% of 22.5p)	14.6p
Leaves	**7.9p**

market earnings, the tax system and the social security system. The phenomenon has a quite distinct and technical meaning. It affects low-paid people in work who are entitled to means-tested benefits such as Family Credit and Housing Benefit. The Family Credit eligibility limits can be regarded as an officially accepted poverty line for low-paid workers with children. However, at the same time that they are considered poor enough for means-tested benefits they are also considered rich enough to pay income tax and National Insurance contributions. The tax and social security systems are working against each other. For the low-paid, a £1 increase in earnings from work can be dramatically reduced by the combined reduction in means-tested benefits and the requirement to pay tax and National Insurance on the increased pound of earnings. As can be seen from Table 9.1, the effective loss of income of 92.1 pence in the pound is much higher than the 40 pence lost by the highest income-earners through the formal income tax system.

The poverty trap may operate over a wide band of earnings resulting in a poverty plateau such that for 'families with earnings in the bottom quartile of the income distribution [it results in] the end of differentials in disposable resources. It does not matter what they earn or what extras they earn, their living standards will be the same as everyone else's' (Walker, 1982: 368.4). This provides a quite different perspective on earnings and incentives from that found in discussions of the formal tax system.

While some industries are partly subsidised by Family Income Supplement (now Family Credit), both employees and employers are to some extent trapped by the arrangements. Workers and their representatives find it more difficult to achieve real improvements in net income, whilst employers find their wage costs increasing without this being reflected in the long-term improvement in the standard of living of their employees. There can be no moral justification for this distribution. If it were widely realised it would surely cause an outrage. 'The poverty plateau is thus not necessarily concerned with work incentives, it is about the morality of governments' encouraging workers to work harder and to claim means-tested benefits, when the combined effect may simply trap them in to poverty' (Walker, 1982: 11).

The combined consequences of sharp reduction in other resources, the stigma and social exclusion, the low take-up, the failure to recognise the compensation element of benefits, and the disincentives of the poverty trap all make means-testing an unacceptable basis for a social right of citizenship.

Furthermore, from a gender perspective, means-testing is incompatible with the notion that a citizen's benefit should relate to needs of the individual citizen, not a couple or a household (Lister, 1992a: 63). For example, the means-testing of unemployed husbands or wives that take into account the income of their spouse often makes it not worthwhile for that spouse to continue in paid employment (Lister, 1990).

Social exclusion and work-based benefits

To the extent that 'as of right' benefits are dependent on contributions for entitlement, they also have a weakness as a citizen's benefit, for they are primarily a worker's benefit. Furthermore, when, as they usually are, they are earnings-related, the inequalities of, and opportunities for, labour market participation become reflected in the benefit system. Working becomes the pre-condition for benefit. It is social class position that takes precedence over status as citizen. Women in particular lose out, as do the other low-paid and insecure workers. Despite the nature of social interdependence outlined in Part One, the inequalities of labour market structure come to determine the life-chances of citizens. Unless there is a base of social class and gender equality in labour market opportunity and reward over the lifecourse, employment-related benefits cannot provide a basis for citizenship. A minimum wage (Bryson, 1989) and equal opportunity might help to provide such a base, but because there is no right to work, and because even if there was, not everyone could exercise that right all the time, then, at best, work-related benefits can only be as secure as labour market reward and participation. And that does not provide a secure basis for a social right of citizenship.

A social right of citizenship that is based on recognition of lifecourse social interdependence would require a *sharing* between those in work and those out of work, at any one time, to provide an optimal level (Doyal and Gough, 1991) of resources for the human development of all. This would be tax-financed. The best embodiment, to date, of this notion of a social right of citizenship is to be found in proposals for a Basic Income. This is discussed below in Chapter 14.

10

THE SOCIAL RIGHTS OF CITIZENSHIP

One approach to social rights is to consider the nature of welfare state provisions in a number of countries (Esping-Anderson, 1990). However, to undertake analysis and make comparisons between states we must first theorise the form and content of social rights to distinguish them from other welfare state forms. As mentioned in Chapter 9, not all welfare state provisions can be considered as providing social rights for citizens. Esping-Anderson has argued that 'the existence of a social programme and the amount of money spent on it may be less important than what it does' (1990: 2). Thus for a programme to be considered a social right we must ask: what does it do? For Esping-Anderson the heart of this question relates to whether the programme de-commodifies social relationships. The same approach is followed here except that in considering actual existing welfare programmes it is necessary to identify greater or lesser tendencies to de-commodification as few programmes fully de-commodify social relationships.

Social rights as de-commodification

Esping-Anderson, in the tradition of Karl Polanyi (1957), takes the view that

> the outstanding criterion of social rights must be the degree to which they *permit people to make their living standards independent of pure market forces*. It is in this sense that social rights diminish citizens' status as 'commodities'. . . . If social rights are given the legal and practical status of property rights, if they are inviolable, and if they are granted on the basis of citizenship rather than performance, they will entail a de-commodification of the status of individuals vis-à-vis the market. (1990: 21; my italics)

In these terms, social rights are a direct challenge to a social class stratified society wherein most people must sell their labour power in the labour market in order to obtain a standard of living. As Marshall (1950) observed, social rights of citizenship should be regarded as providing an equality of status that cuts across social classes. Similarly, Esping-Anderson states, 'one's status as a citizen will compete with, or even replace, one's class position' (1990: 21). Therefore, in these terms, the development of social rights should lead to the breaking down of social class inequalities based upon labour market positions. When social rights are added to civil and political rights we start to move from treating human beings as 'things' to be bought and sold, to a consideration of their essential humanity and its sustenance and development. The individual's isolation in the market is replaced by a concern to maintain the means for the development of his or her individuality as a human being. Thus, social rights of citizenship when added to civil liberties and political democracy may present a major challenge to free market capitalism. It is therefore not surprising that the 1980s saw a resurgence of debate over citizenship in Britain in response to the free-wheeling marketeers in government.

Esping-Anderson reopens an old debate when he poses the 'central question, not only for Marxism but for the entire contemporary debate on the welfare state, [which] is whether, and under what conditions, the class divisions and social inequalities produced by capitalism can be undone by parliamentary democracy' (1990: 11). Though Bismarckian Germany demonstrated that democratic government is not necessary for welfare state programmes to develop, the growth of political democracy in nineteenth-century Britain held out the promise of governments elected to introduce social rights to reduce economic and social inequality. In Britain, this promise was partly fulfilled by the Liberal governments of 1906–11 (without female franchise) and by the Labour governments of 1945–51 (with full adult franchise). Esping-Anderson sharply observes that the 'balance of class power is fundamentally altered when workers enjoy social rights, for the social wage lessens the worker's dependence on the market and employers, and this *turns into a potential power resource*' (1990: 11; my italics). This point is crucial. The power of political democracy can be used to introduce social rights that empower people through the redistribution of resources. Redistributing resources redistributes power and choice. Without the development of social rights, through democratic government, people remain captives of the market and in the power of employers. Thus, insofar as political rights lead to the development of social rights, democratic political power is used to reduce the economic market power of employers. 'Politics not only matters, it is decisive' (Esping-Anderson, 1990: 4). Without such an extension of social rights the balance of power lies in the non-democratic sphere of markets and we are left with a one-armed notion of democratic power. Labour markets treat workers as commodities that are disposable rather than as human beings to be cherished. Yet, it is the essence of democratic politics that each person has equal political power through one person one vote (and that each vote should be of equal worth). As identified in Chapter 2, there is a fundamental tension between political democracy and market economics in their treatment of human beings.

Citizenship is a three-legged stool

As the risks and experience of unemployment are unequally distributed and reflect a person's position in the occupational class structure, this has major implications for the dynamics of class inequality. At any time the labour market may discard a person and declare him or her unemployed and thus place that person (and his or her family) outside the fundamental basis for material well-being and social status in a market economy. At the same time that person remains supposedly equal in power in the system of political democracy. But can that really be so? In the twentieth century Marshall's three elements of citizenship must stand together; civil and political rights must be supported by social rights, otherwise the 'three-legged stool of citizenship' will be unbalanced. Without substantial social rights to material resources (and health and education) the social inclusion and therefore the citizenship of the unemployed person is placed in jeopardy. How may unemployed people claim to be citizens of their society when the economic market system, for reasons unrelated to their actions, treats them as commodities to be discarded? Market treatment of people as commodities threatens their standing as citizens. However, if the treatment of employees as commodities and their periodic unemployment are considered as a *social cost* of labour market operations, then, in a political democracy, the question arises as to who should bear that social cost. Should it be the unemployed person (and his or her family) or the wider society, which apparently benefits from the operations of markets and the periodic unemployment of people? Part of the answer to the question must be found in the extent to which welfare state programmes provide compensation through social rights that de-commodify social relationships. Due to the interdependence of the three elements of citizenship, without social rights the political and civil rights of workers and their families will be more difficult to uphold.

The element of social rights is essential to the emancipatory thrust of citizenship as it unchains people from their dependence on the vagaries of the labour market. Citizens require social resources, health and education not only for economic efficiency but also to participate effectively in furthering their own and other people's civil and political rights, to further their life projects (Gould, 1988). As these are social endeavours which are created and maintained through social relationships they cannot be pursued effectively by isolated individuals and their families but must be pursued by the community as a whole. Each must be the protector and sustainer of the civil, political and social rights – the citizenship – of all. Without this approach society continually faces the risk that the social exclusion of apparent minorities may lead to the situation in Nazi Germany or to 'ethnic cleansing' as in Bosnia-Herzegovina. It is always possible to apply a categorisation to anyone so as to identify them as a minority for social exclusion. Social exclusion was used as a powerful form of sanction and punishment under the New Poor Law in nineteenth-century Britain, and we have lost our sensitivity to its power in the twentieth century. Human beings by their very nature are social beings not isolated individuals and families. Inclusion in a society is essential to our identity and development. To socially exclude is to shrivel the social being. Social rights by eradicating poverty and complete wage dependence have the potential for maintaining social integration that is itself necessary for sustaining civil and political rights.

Any discussion of citizenship is by implication a discussion of power and at the centre of power relations in industrial societies is the system of production and its associated system of distribution. Citizenship, through the element of political rights, implies that relations of power are, to some degree, under democratic control. Democratising power and control must involve reducing inequalities of resource distribution as resources are a crucial form of power in a market society. We may be reluctant to intervene more generally in markets but labour markets are of a different order as they tend to treat human beings as commodities, that is, things. This is not acceptable within a conceptualisation of citizenship that combines civil, political and social rights. Citizens of a democratic polity expect more. If the exercise of power is not democratically accountable then its exercise is likely to be arbitrary and exercised for sectional interests.

The New Right continues to argue that a separation between politics and the economy should be maintained so as to ensure freedom. This conceptualisation, however, was originally formulated in a historical context when state power was held in autocratic hands prior to the emergence of democratic politics. Their continuing insistence on the primacy of market relationships, in the contemporary context of democratic politics, leads them into a problematic circumscription of political action. Furthermore, when the reality of markets is that they are largely composed of oligopolistic corporations, often of a transnational nature, then to limit democratic power is to give enormous power to these unaccountable corporations. When this perspective is added to their objection to social rights it becomes clear that the New Right cannot address the issues of citizenship because they have an inadequate theory of societal power in a democracy. They thus tend to leave power in society concentrated in its pre-democratic centres within industry and labour market relations, and this is profoundly unequal between the buyers and sellers of labour power. Moreover, as Esping-Anderson observes, 'Democracy is an institution that cannot resist majority demands' (1990: 15). In political democracies a democratised form of power tends to be dominant and provides the lead to forms of social and economic organisation. Writing in 1950, T.H. Marshall concluded that in the case of Britain the drive of democratic politics was towards developing welfare state provisions and social rights of citizenship. This path is by no means smooth and automatic and is certainly not evolutionary, and welfare state provisions cannot simply be viewed as automatically establishing social rights. Welfare state forms were in many cases established prior to the emergence of full political democracy, yet, once established, have taken on a dynamic of their own. Welfare state provisions are not automatically, or are only partially, de-commodifying and thus do not necessarily provide a social right for citizens.

A significant feature of Esping-Anderson's (1990) thesis is that the most de-commodifying welfare states develop strong social rights to welfare through the building of class-coalitions. This is an important argument in that such class-coalitions are usually manifested through the operation of democratic political rights. Political rights underpin social rights. It is also notable in Britain that New Right governments have only been able to obtain minority support but have pushed through market policies with the massive parliamentary majorities provided by the lack of proportional representation. The inadequacies of political rights in Britain have led to an increasingly commodified society and dramatic increases in unemployment, poverty and social inequality.

Marshall's (1950) work on citizenship may be criticised for its failure to specify the level, form and content of social rights. Such subsequent specification can, however, be found in the works of Richard Titmuss (1958, 1968). Esping-Anderson has also observed that what we need

is an approach that forces researchers to move from the black box of expenditures to the content of welfare states: targeted versus universalistic programmes, the conditions of eligibility, the quality of benefits and services and, perhaps most importantly, the extent to which employment and working life are encompassed in the state extension of citizen's rights. (1990: 20)

These variable characteristics of welfare states are examined below but in relation to a number of special concerns. First, whether the forms of welfare state provision support a positive self-identity for citizens avoiding stigmatising experiences that threaten their sense of self and result in social exclusion. Second, whether welfare state forms recognise social interdependence, and incorporate measures of compensation for the bearing of the social costs of societal change. Third, what the implications are of particular provisions or the lack of them for the distinctive lifecourse experience of women. We begin, however, with the question of de-commodification.

Commodification, unemployment and de-commodification

It is perhaps easier to identify the processes of commodification rather than to specify welfare state de-commodification. Indeed, in societies where the everyday means to life is intended to be obtained through the selling of labour power, can social relationships be de-commodified in any substantive sense? People are treated as 'commodities in the sense that their survival [is] contingent upon the sale of their labour power' (Esping-Anderson, 1990: 21). In capitalist market economies few citizens have the direct means to live independent of selling their labour power. Some people may have smallholdings that supply them with food and if they have a surplus they might sell it to buy other things they need but are unable to make. In such circumstances, however, their level of living is likely to be dramatically lower than that of those who sell their labour power and benefit from the increased product resulting from the division of labour and use of technology. For most people the benefits of selling their labour are clear and unproblematic: they have a distinctly higher standard of living than if they tried to be self-sufficient. Thus concern with commodification is not a cry for self-sufficiency; indeed, on the contrary, it is to note the social interdependence arising, in part, from the division of labour. At the same time it is to focus attention on the social costs that may fall for varying lengths of time on citizens who are unable to sell their labour power, or are able to sell it only on terms that stunt their self-development and/or leave them with a low level of living compared to most of their fellow citizens.

Problematic features of the labour contract were discussed earlier in Part One. Here we concentrate on problems arising from the inability to sell labour power. Though it is generally accepted as necessary for most people in industrial society to sell their labour power as a means to life, there is in fact no 'right to work'. Although Marshall (1950) lists the right to enter into contracts as a civil right, there is in reality no right to sell your labour power in the sense that someone has to buy it. Therefore it is not appropriate to include a labour contract as a civil right. The right to a labour contract is in reality not a right but an opportunity (Twine, 1992). A society that presumes its members sell their labour as a means to life but takes inadequate steps to ensure they can actually sell their labour power or that labour market reward is sufficient must be regarded as basically callous. The employee, and his or her family, are placed in fear. In fear of being thrust into poverty with its associated threat to self-identify. A person may have worked diligently for many years acquiring and developing skills; establishing a secure family home and a personal reputation as a reliable hardworking person whether as a labourer, craftsperson or professional, and yet become unemployed overnight through no fault of his or her own. Choices made by others in the wider society shift market demand to their benefit, but at the cost of unemployment for others. For example, New Right governments in Britain in the 1980s and 1990s have given priority to reducing inflation at a cost of dramatic increases in unemployment. This in turn, due to inadequate levels of unemployment benefit, has dramatically increased poverty (Oppenheim, 1993). An increase in unemployment has proved to be the quickest way to increase poverty. Indeed, the Thatcher government restricted access to benefits for the unemployed to 'encourage' them to return to the labour market at lower levels of pay (Atkinson and Micklewright, 1989). They were punished for being unemployed though this resulted from government policies declared to be in the national interest. The increased reliance of the unemployed on means-tested benefits and stricter rules of entitlement moved the British social security system away from a social right of citizenship approach to a more means-tested welfare state meant to reinforce the commodity status of workers. The almost complete abolition of Wage Councils furthered this policy by reducing the already limited coverage of minimum wages. In Britain some 60 per cent of the unemployed are partially or solely dependent on means-tested benefits. Through these policies the unemployed are subject to substantial coercion to return to the labour market at lower wages than previously earned. When the numbers unemployed far exceed job vacancies, and thus demonstrate the impossibility of most of the unemployed selling their labour, the cynical nature of this assumption of normally maintaining life through selling labour power is revealed. This has resulted in the UK becoming a more authoritarian and coercive society.

Access to welfare and rules of eligibility

Access to welfare state provisions is seldom unconditional. We can identify a number of commonly used rules of eligibility, contingent rights and contribution rules. Many nations provide a right to benefit based on the contingencies of unemployment, sickness and disability or old age. Eligibility is related to experiencing the contingency and is not related to the income of the person. This is a contingent right. However, such state insurance schemes are also usually based upon contribution records and a minimum number of contributions paid whilst in work. Thus these rules and preconditions are a reflection of labour market security and continuity of employment; having been able to sell your labour power. Under the Beveridge scheme the right to unemployment benefit is mediated by contribution conditions. Where these are not met the unemployed person is thrown into the safety net of means-tested benefits and even the notion of a contingent right to a benefit is lost. As a consequence even 'compulsory state social insurance with fairly strong entitlement may not secure substantial de-commodification, since this hinges on the fabric of eligibility and benefit rules' (Esping-Anderson, 1990: 22) related to employment.

Esping-Anderson's discussion of social rights in terms of de-commodification has stimulated much debate. He suggests, for example, a '*minimal* definition must entail that citizens can freely, and without potential loss of job, income, or general welfare, opt out of work when they themselves consider it necessary' (1990: 23; my italics). This reads more as a *maximum* definition of de-commodification and runs up against the ability of any social security scheme to finance this level of benefit, especially when it depends on the working population to finance it through (supposedly) taxation. There would have to be social control of the circumstances under which Esping-Anderson's definition was operationalised. Similar reservations may be applied to some forms of Basic Income (see later discussion). It is notable, however, that Esping-Anderson's statement can be applied to *some* social groups. He gives an illustration related to sickness benefit which provides 'guaranteed benefits equal to normal earnings, a right to absence with minimum proof and for the duration the individual deems necessary' (1990: 23). These, he notes, are typically provided for academics, civil servants and higher-echelon white-collar employees. This 'social division of welfare' is still generally overlooked in political and many academic discussions of welfare, despite the work of Titmuss (1958), Sinfield (1978), Goodin and Le Grand (1987), Mann (1991) and Twine (1992). Thus, ironically, forms and levels of welfare as a social right are more likely to be applied to secure high-income employees than to the low-paid and vulnerable. This may be regarded as a selective use of social honour applied to those with education and status. Apparently, they can be *trusted* not to abuse the system. What may not be applied to the many is reserved for the few and further bolsters their class position. It is often classified as occupational welfare or private welfare, but is essentially dependent on rules made by the state and, most importantly, on tax subsidies from the Exchequer (see Chapter 11). As argued in the case study of pensions in Chapter 3, these are used to divide workers and weaken political pressure for universal social rights that would apply to all citizens. Esping-Anderson correctly claims that 'the relationship between citizenship and social class has been neglected both theoretically and empirically' and poses the question, 'what kind of stratification system is promoted by social policy?' (1990: 23).

The Beveridge Report of 1942 is sometimes referred to as providing welfare as a social right, but the main benefits, apart from Family Allowance (now Child Benefit), were based upon labour market participation. This had particularly negative consequences for women for Beveridge assumed women would not participate in the labour market for they were seen as 'having other duties' in the home (Lister, 1992b). In one sense, the Beveridge approach of providing an *equal basic benefit to all unrelated to previous earnings* (but requiring minimum flat-rate contributions) might be regarded as providing a citizenship approach. The level of benefit was, however, set too low, certainly as implemented by the 1945 Labour government (Field, 1987), and as shown in the subsequent long drift back to dependence on means-tested social assistance. Esping-Anderson perceptively notes that

> the solidarity of flat-rate universalism presumes a historically peculiar class structure, one in which the majority of the population are the 'little people' for whom a modest, albeit egalitarian, benefit may be considered adequate . . . flat-rate universalism inadvertently promotes dualism because the better-off turn to private insurance and to fringe benefit bargaining to supplement modest equality with what they decide were accustomed standards of welfare. (1990: 24)

It should also be noted, though it seldom is, that the Beveridge proposals left open this possibility in that he believed individuals should be able to build privately upon the state minimum, though he did not envisage its promotion through tax incentives. Thus the Beveridge social security package did not provide the basis for social rights of citizenship.

Whilst Esping-Anderson highlights the dilemma for welfare states of changes in the class structure, the key question remains concerning welfare state responses to labour market insecurity (low pay and unemployment). Significantly, there are no private welfare schemes to cover unemployment and in times of high unemployment its experience reaches up the class structure. This in turn undermines work-related benefits such as occupational pension schemes and any private welfare scheme dependent upon employment for the ability to pay contributions. It is the varied social costs of unemployment for the individual and his or her family that need to be addressed by social rights. Esping-Anderson does acknowledge that 'de-commodifying welfare states are, in practice, of very recent date. . . . The Scandinavian welfare states tend to be the most de-commodifying; the Anglo-Saxon the least' (1990: 23). Therefore we are not very likely to find many examples of de-commodified welfare states in practice. Esping-Anderson's typology of welfare state regimes is considered further in Chapter 12.

Social rights and resources

More than civil and political rights, social rights are crucially resource-dependent, and it is sometimes argued that their range and level cannot be guaranteed in the same way as civil and political rights, though this view is challenged by Plant (1992). The range and level of social rights are, in part, dependent upon the productive capacity of the country and upon secondary mediation by political decisions over public spending priorities. In these circumstances, it is sometimes questioned whether a minimum range and level of social rights can be established and maintained. How crucial is the level of economic growth? Are social rights expenditures to be 'the residual beneficiary of the growth state'? Here, again, we must avoid dichotomous thinking for there is an interdependence between many forms of public expenditure and economic growth. This is shown in education and training, and in the health of citizens, as well as the Keynesian manner in which benefits help to maintain demand during recessions. Furthermore, restricted definitions of public expenditure that exclude tax expenditures (Wilkinson, 1986a) may blinker our thinking as to which range and level of social rights it is possible to finance. We must confront questions of public expenditure priorities emanating from the exercise of political rights.

In the same way as we must consider the range and level of welfare provision in terms of the social rights of citizenship, so we must also consider which form and level of taxation best fits a concept of citizenship. Thus, welfare expenditure must be considered in the wider context of total public expenditure and that in turn must be through an examination of the system of taxation. Most commentators on public expenditure and welfare tend to ignore the private welfare state of tax expenditures. We must be careful that the terminology of the welfare state does not blind us to the social divisions of welfare. It is argued that the private and particularistic welfare state of tax expenditures should have a lower public expenditure priority than the public welfare state of social citizenship. This requires that we undertake an examination of systems of taxation and, because of its relative neglect in social policy debate, that this be done in some detail.

11

SOURCES OF INCOME AND FORMS OF TAXATION

Though some qualification will be required later, we may consider three processes that influence the income of most citizens: labour market reward, taxation and social security. How these processes operate tell us a great deal about the respect and treatment that a nation gives to societal members and the degree of inequality it tolerates. One illustration is the 'poverty trap', discussed in Chapter 9.

In market economies the amount of money a citizen has will be an important influence on the choices he or she is able to make. Therefore the initial or primary distribution of income is an important source of power and has an important influence on our choices as to the kind of person we or our children may become. Due to the centrality of wage labour and the labour market in the lifecourse of people, as was argued in Chapter 2, the manner in which labour market inequalities are mediated through the tax and social security system becomes a central aspect of the social rights of citizenship. Fundamental to a conceptualisation of citizenship within any nation will be the structure of its taxation system, but before we examine taxation systems it is important to consider the distribution of earnings against which the tax system operates. The examples are taken from the UK. Along the way some conceptual points are clarified.

The distribution of earnings: patterns of labour market reward

Britain has a highly complex system of income provision that interweaves the influences of labour market earnings, National Insurance, the tax system, fringe benefits and the social security system. In a variety of ways the interweaving of these influences incorporates different rules, customs and practices. They reflect what it is about a person's 'work' or contribution to society that should be rewarded, as well as the assumed needs of individuals and their family members. It is therefore important to take a wide perspective on what constitutes 'income'. We focus on three aspects of this complexity here: labour market earnings, special additions to labour market earnings, and the taxation of labour market earnings.

There are, in turn, three main aspects of labour market earnings that make up the 'effort bargain' – what we have to do for the money we get:

1   the level of pay,
2   the hours worked, including holidays, and
3   the conditions in which work is carried out and the opportunities for self-development and control of work.

In April each year since 1970 the UK Department of Employment has carried out a New Earnings Survey. The following analysis uses data based upon the average earnings for full-time employees on adult rates, whose pay was not affected by absence in April 1992 (Department of Employment, 1992). These might be regarded the 'core workforce', though we should note that this core workforce is slowly shrinking as part-time work, especially among women, grows in importance. These figures would tend, therefore, to under-estimate the scale of low pay, identified by the Low Pay Unit (1993) as two-thirds of median male earnings or £197.30p per week in 1992. A basic snapshot of class and gender differences in average earnings is provided in Table 11.1. Male manual workers received 67.0 per cent of the earnings of non-manual workers, whilst female manual workers received 66.3 per cent that of non-manual workers. Turning to gender differences, amongst manual workers women earned 63.4 per cent of that earned by men; and amongst non-manual workers, women earned 64.1 per cent of that earned by men. In the early 1980s, women's earnings were a higher proportion of men's.

One factor hidden in these averages is the variable impact of overtime working by class and gender. Overtime is most significant

Table 11.1   *Average gross weekly earnings (£) of adults working full time in April 1992*

Male manual	Male non-manual	Female manual	Female non-manual
268.30	400.40	170.10	256.50

Source: Department of Employment, 1992: Part A, Table 1

Table 11.2 *Distribution of total hours worked, percentage of
employees, April 1992*

Hours per week	Male manual	Male non-manual	Female manual	Female non-manual
36 hours or less	2.5	23.2	15.3	35.1
40 hours or less	46.9	80.9	75.8	92.5
More than 40 hours	53.1	19.1	24.2	7.6
More than 48 hours	23.9	5.0	6.5	1.2

Source: Department of Employment, 1992: Part A, Table 1

in raising the pay of male manual workers; it made up 14.1 per cent
of their average earnings. The opportunity to work overtime is an
important way of raising total earnings for those on low rates of pay.
Not everyone, however, works overtime. For example, of all male
manual workers, 52.4 per cent worked *some* overtime; this averaged
10.1 hours per week, increasing earnings on average by £72.40. A
picture of the structure of overtime working in April 1992 is
provided in Table 11.2.

From Table 11.2, and assuming an average working day of 8
hours, we can make the following comparison. Some 23.2 per cent
of male non-manual workers worked the equivalent of only 4.5 days
per week, whereas 23.9 per cent of male manual workers worked
the equivalent of *more than* 6 days per week. These are quite
dramatic differences. We should note, however, that some professional workers work long hours without overtime pay, for
example teachers. The European Community directive to limit
weekly hours worked to a maximum of 48 hours would affect nearly
a quarter of male manual workers in the UK and, now that the UK
has almost no minimum wage protection, might have particularly
negative consequences for the low-paid. Considerable injustice
might occur if hours were reduced in the absence of a minimum
wage.

There are further differences between the worlds of work for
manual and non-manual workers. Manual work is more likely to be
boring and routine with less opportunity for self-fulfilment and the
exercise of initiative; in many cases it will be physically and
aesthetically disagreeable or downright dangerous. However, an
awful lot of office work is also boring and routine, especially for
women. These aspects of work seem to find little reflection in the
payment system. Indeed, some kinds of work may cost the worker
dearly. The most recent figures show around 1.6 million industrial
accidents a year in the UK, and 18 million lost working days as a

result. Some further 11.5 million days were lost through work-related ill-health. Each year, 5,000 people have to leave work permanently as a result of accidents, and 16,000 retire early (Milne, 1994; see also Davies and Easdale, 1994). These figures are another illustration of the social costs of economic activity. The Black Report (Townsend and Davidson, 1988) on health inequalities shows a clear 'class gradient' for experience of industrial injury and illness.

Other differences in work experience can be briefly noted. Manual workers tend to: start work earlier in the day; work under greater supervision; 'clock in and out'; have greater difficulties in taking time off for personal reasons without loss of pay; and have fewer weeks of holiday and are less able to choose when to take their holiday. In private as compared to public employment, manual workers are less likely to be in occupational pension schemes. This, along with lower pay that affects earnings-related pensions, means they have greater risk of eventual poverty in old age; this is especially true for women.

We tend to think of equity in terms of 'equal percentage' increases in pay, yet this results in unequal 'money increases' that help to perpetuate inequalities in well-being and life-chances between occupations. Income policies during the 1960s and 1970s were premised on equal percentage increases related to an average percentage rate of inflation. This resulted in higher-income groups obtaining a larger *money* increase in income than the lower-paid, thus income inequalities tended to widen. Over the lifecourse these differences may be widened further by some employees, mainly non-manual workers, receiving annual increments to their pay along with any negotiated pay increases. The reason why some workers but not others receive automatic annual incremental increases remains obscure.

Differences in earnings by occupation and gender are shown in Table 11.3. All the examples show women's average earnings lower than those of men in the same occupation. This may reflect differences in overtime opportunities, broken career paths for women due to childbirth and child-rearing, differing promotion opportunities or just plain discrimination against women. We can also observe the relatively high pay of police. Their pay has improved substantially in the 1980s and 1990s, whereas that of teachers has tended to fall in relative terms.

The lowest-paid males and females are found in shops and restaurants (and women in hairdressing). Until 1993, adult workers in these industries (those under 21 were excluded in 1986) were

Table 11.3 *Occupational earnings (£), April 1992*

Male occupation	Average weekly earnings	Female occupation	Average weekly earnings
Medical practitioner	755.6		
Solicitor	623.6		
		Medical practitioner	615.1
University teacher	533.1		
Electronic engineer	473.0		
		Solicitor	459.3
Secondary teacher	435.5		
Police sergeant	419.0		
Primary school teacher	413.7		
		Secondary school teacher	382.4
		Primary school teacher	362.0
		Police: sergeant and below	360.1
Electrician	334.5		
Coal miner	331.9		
Social worker	330.9		
Fire officer	321.8		
Nurse	320.2		
Draughtsman	316.7		
		Nurse	293.2
		Social worker	283.7
Lathe operator	280.1		
Motor mechanic	261.6		
Bricklayer	237.7		
Bus drivers	234.7		
Refuse collector	228.4		
Road sweeper	216.3		
		Clerks	200.5
		Typist, WP	196.6
Farm workers	198.4		
Sales assistant	190.2		
Waiter	169.0		
		Sales assistant	149.0
		Waitress	138.3
		Hairdresser	127.7

Source: Department of Employment, 1992: Part A, Table 8

'protected' by legally enforceable minimum wage legislation through Wages Councils. Unlike other countries of the European Community which provide minimum wages, Britain now has only an Agricultural Wages Board. Wages Boards were originally established in 1909 to protect workers' wages in industries where there was fierce competition leading to the 'competitive down-bidding of wages'. Introducing the legislation in 1909, Winston Churchill, at the time a Liberal MP, stated,

> It is a serious national evil that any class of His Majesty's subjects should receive less than a living wage in return for their utmost exertions. It was formerly supposed that the workings of the laws of supply and demand would naturally regulate or eliminate this evil . . . but where you have no organisation, no parity of bargaining, the good employer is undercut by the bad and the bad employer by the worst . . . where these conditions prevail you have no condition of progress, but a condition of progressive degeneration . . . this degeneration will continue, and there is no reason why it should not continue in a sort of squalid welter for a period which compared with our brief lives is indefinite. (Hansard, 28 April 1909: Col. 388)

Wages Council rates, nevertheless, remained low and governments were not very active in their pursuit of employers who broke the law by paying below the minimum (Bryson, 1989).

Following the abolition of Wages Councils we might expect earnings in these sectors to fall even lower. For the first time in over eighty-five years Britain has almost no minimum wage legislation (Minford, 1991). The issue of a national minimum wage in Britain also revolves around the present Conservative government's intention to exclude Britain from the Social Charter of the Maastricht agreement; this requires member states to protect their workers from the competitive down-bidding of wages. The government argues that Britain's exclusion will allow industry to be more competitive by paying lower wages but at the same time creating more jobs and thus reducing unemployment.

From the above discussion it is apparent that there is seldom a free market for labour. There is always some framework of rules, affecting labour markets, which varies over time, set by democratically elected governments. This, of course, affects the balance of power between buyers and sellers of labour power.

It is useful to be aware that analysis of earnings figures in terms of 'averages' may distract attention away from the distribution around the average. In Table 11.4 we can see details of these distributions. The first point to note is that in all cases the mean is more than 100 per cent of the median. Thus more than 50 per cent of workers earn below the mean or average. Though not shown in Table 11.4, the original source shows that over the past ten years the distribution around the median has widened for all four groups of workers. During the same period part-time working, especially among

Table 11.4 *The distribution of earnings, April 1992 (percentage of the corresponding median)*

Group	Lowest decile	Lower quartile	Upper quartile	Highest decile	Mean
Male					
manual	62.8	78.7	126.3	158.5	107.0
non-manual	53.2	72.9	133.9	181.4	113.3
Female					
manual	67.5	80.8	127.2	161.8	108.6
non-manual	61.7	76.6	138.8	176.5	112.7

Source: Department of Employment, 1992: Part A, Table 15

women, has increased dramatically and unemployment has been at very high levels. Thus, those in full-time work at the upper end of the distribution have done very well in the 1980s and 1990s, and they have also been the main beneficiaries of the cuts in personal income tax (Elliot and Kelly, 1994). For them, increased pay has combined with lower income tax to boost their material well-being.

We turn now to additions to labour market earnings. These can be dealt with more briefly and placed into three broad categories of welfare that were identified by Richard Titmuss (1958) in his discussion of the 'social division of welfare'. They are state welfare, occupational welfare and fiscal welfare.

Focusing only on additions to labour market earnings, *state welfare* benefits can be divided into two broad categories. First, benefits to which people are entitled as a right of citizenship, such as Child Benefit, or some disability benefits. Second, 'means-tested' benefits which require a test of other income and involve problems of stigma and take-up. Examples are Housing Benefit paid to those on lower incomes paying rent, or Family Credit paid to those in low-paid jobs who have children (Barr and Coulter, 1991).

Occupational welfare varies greatly, within and among firms, as it comes through particular employment contracts. Occupational welfare is a 'civil opportunity' open to some workers but not others, which varies among the occupations covered and is dependent upon staying with that employer. Generally there is differential treatment of manual and non-manual workers, and men and women. Occupational welfare ranges from luncheon vouchers to company cars (unrelated to work needs), private health care and occupational pension schemes providing for deferred income in retirement. Occupational welfare is commonly referred to as 'fringe benefits', but this peripheral imagery disguises their substantial impact on income differentials (Smail et al., 1984; OECD, 1988). Occupational welfare, by making employment conditions more attractive, enables employers to attract and hold staff. Furthermore, as 'income in kind', fringe benefits are treated more generously for tax purposes than the equivalent amount of income. Thus, occupational welfare and fiscal welfare are linked. Company cars are taxed at a lower rate and at less than their real value, though we should note that this has been made less generous in recent years. This subsidy to company cars also increases road traffic and reduces demand for public transport. Lower-income groups, such as pensioners, are more dependent on public transport, as are most women. Medical insurance provided free to employees by their employer has become of increasing significance in debates over the growth and encouragement of private medical care. Overall, these fringe benefits, which go disproportionately to higher-income groups, make up 20 to 25 per cent of labour costs. Media discussion of labour costs seldom pays attention to the costs of occupational welfare benefits.

Fiscal welfare refers to tax reliefs such as those on mortgage interest payments, or linked to occupational welfare through tax relief on employee and employer contribution to occupational pensions (Wilkinson, 1986a). Two key points may be made about fiscal welfare.

First, it usually brings most benefit to those with higher incomes paying the higher marginal rates of tax. In the autumn budget of 1993, however, the UK Finance Minister reduced mortgage interest relief to a flat rate of 20 per cent, with a promised future reduction to 15 per cent. Similar changes were not made to tax relief on payments to occupational pensions, and these remain unrelated to income, unlike means-tested benefits for the poor.

Second, as fiscal welfare is not regarded as public expenditure it tends to be open-ended regarding the total amount forgone by the Treasury. For example, in 1991–2 tax relief on mortgage interest cost the Exchequer £6,100 million in revenue forgone (Table 11.6). Comparisons of pre- and post-tax income in the UK for the years 1979 and 1988 are shown in Table 11.5. What is most noticeable is the growth of income inequality in both pre- and post-tax incomes, with quite dramatic increases in income in the top fifth of households. We can also see that the proportion of post-tax income going to the bottom fifth of households has declined during the period. Indeed, 80 per cent of households experienced a decline in their share of post-tax income between 1979 and 1988. Income inequalities in the UK have significantly widened in the past decade.

Table 11.5 *The distribution of household income before and after tax in the UK*

	Quintile groups of households ranked by equivalised disposable income				
	Bottom fifth	Next fifth	Middle fifth	Next fifth	Top fifth
Equivalised original income					
1979	2	10	18	27	43
1988	2	7	16	25	50
Equivalised post-tax income					
1979	10	13	18	23	37
1988	7	11	16	22	44

Source: Central Statistical Office, 1992: Table 5.19

Citizenship and structures of income tax

Having outlined some key aspects of income and earnings patterns we turn to ways in which they may be taxed. This is an important, but neglected, issue. Though public revenues provide the fundamental source of funding for social rights, they are little understood by the majority of citizens. Politicians seem reluctant to discuss structures of taxation in detail for fear that this will lead to greater *visibility* of the tax system and public resistance to payment. As citizens in a democracy ultimately have to give support to structures of taxation, it should be done openly and with understanding. Ignorance of such matters must be considered an unacceptable constraint on the exercise of political rights. If we wish strong social rights to be firmly established through the support of citizens, then, ultimately, we must trust in the informed judgements of citizens. Social rights of citizenship ultimately rest upon the values and understanding of citizens as expressed through democratic political forms. It is suggested that much of the following discussion of taxation is not yet understood by a majority of citizens in any nation.

Due to the image of taxation as a burden, we are not encouraged to appreciate its powerful role in sharing costs over the lifecourse. The New Right claim that high income is simply the result of personal effort rather than being, in part, a consequence of benefiting from the externalities of social change in a socially interdependent world. Most discussions of social policy do not usually include consideration of the system of taxation, yet it remains one of the most powerful instruments of social policy. The questions of how money is raised and how money is spent are of central concern for any democratic government. The tax structure is the bridge between market income and public expenditure. The earlier section considered the pattern of market income and some of the ways in which democratic governments might influence its level and distribution. The tax system operates on those various sources of income to raise the monies that governments spend for a wide range of public purposes. However, most studies of social policy are concerned with how this money is spent on social programmes rather than the manner in which it is raised. Yet how the 'burden' of taxation falls across the population and its distributive character is itself a major social policy programme and should be seen as such. Nevertheless, most citizens have less knowledge and understanding of the tax system and the pattern of tax falling on them and their fellow citizens than they do of the activities of pop stars, footballers or members of the Royal Family. Such widespread ignorance must be considered a significant barrier to 'fairness' in social policy outcomes in a political democracy.

The 'fairness' of any tax system must be reckoned a key political issue yet it is seldom discussed in any detail, and seldom as a whole. In consequence many citizens may believe they are paying less tax at a time when total taxes have in reality increased, as in the UK in the 1980s and 1990s. Thus it seems appropriate to consider whether we can identify principles of citizenship that might be employed in analysing tax systems. This is not so easy as it might seem. It is possible to describe and compare tax systems, as has been done in the lucid accounts by Peters (1991) and Hills (1988). I am indebted to both these works. Is it possible to say, however, that a particular aspect of a tax structure is to be regarded as more conducive to citizenship whilst another is less so? This question will be explored through examination of a number of common aspects of tax systems in terms of 'fairness', though other considerations will also have to be taken into account.

We start with the assumption that in modern democratic societies governments and their electorates will wish to raise monies for public expenditure, and that these monies should be raised in ways that are considered 'fair'. We shall consider these questions 'in principle' regarding citizenship, recognising that 'in practice' they may not, for a number of reasons, be fully realisable.

An initial question is whether all of a person's income is taxable. This is a pivotal question. If only half of all personal income was taxable, the government, to raise a given amount of money, would have to tax that half of income at twice the rate than if all income were taxable. Thus, the size of the 'tax base' is an important factor influencing the tax rate. To raise a given amount of revenue, marginal rates of tax will tend to be higher the smaller the tax base, and vice versa. A central influence on the size of the tax base is the extent to which tax allowances and reliefs reduce the proportion of total income upon which a person pays income tax.

Tax allowances are normally applicable to all persons in similar circumstances, and under the British tax system taxpayers are allocated personal allowances that are tax-free. For example, the basic personal allowance was £3,445 for the tax year 1992–3. *Tax reliefs* differ from tax allowances in that they are specifically related to how the taxpayers spend their money. They are an incentive to spend money in ways that attract tax relief. In Britain, for example, people buying a house obtain tax relief on mortgage interest up to a maximum mortgage of £30,000. Similarly, others, often the same people, obtain tax relief on their contributions to occupational pension schemes. The scale of tax forgone by the British Exchequer in 1991–2 as a result of these main tax reliefs is shown in Table 11.6.

Significantly, and regressively, for the individual taxpayer, allowances and reliefs are worth more the higher an individual's marginal rate of tax, that is, the tax he or she pays on the last pound of income. For example, tax relief on £1,000 is worth £250 to someone with a marginal tax rate of 25 per cent, but £400 to a person whose marginal tax rate is 40 per cent. This may be regarded as doubly unfair. The tax relief is not only worth much more to the higher-income taxpayer but at the same time it reduces the tax base upon which tax revenue is levied and will tend to push up marginal tax rates for all taxpayers. Lower-income persons may lose twice in that they are unable to afford expenditures that attract tax relief and pay higher taxes to pay for the revenue forgone to the Exchequer through tax reliefs to higher-income earners. This is another example of social interdependence that becomes visible once we

Table 11.6 *Cost to the Exchequer of main tax reliefs, 1991–2*

Type of tax relief	£ million
Occupational pension provision	7,700
Contribution to personal pensions (including retirement annuity premia and FSAVCs)[1]	1,500
Qualifying interest on loans for purchase or improvement of owner-occupied property	6,100

[1] Free Standing Additional Voluntary Contributions.

Source: Extracted from Statistics and Economics Office, 1992: Table 1.8

examine the structures of society rather than limiting our vision to isolated individuals. Thus, tax reliefs on specific expenditures for selected individuals may be regarded as going against the principles of citizenship, and especially if their value is greater to those with higher incomes. As was noted above, however, recent UK tax changes with effect from April 1994 have provided, for some purposes, a single rate for relief affecting all income ranges.

As tax reliefs are often attached to 'fringe benefits' (income in kind) they may be regarded as forms of tax avoidance open to some citizens but not others. Such income and tax privileges are not conducive to citizenship. Furthermore, in Britain, these 'tax expenditures', that is, revenues forgone, are not counted as public expenditure. Thus they remain relatively invisible in decisions over the control of public expenditure and the total revenues to be raised through the tax system. For example, on the one hand, expenditure on Housing Benefit to low-income tenants is more visible and means-tested and subject to regular constraint by government. On the other hand, tax forgone on mortgage tax relief is less visible, not means-tested, nor is the total amount forgone by the Exchequer constrained other than by the £30,000 upper limit to individuals. The first is regarded as public expenditure the second is not. Therefore, during the 1980s and 1990s tax relief on mortgage interest has become a growing and major subsidy (Table 11.6) to owner-occupiers, and whilst Housing Benefit to those who rent has also grown in total due to rising rents, its generosity to individuals has declined. (From 1992, tax relief on mortgage interest was reduced to the standard tax rate of 25 per cent, and in 1994 was further reduced to the new minimum tax rate of 20 per cent.) Due to differences in treatment as public expenditure and related differences in public and political visibility the balance of public expenditures on housing has changed dramatically in the 1980s and 1990s. We can add to this price discounts under the 'right to buy' public rented housing policy, and reductions in loan sanctions to local authorities to build for rent (Gibb and Munro, 1991). When this is done we may conclude that changing housing expenditure in Britain, at a time of dramatic increases in homelessness (Greve and Currie, 1990), does not reflect citizenship priorities. They lead to the social exclusion of the poor from housing.

In Britain, the second significant example of tax relief is on income spent on occupational pensions. This was discussed in the case study in Chapter 3.

Two generalisations can be made:

First, that the proportion of standard allowances tend to fall (as a proportion of tax) when income rises in almost all countries, since generally these allowances are fixed amounts independent of the income level. Second, that non-standard allowances (tax reliefs) almost universally increase as a proportion of income subject to tax as income increases (with Germany as the clearest exception) (Peters, 1991).

Thus we may conclude that an important determinant of fairness in personal income tax systems is the way *taxable* income is defined or delimited from broader income concepts. Thus, statutory tax rates taken alone do not give an accurate picture of the degree of progressivity of the system. If citizenship is to involve notions of fairness, then the use of the tax system as a relatively privileged route to welfare must be the subject of substantive scrutiny. Most people are unaware of the inequalities built into these fiscal elements of welfare.

A further key question in judging the 'fairness' of a tax system is the equity of the tax burden. How progressive or regressive is a nation's tax structure? Hills sets out clearly some basic distinctions on this question:

> [The] burden imposed by taking £1 from a high income is clearly less than that imposed by taking the same amount from a low income. . . . Such arguments imply that the tax system should be *progressive* – i.e., the proportion of income taken in tax should rise with income . . . a tax which takes a greater proportion of low than high income is *regressive*. . . . Finally, a tax which takes the same proportion of all incomes is *proportional*, but this bears more heavily on the poor than on the rich. One complication of tax analysis is that taxes can be progressive over one income range but proportional or regressive over another. (1988: 8)

We may assert that citizenship requires the maximisation of progressivity and the minimisation of regressivity with proportionality being a second best to progressivity. However, a word of caution is required here. As a central purpose of taxation is to raise money for public expenditure, then a chosen tax structure must be able to bring in the money. The most beautifully progressive tax structure will fail if it has such a disincentive effect that revenues are reduced. Usually economists (Heady, 1993) seek an optimal tax system that provides a compromise between fairness (equality) and incentives (efficiency), though administrative costs may also be a concern. Heady acknowledges, however, that it is difficult for models of the tax system to incorporate the real-world complexities of disincentives and labour market supply. With most of these models,

> Perfect competition is usually assumed, as is the absence of environmental effects and other externalities. The dropping of these assumptions

would alter the optimal pattern of taxes but would greatly increase both the complexity of these models and their data requirements. The application of optimal tax results in situations where imperfect competition or externality problems are significant therefore requires considerable care. (Heady, 1993: 24)

As imperfect competition and externalities are commonplace it seems that optimal tax results will remain problematic. Furthermore, concern with labour market disincentives often overlooks that people may prefer to be taxed to fund a National Health Service collectively than to buy private insurance through their labour market income. People's assessment of the benefits of public expenditure made possible through taxation are often left out of the economists' equation.

To continue the exposition. Once the proportion of income free of tax has been decided with allowances and reliefs, the next issue is at what rate to tax the first slice of taxable income and how many tax bands to use. Hills notes that, 'The UK system is unusual in Europe in having a wide band of income subject to a single rate. In most other countries income tax generally starts at a lower rate and the bands subject to each rate of tax are narrower' (1988: 15–16). In Britain in tax year 1992–3 there were only three income tax bands: a 20 per cent rate on the first £2,000 of taxable income, introduced in 1993 (increased to £3,000 in 1994); then a basic rate of 25 per cent up to £23,700 of taxable income; with the highest rate of 40 per cent payable on all taxable income over £23,700. Only about 7 per cent of taxpayers pay the 40 per cent rate of tax. With most people paying 25 per cent on most of their taxable income, this wide band means income tax in Britain is hardly progressive at all, although some progressivity is introduced through the additional three levels of earnings-related National Insurance contributions of 5, 7 and 9 per cent. However, there is an upper income limit on the payment of the 9 per cent contribution set at £390 of weekly income in 1992, which makes it regressive overall. The upper rate of National Insurance has been raised to 10 per cent in 1994.

Perceptions of fairness: marginal and average rates of tax

The ignorance of income tax structures may lead citizens to distorted conclusions as to their operation. Such misunderstandings may be played upon by politicians during election campaigns. One confusion relates to perceptions of the 'tax burden' and how heavily people *believe* they are taxed. The confusion surrounds the distinc-

Table 11.7 *Aggregate average tax rates*

Country/year	Method by which basic relief is mainly given[1]	Taxable income as a % of income subject to tax	Aggregate average tax rates as a % of income subject to tax
Australia 1987/8	Z	89.8	21.0
Austria [2, 4] 1982	C	78.0	12.8
Belgium [2*] 1987	Z	72.1	23.0
Canada [2] 1986	A	61.2	17.6
Denmark [2, 3] 1987	C	76.6	30.9
Finland [2, 3] 1985	Z	70.4	28.2
France 1987	Z	70.5	7.8
Germany [2*] 1987	A	78.3	19.8
Greece 1987	C	69.0	10.8
Ireland 1985/6	A	57.7	23.2
Italy [2*] 1985	C	95.0	18.6
Netherlands 1988	A	50.0	13.7
Norway [2, 3] 1987	Z	75.1	25.6
Spain [2] 1987	C	92.8	14.5
Sweden [2, 3] 1987	A	74.4	32.2
UK 1986/7	A	56.5	17.1
USA [2*] 1988	A	65.9	13.0

[1] A = Allowance. C = Credit. Z = Zero-rated first bracket.

[2] Countries with personal income taxes at subordinate levels of government. An asterisk refers to cases in which local income taxes are very small.

[3] Countries where social security contributions are financed by income taxes.

[4] Includes pension income for persons without additional employment income.

Source: Based on OECD, 1990: Table 1.1

tion between marginal and average rates of income tax. The marginal tax rate is the amount people pay on their last pound of taxable income, whereas the average rate is calculated by dividing *all* income (whether taxed or not) by the total amount of tax actually paid. Due to tax allowances and numerous tax reliefs, UK average tax rates are substantially lower than marginal rates. Citizens are much more aware, however, of levels of marginal than average tax rates. With marginal tax rates ranging up to 85 per cent in the early 1980s, it could be claimed that Britain was heavily taxed compared to other European nations where marginal tax rates were lower. This conclusion, however, did not take into account that other European nations did not have the same extensive range of tax allowances and reliefs, thus average tax rates in Britain were lower than in many European nations (Table 11.7). A citizenship perspective on taxation would suggest that if high marginal rates of taxation were reduced, so should the generosity of tax reliefs. This would widen the tax base and increase the progressive character of the tax structure. As it was, the reductions in marginal rates of income tax in the 1980s quite disproportionately benefited those with high incomes. However, reductions in some tax reliefs in the early 1990s suggest that some action is being taken on this point.

Average tax rates vary significantly between countries, with Denmark, Finland, Norway and Sweden at the top end with over 25.0 per cent; Australia, Belgium, Germany, Ireland, Italy and the UK in the middle range of 15–25 per cent; Austria, Canada, Greece, Netherlands, Spain and the USA below 15 per cent; and with France at the very bottom with 7.8 per cent. To some extent these variations reflect different concepts of income (OECD, 1990: 77), but also methods other than direct income tax for raising revenue.

In making comparisons between tax structures we must, as Peters (1991) noted, have a consistent data set. Following Peters, this is provided through the OECD and the following tables are those most recently available since his work was published. In establishing a comparable data set the OECD (1990) used the following three definitions of income:

1 'Taxable income' refers to the base to which the tax rate schedule is applied.
2 'Income subject to tax' is defined as taxable income plus all standard and non-standard tax allowances. This is the concept most used by the OECD. Standard allowances are usually unrelated to the actual expenditures incurred by the taxpayer and are automatically available to all taxpayers who satisfy the eligibility rules. Non-standard allowances are wholly determined by reference to the actual expenses incurred. They are neither fixed amounts nor fixed percentages of income (though they may be subject to a ceiling, as with the £30,000 mortgage limit for mortgage interest tax relief in Britain).
3 'Gross income' is defined as income subject to tax plus tax exempt income.

Although a common conceptual framework and methodology have been established to analyse and compare the income tax base and average tax rates in OECD countries, we need to be cautious in making simple comparisons. Variations often reflect the alternative role of income tax and ways of achieving the desired degree of progressivity. Table 11.7 shows significant variation between nations in the size of their tax base and in the average rates of income levied on that base.

The choices made by different countries regarding tax levels and how far they are going to rely on the personal income tax system, may provide some explanations for different national patterns. A later section considers patterns of public expenditure for social policy purposes and whether this does or does not redistribute income in addition to the tax system.

Taxation as a proportion of GDP

It is sometimes argued that if tax revenues exceed a given percentage of gross domestic product (GDP, that is, GNP less income from foreign investments) a nation will increasingly run into economic difficulties. The relationship of tax levels to GDP is examined in Table 11.8. These levels are likely to be influenced by the extent to which income tax receipts are used to finance social security and local government expenditure. Social security contributions levied on an income tax base are included in the data whereas those levied on other bases are excluded. We can see that total taxes as a percentage of GDP varies significantly between 30.0 per cent for the USA up to 56.7 per cent for Sweden, suggesting there are considerable possibilities for choice. We may conclude that overall levels of taxation depend on the values of societal members as manifested through the exercise of political rights rather than there being some technical maximum that *must* not be exceeded.

Table 11.8 also illustrates national variations in forms of tax-raising that Peters uses later in developing his typology of tax clusters, especially national variations in the balance between direct income tax, social security payments and indirect taxes on consumption. With the exception of the USA, the data include income taxes levied at subordinate levels of government, which, as in the Nordic countries, are more important than the central government income tax. As the OECD Report observes,

> this may have two effects; first those [nations] which rely considerably on income taxes for revenue sources at subordinate levels of government may have a greater total income tax burden than those relying more on other revenue sources such as property or consumption taxes for financing lower levels of government. Second, because central government income taxes have progressive rate schedules whereas local taxes tend to have proportional or less progressive schedules [or even regressive schedules, as with the British Community Charge] the total progressivity of the income tax system may be affected. (1990: 23)

In terms of financing social welfare programmes it is important to isolate specifically social expenditure from all expenditures, and

Table 11.8 *Taxes as a percentage of GDP, 1987*

Country	Total tax	Personal income tax			Social security	Consumption taxes	Other taxes
		Total	Central or federal	Other			
Australia	31.3	**14.2**	14.2	–	–	**9.3**	7.8
Austria	42.3	**9.6**	5.3	4.3	13.7	**13.7**	5.4
Belgium	46.1	**15.1**	13.6	1.5	15.6	**11.4**	4.0
Canada	34.5	**13.4**	8.3	5.0	4.6	**10.0**	6.6
Denmark	52.0	**25.6**	12.1	13.5	1.9	**17.6**	6.8
Finland	35.9	**16.4**	6.2	10.2	3.2	**13.7**	2.6
France	44.8	**5.7**	5.1	0.6	19.2	**13.1**	6.7
Germany	37.6	**10.9**	4.4	6.5	14.0	**9.6**	3.1
Greece	37.4	**4.6**	4.6	–	12.2	**17.4**	3.2
Ireland	39.9	**13.8**	13.8	–	5.6	**16.9**	3.6
Italy	36.2	**9.5**	9.4	0.1	12.4	**9.6**	4.7
Netherlands	48.0	**9.5**	9.5	–	20.5	**12.5**	5.6
Norway	48.3	**12.8**	2.7	10.1	11.4	**19.4**	4.8
Spain	33.0	**7.0**	6.5	0.6	11.9	**10.0**	4.0
Sweden	56.7	**21.1**	5.9	15.2	13.7	**13.7**	8.2
UK	37.5	**10.0**	10.0	–	6.8	**11.8**	9.0
USA	30.0	**10.9**	9.0	1.9	8.6	**5.0**	5.5

Figures have been rounded up and down.

Source: Based on OECD, 1990: Table 2.2

Table 11.9 compares social expenditure with total taxes as a percentage of GDP and provides a ratio of one to the other.

First, we should note that there is no simple relationship between total taxes as a percentage of GDP and social expenditure as a percentage of GDP, therefore simple cross-national comparisons of social expenditure have limited value. This is why writers such as Esping-Anderson (1990) have moved the debate on to the comparison of welfare state regimes, discussed later. Second, and most importantly, we should note the relationship between total taxes and social expenditure does not include 'tax expenditures' that subsidise private social welfare. They reduce total taxation by providing hidden welfare for those social groups with particular patterns of expenditure on owner-occupied housing and occupational and personal pension plans. On the other hand, social expenditure does include Housing Benefit to tenants, and basic state and SERPS pension payments, in the case of the UK. Therefore, interpretations of the ratio calculation must be undertaken with some care. Furthermore, we can see that social expendi-

Table 11.9   *Total taxes and social expenditure as a percentage of GDP*

Country	Total tax as % of GDP (1988) (1)	Social expenditure as % of GDP (1985) (2)	(2) as % of (1) (3)
Australia	31.3	18.4	58.8
Austria	42.3	28.8	68.1
Belgium	46.1	35.8	77.7
Canada	34.5	22.7	65.8
Denmark	52.0	33.9	65.2
Finland	35.9	22.8	63.5
France	44.8	34.2	76.3
Germany	37.6	25.8	68.6
Greece	37.4	19.5	52.1
Ireland	39.9	25.6	64.2
Italy	36.2	26.7	73.8
Netherlands	48.0	30.7	64.0
Norway	48.3	23.5	48.7
Spain	33.0	15.2	46.1
Sweden	56.7	30.2	53.3
UK	37.5	20.9	55.7
USA	30.0	18.2	60.7

Sources: OECD, 1990: Table 2.2; OECD, 1988: Table 1

ture as a percentage of GDP cannot be used as a measure of 'social burden' as it clearly varies considerably with respect to total taxation. It may well be that other expenditures such as defence are the 'real' burden. Social expenditures will of course vary with their generosity as well as the size of client groups, such as those of school age, numbers unemployed and those over retirement age. The latter two have tended to increase whilst the former decreased during the 1980s (OECD, 1988).

We can home in, however, on some specific areas of lost taxation following on from the earlier identification of the importance of 'income in kind' or fringe benefits.

The taxation of fringe benefits

Earlier discussion of patterns of income distribution highlighted the significance of fringe benefits in increasing the overall inequality of income distribution. We consider now how differential tax treatment of fringe benefits (income in kind) further affects the post-tax distribution of income and the manner in which the tax burden is shared. The peripheral imagery of 'fringe benefits' should not deceive us, though it seems intended to divert attention away from their importance for certain social groups. At times of income policies or in an attempt to hold or attract labour, income in kind may significantly increase a person's real income. How or whether fringe benefits are subject to tax is therefore an important aspect of 'fairness' within a tax system. This is especially so as the value of fringe benefits tends to increase with monetary income, which is usually progressively taxed. As the OECD has noted, 'The increasing use of fringe benefits which qualify for a favourable tax treatment reduces tax revenues and the fairness of the tax system' (1988: 7).

If the value of income in kind is treated more favourably than cash income, then there is the potential for tax avoidance and reduction in the progressivity of the tax system. This is especially so as fringe benefits go disproportionately to higher-income groups. Some citizens can use their stronger position in the labour market, and through civil rights (opportunities) obtain contracts of employment that provide not only privileged access to 'income in kind', but also favourable tax treatment. Such forms of privilege are relatively invisible to most citizens in their perceptions of the distribution of reward, yet visibility is essential for informed political citizenship and choice of social objectives and priorities. As income in kind that is either not taxed or receives favourable tax treatment, many fringe benefits must be regarded as a means of tax avoidance. This benefits both employer and employee in that, due to this more favourable tax treatment, income in kind is a more valuable form of payment, e.g. a company car. Furthermore, in some countries employees may avoid some element of the social security contributions they have to pay as income in kind is not included in the calculation of contributions (OECD, 1988).

In addition to reducing the employer's liability to pay social security contributions, 'income in kind' is also used as a method to circumvent government incomes policy. Thus, while democratically elected governments may impose incomes policies upon the community as a whole, 'income in kind' may reduce the social obligations of groups of employers and employees. As fringe benefits are usually deductible under corporation tax the Exchequer is thus also providing a tax subsidy to employers who make such provision. Revenues from consumption taxes may also be reduced by 'income in kind' by the avoidance of VAT (Denmark) and excise duty or sales tax (OECD, 1988). Fringe benefits, therefore, are a way of reducing the tax base and may be a way of reducing the marginal and average tax rate of higher-income groups.

We may also note that 'income in kind' is a less flexible form of payment and may be used to 'hold' employees in their present job. This may be particularly true of occupational pension schemes whose level of final pension depends on the number of years in the company scheme. A further advantage to employers of 'income in kind' payments is that they are worth more to their employees and thus raise the real value of the remuneration package. This results from the effective tax subsidy that goes to 'income in kind' which is not taxed in the normal way. Income in kind reduces the tax base, and this tax forgone by the Exchequer reduces the total tax taken and means that levels of taxation will have to be higher in the tax system due to this loss of tax income. Thus, 'income in kind' is an effective tax transfer to those who receive 'income in kind' from those who do not. In the interdependence of income definitions and taxes levied we once again observe the interdependence of modern society embodied, in this case, in systems of remuneration and taxation. Just as fringe benefits are the less visible part of the income package, so taxation of fringe benefits is the less visible part of the tax system. They both multiply the inequalities of resource distribution.

Considering the above observations, one may ask why governments provide favourable tax treatment for 'fringe benefits'. An important reason may be the furtherance of other government policies, such as the provision of private pensions, sickness benefits or the encouragement of domestic vehicle production through limited taxation of company cars (though this may just subsidise company cars in general where imported cars also attract tax subsidy). It must be concluded that the generous tax treatment of 'income in kind' should be regarded as an important aspect of social policy, especially where tax expenditures are not subject to public expenditure controls. Viewed from the citizenship perspective developed above, this results in interesting policy conflicts for governments. This was well stated by the OECD study:

> The main problem posed to governments by the spread of fringe benefits is that so far as they are subject to a favourable tax treatment the tax base is eroded (especially in France) and revenues are reduced below what they would have been if the payment had taken the form of fully taxable wages and salaries, or fringe benefits that are subject to normal taxation. This, in turn, may force governments to increase rates of income tax, thereby providing even greater incentives for taxpayers to substitute fringe benefits for wages and salaries. (1988: 15)

It seems doubtful that the collectivity of citizens would support these arrangements were they fully understood and more visible than they are. The fundamental citizenship issues raised by 'income in kind' are those of fairness and equity. Horizontal equity requires that taxpayers receiving equivalent remuneration should pay similar amounts of tax no matter what sort remuneration package they have. If this is not so citizens may feel they are justified in tax avoidance or evasion. The legitimacy of the way in which the community raises its funds may be undermined. Similarly, vertical equity requires that average rates of tax increase as the incomes of taxpayers increase. Income in kind reduces the progressivity of the tax system.

The main method used to measure, in aggregate, the cost of 'income in kind' is the revenue forgone by the Exchequer (Table 11.6). As information is limited for many countries, the UK is chosen for detailed examination and to exemplify the costs of income in kind. According to the OECD study, 'fringe benefits have provided higher income level employees with an increasingly greater proportion of their total remuneration in relation to lower income employees' (1988). There were about 1.35 million persons in 1983/4 receiving income in kind that was liable to tax; of those, 850,000 had a company car (500,000 also received free fuel from their employer). A further 400,000 employees were estimated to have company cars but were below the £8,500 earnings threshold for tax on company cars. About 6 per cent of all UK employees (including directors) had a company car. The earnings threshold has been held at £8,500 since 1979, thus more people are being brought within the regulations. The tax value of a company car is affected by a combination of factors: its age – over or under four years; its engine size; a person's business mileage; and the car's value. For example, a car of under four years, with a value up to £19,250, of 2,000 cc engine size and with business miles of 5,000 is given a taxable value of £2,770. Private medical insurance wholly or in part paid for by their employers covered some 530,000 persons, with a further 270,000 below the income threshold for tax. What are the implications for citizenship of providing a tax subsidy for people to be members of private insurance schemes when everybody is covered by the National Health Service? It is basically to jump the queue for treatment on the basis of need; an individualistic solution to a social problem of overall under-funding of the NHS.

The total value of fringe benefits to directors and higher-paid employees (those earning over £8,500) was nearly £1,000 million in 1983/4 – an average of £700 per person (OECD, 1988: 22) – whilst only £370 million was raised in tax on fringe benefits. Some 75 per cent of the total taxable value of expenses and benefits was made up of cars, fuel and private medical insurance. Employees are not liable for any tax on a number of fringe benefits. Some examples are: employer's contributions to an approved pension scheme; the first 15p of Luncheon Vouchers each working day; workplace nurseries provided by the employer; employee shares through an approved profit-sharing or SAYE scheme or executive share option scheme. These add substantially to a person's income package yet remain outside the tax base. Furthermore, almost all countries allow employers to deduct the actual cost of providing fringe benefits to their employees, where such costs are incurred exclusively and legitimately for the purpose of the business. This adds further to the revenue forgone and requires the Exchequer to raise more money from other sources.

The OECD (1988) concluded that fringe benefits are now widespread in most countries, their monetary value tends to increase as income increases and the cost of favourable tax treatment is significant. However, Peters states that 'Tax reforms of the past ten years . . . have tended to reduce or eliminate many of the tax privileges granted to special interest groups and this has permitted a broadening of the tax base' (1991: 13).

The balance between direct and indirect taxation

So far discussion has focused on direct taxation, the taxation of income. Nations vary considerably, however, in their balance of revenues from income tax, which tends to be progressive, and from indirect taxes on expenditure, which are regressive (Peters, 1991). This balance crucially affects the visibility and public perception of the taxes levied. The balance between revenues raised by direct and indirect taxes is thus another basis for considering whether revenues are raised on principles of citizenship. In this context it is noteworthy that much taxation debate in the 1980s was concerned with changing the balance in favour of indirect taxation and away from direct taxation (Meade, 1978), and in the UK this was done with the effect that the overall 'burden' of taxation increased, even as marginal rates of income tax were reduced. In April 1994, however, the UK government introduced VAT on fuel, with a further increase planned for April 1995. Contrary to a number of observations above this move has had high political visibility and has provoked widespread opposition. Nevertheless, it continues the move towards more indirect taxation. Sources of taxation revenues in Britain for 1988/9 are shown in Table 11.10.

The split between direct and indirect tax was 57:43, suggesting that the source of revenues is only slightly balanced towards

Table 11.10   *Tax revenues, 1988–9 (Budget forecast)*

	billion	%
Direct taxes		
Income tax	42.1	24.4
National Insurance contributions	31.6	18.3
Corporation tax	17.3	10.0
Capital taxes	4.7	2.7
Other (mainly North Sea oil)	2.6	1.5
Total	**98.3**	**56.9**
Indirect taxes		
Value added tax	26.2	15.2
Rates	19.0	11.0
Excise duty	17.9	10.4
Other (car tax, stamp duty, customs, etc.)	11.4	6.6
Total	**74.5**	**43.1**

Source: Financial Statement and Budget Report 1988 (the Red Book), taken from Hills, 1988

possible progressivity. Further, once the tax rates within direct taxation are also considered, then the UK tax system cannot be regarded as very progressive. In comparing the tax structure of nations, the national balance between direct and indirect taxes may be used as a primary indicator of 'citizenship taxation'; then, within direct taxation, the size of the tax base and the progressivity of the tax rates may be used as a secondary indicator. This might enable us to construct a typology of tax regimes in terms of principles of citizenship. In most countries, however, the tax system is dispersed with a number of tax instruments employed. Basically, tax systems of this kind are intended to reduce expected political opposition to the total amount of revenues raised. It makes some taxes less visible, e.g. taxes on consumption; it multiplies the variety of ways taxes may be collected and therefore reduces tax avoidance as taxes are spread over different activities people are involved in and the sources of their income. Though personal income tax is the largest single source of revenue it seldom exceeds half, and averages about a third, of all tax revenue. And sometimes it is levied at more than one level of government, for example in Sweden. Interesting examples of taxes on expenditure relate to customs and excise. Customs duties are levied on goods imported from abroad while excise taxes are levied on specific commodities. These are often placed upon commodities which may be popular but thought less desirable in some way, such as luxury imports of perfume and furs, or consumption of drink and tobacco, where reduced consumption due to taxation is not thought to be a hardship or may be desirable on health grounds. This highlights sharply how taxes may embody particular values and be used to modify and control behaviour. All tax systems embody value choices and that is a central argument for their greater visibility in a political democracy.

Though they are little used outside Britain and America, wealth taxes raise further issues for citizenship. Research into the distribution of wealth in Britain concluded that on average 40 per cent of personal wealth was inherited and amongst the richest 1 per cent as much as 75 per cent came from inheritance (Royal Commission on the Distribution of Income and Wealth, 1977; 1979). It is interesting that the rules of inheritance have survived so strongly in Britain despite a full adult franchise and widespread support across all political parties for the notion of 'equality of opportunity'. It is difficult to see how the rules of inheritance that pass on privilege to the sons and daughters of the rich can be squared with the meritocratic notion of equal competition for highly rewarded positions in society. Inheritance does seem to provide a flying start in the race. Thus, many so-called 'self-made men' are really made, in more senses than one, by their parents, not to say their grandparents and great grand-parents. Furthermore, to a certain extent wealth may accrue to individuals not so much through their own efforts as as a result of the needs and activities of the wider society. For example, those who had long held agricultural land around Aberdeen in Scotland suddenly found as a result of the discovery and development of North Sea oil the land's value increased dramatically through no effort of the owner. This has led to arguments not for taxing the wealth of the rich whilst they are alive but taxing those who receive gifts of wealth through inheritance.

In Part Three argument was made in favour of devolved systems of government in terms of the principle of 'subsidiarity', that decision-making should take place at the lowest possible level of government and closest to those affected by the decisions. It has also been argued in the context of the debate over Scottish devolution that it was essential that any Scottish Assembly should have fund-raising powers to give it accountability and responsibility. Thus, the governmental level at which taxes are raised is also a debate about the devolution of power in a democratic state and the degree of independence of sub-national governments from central control. This is an important element of the argument for the creation and maintenance of diverse milieux for the development of the 'social self'. The degree of central government funding of sub-national government in selected countries is shown in Table 11.11. The lower the figure the greater local autonomy there is in fund raising; for example, the low figures for Germany and the USA reflect their strong federal structures.

Progressive taxation

So, can countries be grouped according to the progressivity of their tax system? Shifting tax burdens from direct to indirect taxes will be regressive, thus less visibility and less political openness work against citizenship in terms of both democratic politics and progressive taxation. Restricting debate on taxation to élite groups without endeavouring to educate electorates as to the workings of tax systems undermines the values of citizenship in both politics and social policy. Due to a number of conceptual and statistical problems relating to international comparisons of income distributions in the OECD data, income distribution comparisons are restricted to comparisons *within* each country as a basis for the measurement of progressivity. The OECD data use Gini coefficients as a basis from which some

> broad cross-country generalisations [can] be made. [First,] there is generally an element of progressivity in the way taxable income is

Table 11.11 *Central funding of sub-national government, 1985*

Country	Central government grants as % of total revenues
Austria	17.6
Belgium	59.9
Denmark	43.7
France	39.0
Germany	8.5
Greece	42.5
Ireland	73.4
Italy	84.3
Luxemburg	50.7
Netherlands	83.8
Norway	40.1
Spain	40.3
Sweden	21.9
UK	48.7
USA	12.6

Source: International Monetary Fund Yearbook 1987, adapted from Peters, 1991: 47

Table 11.12 *Measures of progressivity*

Country	Income subject to tax		
	Musgrave	Suits	SPLIT
Australia	1.08	0.45	39
Austria	1.04	0.45	39
Belgium	1.08	0.38	67
Canada	1.15	0.82	70
Denmark	1.05	0.19	20*
Finland	1.08	0.32	42
France	1.03	0.55	13
Germany	1.05	0.56	23
Greece	1.04	0.44	14
Ireland	1.08	0.53	98
Italy	1.03	0.21	40
Netherlands	1.05	0.51	5
Norway	1.07	0.27	21
Spain	1.05	0.45	1*
Sweden	1.08	0.24	96
UK	1.06	0.72	84
USA	1.03	0.66	16

* indicates a negative measure.

Source: Extracted from OECD, 1990: Table 6.5

defined. [Second,] income minus taxes is in general more equally distributed than other income measures. This effect includes the impact of another progressivity factor; the use of a progressive tax rate schedule in determining tax payments. (1990: 62)

In most countries there are two determinants of progressivity in the tax system: first, the way taxable income is generally defined, delimited from broader income concepts through the use of exemptions and allowances; and second, the application of a progressive tax rate structure to taxable income. It is the interaction of these two factors that largely determines the progressivity of a tax system.

A number of measures of progressivity from the OECD (1990) study are presented in Table 11.12. The Musgrave measure registers the proportionate change in the equality of income distribution between pre- and post-tax income; a value higher than 1 signifies a progressive tax system. The Suits measure is identical to the Gini coefficient for taxes set against pre-tax income; a value higher than zero signifies a progressive tax system. Tax systems in all countries are clearly progressive, but the degree of progressivity (given by the ranking of countries) very much depends on the specific measure used. Different measures capture different aspects of progressivity.

It should also be noted that the structure of pre-tax distributions may in themselves influence the calculated values. Finally, the SPLIT measure in Table 11.12 indicates the relative importance of the way taxable income is delimited by allowances compared to the total progressivity effect.

The OECD study concluded

> that governments have chosen very different means of achieving the actual level of overall progressivity: especially in Denmark, the move from income subject to tax to taxable income has a regressive impact, the progressive impact of the total system being generated only by the progressive rate scale. In Austria, France, Greece, the Netherlands and the USA, only a small proportion of the total progressivity is caused by the definition of taxable income, the major part being caused by the progressive rate schedule. At the other extreme, the total progressivity in Ireland and Sweden is due almost entirely to the definition of taxable income, the rate schedule having only a negligible effect. (1990: 67)

We may conclude that measurement of progressivity of national income tax systems as a criterion for citizenship funding and comparisons between national income tax systems is not an easy matter. We may, however, begin to identify aspects of income tax structures which may be regarded as supportive of a citizenship approach to raising public revenues:

1 There should be a broad base for taxation, with minimal allowances and especially tax reliefs.
2 Taxes on income should bring in more revenues than taxes on expenditure.
3 Those with higher incomes should pay a larger proportion of that income in tax than those on lower incomes. Tax schedules should be progressive.
4 Those on higher income should not be treated, due to different marginal rates of tax, more generously through tax reliefs and allowances than lower-income groups.
5 Fringe benefits, income in kind, should be taxed on the same basis as money income.
6 Those considered poor enough to receive means-tested benefits should not at the same time be taxed on their income: the 'poverty trap'.

This section has critically examined differing structures of taxation and sought to identify some principles of taxation that seem conducive to citizenship. Taxation is a neglected yet crucial aspect of citizenship for it entails all three elements of citizenship: civil, political and social rights. Political judgements over tax structures crucially affect the distribution of resources in society and the extent to which they depend on civil rights (civil opportunity) of markets and labour contracts or social rights to state-provided welfare financed through the taxation of market rewards. Through their chosen systems and structures of taxation democratic states obtain the revenues through which citizens may be provided with social rights.

In the next section we examine the typology of tax regimes constructed by Peters (1991) and assess whether tax revenues are raised in ways supportive of citizenship.

Tax regimes

It is not easy to bring the above diversity of tax systems together in summary form but this has been attempted by Peters (1991). His work is particularly valuable for the way in which it argues the political character of taxation policy rather than the economic: that taxation is concerned not simply with raising revenue but also with achieving a variety of other social and political goals, for example reducing social inequalities that arise from labour market processes. He examined the pattern of taxation found in OECD countries in 1965 'based on the percentage of total tax revenue for all levels of government derived from each of eleven types of taxes'.[1] It is thus concerned with the ways in which revenue is *raised* rather than its pattern of expenditure. Through cluster analysis he identified four clusters of nations:

1   the Anglo-American cluster contains the UK, the USA, Canada, Australia, New Zealand, Japan and Switzerland;
2   the Latin cluster includes France, Greece, Italy, Portugal and Ireland;
3   the broad-based tax cluster contains Austria, Belgium, Luxemburg, the Netherlands, Spain and West Germany (pre-unification); and, finally,
4   the Scandinavian cluster includes Sweden, Norway, Denmark and Finland.

In 1965, the 'Anglo-American cluster' was 'characterised by much higher than average reliance on property tax, as well as on corporation taxes, and a somewhat higher than average reliance on personal income tax' (Peters, 1991: 62). Employers and employees roughly made equal contributions to social insurance, and these nations tend to have lower than average consumption taxes.

Countries in the 'Latin cluster'

rely heavily on indirect taxation, including customs duties, employers' social security contributions, and consumption taxes (general and specific) to meet their revenue needs. [Personal income tax revenue is especially low in France, Peters observes.] The pattern of taxation . . . is often argued to reflect the difficulties of their governments in collecting taxes directly from citizens. The tax system tends to be regressive, but has been the only effective means of generating revenue in these societies. (1991: 63–4)

It seems ironic that reluctance to pay progressive direct taxation results in the development of regressive tax systems that fall disproportionately on the lower-income members of society. How conscious of this are the citizens of France and Italy?

Countries in the 'broad-based tax cluster'

tend to use all tax instruments at their disposal, but to do so in moderation. . . . at the mean level for all OECD countries. . . . This level is not selected consciously by the governments, but appears rather to emerge from the political and economic systems within which the policy choices are made. This pattern of taxation tends to reduce the visibility of the tax system to citizens. . . . All these countries have had, or developed, corporate structures for the management of relationships between the public and private sectors. (1991: 63)

Private interest accommodation may thus explain the use of multiple tax instruments to spread tax burdens.

The 'Scandinavian cluster' had a

heavy reliance on personal income tax but relatively low corporate income taxes. They also tend to use the employers' social insurance contribution extensively, but to extract relatively little, or nothing, as the employee's contribution to social insurance. Both citizens and their employers contribute to the tax systems, but in different ways. The manner selected may conform to social democratic ideology, but also tend to make the tax system rather visible to citizens and may be in part to blame for tax revolts in Denmark. (1991: 62)

However, in terms of democratic openness such tax visibility should be regarded in positive terms rather than having the reality of the tax system hidden away from electors and thus reducing their ability to judge matters. Scandinavian countries also 'extract high consumption taxes, both general consumption taxes and excises. Excise duties on tobacco and alcohol are very high . . . in an attempt to deter consumption' (1991: 62).

Remembering that Peters was examining patterns in 1965, what changes have taken place since then? '[Very] little has changed in the tax policies of these countries. The same clusters identified in 1965 persist, with few . . . changes . . . until 1987'. This observation requires an important qualification: 'the much vaunted tax reforms of the 1980s and 1990s have done little to alter the distribution of *revenue* derived from the various taxes. The reforms have had a great deal of impact on *who pays the income tax* but little on what proportion of total revenues come from that source' (1991: 67; my italics). Since 1987, the general direction of tax reform 'has been toward a more broad-based taxation of the type found in cluster [3]'; dramatically, France has left the Latin cluster and joined the broad-based cluster. Peters further concludes that 'the four clusters had moved closer together . . . the OECD countries are becoming much more alike in tax policies than they have been' (1991: 67).

Governments have been less than open with their electors, effectively making taxes less visible to their citizens to reduce actual or expected discontent, or in the case of Britain to disguise an actual increase in total taxation as a decrease. Lack of information and understanding of these issues considerably strengthens the power of economic and political élites. Whilst visible income taxes in Britain declined substantially in the 1980s, less visible direct taxes in the form of social security contributions and indirect taxes in the form of VAT increased considerably. However, in contrast to making taxes less visible, the Thatcher government's ideological overdrive led it to introduce the highly visible and highly unpopular 'poll tax'. The poll tax was a flat-rate charge levied on all adults in a local authority district. It replaced local property rates levied on house-holders as a means of financing local government services. This was socially regressive as it was not related to income or ability to pay (McCrone, 1991). Hills has calculated that, 'Until their abolition, domestic rates roughly counterbalanced the subsidies and tax concessions to housing' (1991b: 5). In Scotland, a mainly owner-occupied housing area in Aberdeen found itself paying £1 million less than under the poll tax, whilst a mainly local authority housing area paid £1 million more. Due to widespread public opposition this flagship policy had to be dramatically reversed when Thatcher was removed from the party leadership.

In Britain the tax treatment of owner-occupied housing has only recently emerged as a major policy issue related to the tax sub-sidising of wealth accumulation for owner-occupiers (Forrest et al., 1990) and to the growth in credit (McLennan et al., 1991). One dimension of the issue is whether a country taxes imputed rental income. Such income is usually calculated as a percentage of the capital value of a house (generally much below the market value). Outlays on maintenance and current repairs are taken into account. Property tends to be undervalued, deductions are generous and the rates of tax do not reflect market rates of return on the property.

Interestingly, Peters suggests that 'One of the most important pressures [for tax harmonisation across the OECD countries] has been the strong desire of many governments to reduce the impacts of direct personal and corporate income taxes on their citizens as a means of encouraging economic growth' (1991: 68). It is perhaps better to consider this in terms of economic ideology rather than for its effectiveness in bringing about economic growth. The record in the UK has been singularly unsuccessful, average economic growth being lower in the 1980s than 1970s. The 'increasing internationalisation of business and finance' (1991: 68) has further contributed to a degree of harmonisation between nations, especially within the European Community. Therefore, the future development of citizenship principles in taxation will need to be considered at a level beyond the nation state. Whether the changes Peters identifies should be considered a trend remains to be seen.

Further analysis of tax regimes is undertaken in Chapter 12, where they are linked with Esping-Anderson's welfare state regimes. From this comparison, tax–welfare state clusters are identified in terms of their production of social rights of citizenship.

Note

1 From Table 2.1 in Peters (1991) the eleven types of tax were: personal income, corporate income, employee and employer social security contributions, payroll, property, general consumption, specific commodities, estate and gifts, customs, wealth and other.

12

WELFARE STATE REGIMES

Though Esping-Anderson's (1990) typology of welfare state regimes has generated substantial discussion (Langan and Ostner, 1991; Liebfried, 1991b; Mitchell, 1991; Taylor-Gooby, 1991; Lewis, 1992) it is not my intention to enter that debate at this point, but, rather, to outline his typology as a suitable starting point for distinguishing national welfare regimes. This then provides a basis for comparison with national tax regimes as outlined by Peters (1991). Esping-Anderson, whilst acknowledging that there is 'no single pure case' (1990: 28), identifies three clusters of welfare state regimes: 'liberal', 'corporatist' and 'social-democratic'. His clusters are based upon the total combined de-commodification scores of programmes for old-age pensions, sickness and unemployment insurance. 'We are capturing the degree of market-independence for an average worker' (1990: 50).

He characterises 'liberal' (low de-commodification) regimes by predominance of

> means-tested assistance, modest universal transfers, or modest social insurance plans. . . . Benefits cater mainly to a clientele of low-income, usually working-class, state dependants. . . . it is one where the limits of welfare equal the marginal propensity to opt for welfare instead of work. Entitlement rules are therefore strict and often associated with stigma; benefits are typically modest. . . . the state encourages the market by either [a low state] minimum or by subsidising private welfare schemes. [It] minimizes decommodification effects. (1990: 26–7)

The nations that compose this cluster are the USA, Canada and Australia and, to a lesser extent, the UK.[1] Second, is the 'corporatist' (medium de-commodification) cluster, in which

> the liberal obsession with market efficiency and commodification was never pre-eminent and, as such, the granting of social rights was hardly ever a seriously contested issue. What predominated was the preservation of status differentials; rights therefore were attached to class and status. [As this corporatism was subsumed under the state] private insurance and occupational fringe benefits play a truly marginal role. On the other hand . . . its redistributive impact is negligible. [Such regimes are] typically shaped by the Church (1990: 27)

Within this cluster, we find France, Germany, Finland and Italy.

Austria, which might be expected to be in this cluster, just squeezes into the next, his third, and smallest, cluster of regimes, which is of the 'social-democratic' (high de-commodification) kind. These are nations

> in which the principles of universalism and de-commodification [through] social rights were extended to the new middle class. Rather than tolerate a dualism between state and market, between working class and middle class, the social democrats pursued a welfare state that would promote an equality of the highest standards, not an equality of minimum needs as was pursued elsewhere. . . . services and benefits [are] upgraded to [meet the expectations of the middle class and workers are guaranteed] full participation in the quality of rights enjoyed by the better off. . . . a mix of highly de-commodifying and universalistic programs. . . . all strata are incorporated under one universal insurance system, yet benefits are graduated according to accustomed earnings. All benefit, all are [inter]dependent; and all will presumably feel obliged to pay. (1990: 27–8)

The nations found in this cluster are Sweden, Norway, Denmark, Netherlands, Belgium and Austria. Finland, which we might expect to be in this cluster, is on the edge of the previous corporatist cluster. Importantly, it is those welfare regimes that are most de-commodifying that place emphasis on full employment. The social-democratic regimes, unlike the other two,

> espouse full employment. It is at once genuinely committed to a full-employment guarantee, and entirely dependent on its attainment . . . the right to work has equal status to the right to income. . . . the enormous costs of maintaining a solidaristic, universal and de-commodifying welfare system means it must minimise social problems and maximise revenue income. (1990: 28)

We should note a further distinction, to which we return later, that in the corporatist tradition 'women are discouraged from working; [and] in the liberal ideal, concerns of gender matter less than the sanctity of the market' (1990: 28).

In explaining the causes of these clusters Esping-Anderson emphasises three factors: the historical legacy of regime institution-alisation, the nature of class mobilisation and, most importantly, class–political coalition structures (1990: 29). Class–political coalitions are particularly important if social rights of citizenship of an inclusionary kind are to be developed. In this context it will be interesting to see whether recent elections in Italy lead to new class–political coalitions and whether Italy moves its position within the typology in Table 12.2. Having outlined Esping-Anderson's clusters of welfare state regimes we may now identify some interesting relationships with Peters' (1991) tax regimes. Some of this ground was covered earlier but is repeated here for ease of comparison.

Linking tax and welfare state regimes

Peters' typology is 'based on the percentage of total tax revenue for all levels of government derived form each of eleven types of tax: personal, corporate, employers' and employees' social security contributions, payroll, property, general consumption, specific commodity taxes, estate and gifts, customs, wealth and other' (1991: 58 and Table 2.1). It is essentially based upon comparisons of the 'way in which [OECD nations] raise revenues' (1991: 59). His initial analysis was for 1965 and then updated to 1987, with the only difference being France moving from the Latin cluster to the broad-based cluster. It is the updated clusters which are compared with Esping-Anderson's welfare state clusters.

Peters' first cluster of tax regimes is titled 'Anglo-American'. These have much higher than average reliance on property tax, corporation tax, and a somewhat higher than average reliance on personal income tax. On the other hand, they have lower than average consumption taxes. Both employer and employee contribute to social insurance (1991). The USA, UK, Australia, Canada, New Zealand, Japan and Switzerland are placed in this cluster.

The second cluster is described by Peters as the 'Latin cluster'. These nations rely heavily on indirect taxation, including excise, employers' social security contributions and consumption taxes. This significantly reduces the 'visibility' of the taxes levied. In these nations it is often difficult to collect taxes, due in part to high numbers of self-employed and/or rural workers. Tax is levied in a highly centralised manner. This cluster contains Italy, Ireland, Greece and Portugal.

The third cluster of nations has 'broad-based taxation'. They tend to use all tax instruments in moderation at around the mean level for all the OECD countries. This reflects to some extent their corporatist traditions, and reduces 'visibility' of the overall level of taxation. In this cluster we find Germany, France, Austria, Belgium, the Netherlands, Luxemburg and Spain.

The fourth and final cluster relates to the 'Scandinavian countries'. Here there is heavy reliance on personal income tax but relatively low corporate income tax. There is extensive use of employers' social insurance, together with high consumption taxes and excise duties. This a highly 'visible' system of taxation. The nations are Sweden, Denmark, Norway and Finland.

Table 12.1 provides comparisons of tax and welfare state clusters, in which Esping-Anderson's medium de-commodification cluster is split for comparison with that of Peters. Certain nations in square

Table 12.1   *Comparing tax and welfare state clusters*

Tax clusters[1]	Welfare state clusters[2]
Characteristics of tax clusters, in 1987.	Characteristics of welfare state cluster by de-commodification score in 1980.
1 *Anglo-American* Much higher than average reliance on the property tax, corporation tax, and a somewhat higher than average reliance on personal income tax. Lower than average consumption tax. Employer and employee social insurance contributions.	*Low de-commodification* Means-tested assistance, modest universal transfers or modest social insurance plans, clientele low-income, usually working class. Entitlement rules strict, often associated with stigma; benefits are typically modest.
UK, US, Canada, Australia, NZ (Japan, Switzerland)	**UK, US, Canada, Australia, NZ** (Ireland)
2 *Latin cluster* Rely heavily on indirect taxation, including excise duties, employers' social security contributions and consumption taxes. High degree of centralisation. Difficulty of collection. Least 'visibility'.	*Medium de-commodification* Preservation of status differentials; rights therefore attached to class and status. Church-influenced. Little redistribution.
Italy (Ireland) [Greece, Portugal]	**France, Italy**
3 *Broad-based taxation* Tend to use all tax instruments in moderation at around the mean level for the OECD. Corporatist traditions. Reduced 'visibility'.	*Medium de-commodification* Preservation of status differentials; rights therefore attached to class and status. Church-influenced. Little redistribution.
West Germany, France (Austria, Belgium, Netherlands) [Luxemburg, Spain]	**West Germany** (Finland, Japan, Switzerland)
4 *Scandinavian countries* Heavy reliance on personal income tax but relatively low corporate income tax. Extensive use of employers' social insurance. High consumption taxes and excise duties. A 'visible' system.	*High de-commodification* Universalism and de-commodification through social rights extended to the new middle class. Equality of the highest standards, one universal insurance system, yet benefits graduated according to accustomed earnings. All benefit, all are interdependent.
Sweden, Norway, Denmark (Finland)	**Sweden, Norway, Denmark** (Austria, Belgium, Netherlands)

Sources: Derived from (1) Peters, 1991, and (2) Esping-Anderson, 1990

brackets [ ] appear only in the tax clusters and are omitted from comparison. Other nations appear in round brackets ( ), which indicates a disjuncture between their placement within the two clusters. Those nations which 'fit' comparisons across clusters are shown in bold.

Linking tax and welfare state regimes

This section compares Peters' (1991) clustering of tax regimes with Esping-Anderson's (1990) clustering of welfare state regimes shown in Table 12.1. There are remarkable parallels between the two clusters. We may clearly identify seven *joint* tax–welfare clusters, though most nations fit into four. (These seven tax–welfare regimes are shown in Table 12.2.)

There are two low de-commodification joint clusters. First, we can identify an 'Anglo-American tax, low de-commodification' group of nations: the USA, UK, Australia, Canada and New Zealand. This joint grouping seems least to fit the criteria of citizenship for both tax and welfare highlighted above. Second is a 'Latin tax, low de-commodification' cluster containing only Ireland.

There are three medium de-commodification clusters. First, we have a 'Latin tax, medium de-commodification' group consisting of Italy. Second is a 'broad-based tax, medium de-commodifaction' cluster, containing Germany and France. And third is a 'Scandinavian tax, medium de-commodification' cluster containing Finland. In these three clusters we find more complex relationships between tax and welfare systems.

Finally, there are two high de-commodification clusters. The first is a 'broad-based tax, high de-commodification' cluster containing Austria, Belgium and the Netherlands. Second is a 'Scandinavian tax, high de-commodification' group of nations that includes Sweden, Denmark and Norway. Here the latter have high direct tax regimes with a high de-commodification welfare state, where taxes are highly visible and the welfare regime incorporates all social classes. This seems best to fit the criteria for citizenship highlighted in the earlier discussion of both tax and welfare systems, as well as being 'visible' to its citizens. We can see, however, the possibility for a broad-based tax regime to also coincide with high de-commodification. This flexibility is an extremely hopeful phenomenon for later discussion of the future of welfare and social rights within the European Community.

In conclusion, we can observe that different tax regimes 'bridge' different welfare state regimes. The Latin tax regime bridges low and medium de-commodification, whilst broad-based tax regimes

Table 12.2 *Joint tax–welfare state regimes*

Joint tax–welfare state regimes	Nations
1 Anglo-American tax, low de-commodification welfare states	UK, US, Australia, Canada, New Zealand
2 Latin tax, low de-commodification welfare states	Ireland
3 Latin tax, medium de-commodification welfare states	Italy
4 Broad-based tax, medium de-commodification welfare states	Germany, France
5 Broad-based tax, high de-commodification welfare states	Austria, Belgium, Netherlands
6 Scandinavian tax, medium de-commodification welfare states	Finland
7 Scandinavian tax, high de-commodification welfare states	Sweden, Denmark, Norway

bridge medium and high de-commodification welfare state regimes. Thus we can identify a clear gradation from Anglo-American tax, low de-commodification joint regimes to Scandinavian tax, high de-commodification joint regimes. Thus, joint tax–welfare regimes enable us to make links between forms of welfare states and the manner in which those nations raise their tax revenues. We may conclude that, to a large extent, the 'jointness' of the regimes is a reflection of common ideology influencing both tax and welfare systems. This is at the same time an indication of the openness of choice that is available to nations, and possibly to a future expanded European Community.

Having explored, compared and related the complex structures of taxation to the very differing types of welfare state regimes, in Part Five we daringly consider the prospects for the development of social rights of citizenship at a European Community level.

Note

1 Mitchell (1991) suggests 'in terms of the poverty gap and the level of income inequality [in 1980], the *outcomes* of the UK system are closer to the corporatist group of countries' (my italics).

PART FIVE
TOWARDS EUROPEAN
SOCIAL RIGHTS

In the move towards a Single European Market (SEM) a 'social dimension' has been identified as necessary to protect workers whose lives will be disturbed and disrupted by the increasingly free movement of goods, services and people. The European Community, it is argued, must be seen as pursuing more than the economic interests of industry and citizens as consumers. During the considerable restructuring that will result from the development of an SEM, workers and their organisations will expect their employment and social rights to be maintained and even improved. Kleinman and Piachaud have summarised the situation well when they observe,

> 'Convergence' between the member states has come to mean the acceptance of tight inflation and exchange rate targets, and the abandonment of deficit spending as a major tool of macro-economic management. Social policy is thus the handmaiden, not an equal partner, of economic integration. Its role, at present at least, is secondary (although nonetheless important): to ease the transition into the internal market by reassuring workers that there will be a social dimension; and to assist the casualties of the process of economic restructuring which is at the heart of the whole integration project. (1993: 10)

Thus the social dimension can be seen as in the German tradition of compensating workers for the social costs of change that will arise from economic integration. However, it is not at all clear that sufficient resources are being devoted to social policy to compensate those who will bear the social costs of this economic restructuring. As suggested earlier, the 'success' of economic integration is likely to be exaggerated by failure fully to recognise the costs of economic change. 'This meagre level of resources devoted to redistributional policy [through the Community's Structural Funds], accompanied by a lack of serious forecasts of who and where will lose and gain from the single market is probably the most worrying aspect of current development' (Kleinman and Piachaud, 1993: 11). Most crucially it seems to be assumed that unemployment resulting from economic restructuring will automatically be absorbed through the economic growth released by the restructuring, but no evidence is provided, and in 1994 rising unemployment across the Community looks increasingly to threaten restructuring itself, as nations start to look to national solutions to the problem. However, looking beyond immediate problems of unemployment, or possibly in response to them, what are the prospects for the development of European social rights?

13

SOCIAL CITIZENSHIP IN EUROPE: THE EUROPEAN SOCIAL CHARTER

The first scenario for the development of social rights is through nation states steadily internalising European Community policy through the 'basic social rights' found in the 'Social Charter'. However, as its title suggests, 'The Community Charter of Fundamental Rights of Workers,' is directed at the interests of workers rather than all citizens. Indeed, its function is to compensate workers for the costs of economic restructuring, but, clearly, the more generously it compensates the more difficult it may be to justify such economic restructuring. Therefore we may expect the resources provided under the Charter to be limited. We are again confronted with the questions posed in Chapter 6: who bears the costs of social change, and how much are they compensated? Doogan has observed that although the Charter 'maps out a formidable area of policy making in which to establish social rights [, the] Community's 15 million unemployed [in 1992, now nearer 21 million in 1994], of whom roughly half are long-term unemployed, fail to provide a focus for policy making in this arena' (1992: 168). Although the long-term unemployed are a priority under the Structural Funds, they are not given 'fundamental social rights' because there is no right to work. The Social Charter does not address the fundamental social relationship of industrial society, the need to sell one's labour power as a means to life. Setting that important point aside, what is the status of the Charter? The complexity and uncertainty surrounding the legal basis of the Charter have been concisely summarised by Doogan.

> In the first instance it is difficult to locate the Charter in the armoury of legal provisions at the disposal of the Commission. It falls *outside* the two groups of measures, one of which of which is *legally* binding and takes the form of Regulations, Decisions and Directives and the other set of Community instruments which are *not legally* binding including Memorandums, Communications, Opinions, Recommendations and Resolutions. The measures of the Social Charter's Action Programme, which has been produced to give effect to the declarations of the Charter, are

more easily classified. The programme involves a package of some 47 proposals which are currently in the various stages in the process of formulation, consultation and negotiation. Approximately half of the action programmes will be non-legislative and half will involve new legislative measures of differing legal status. In all they comprise 23 directives (specifying outcomes but *not* process) in the social field, including 11 in the field of health and safety and five measures currently described as 'Community instruments'. There are, in addition, five recommendations and 20 other measures. They also *vary in the specificity and generality of their application.* (1992: 169; my italics)

Due to this complexity and lack of clarity we may expect progress to establish social rights, even to workers under the Charter, to be a slow process. One example of controversy, for example, concerns limiting the maximum number of hours to be worked to 48 in any one week. It was highlighted earlier in Table 11.2 that nearly a quarter of male manual workers in Britain worked more than 48 hours a week in April 1992. This proposal is being progressed as a health and safety measure that requires a qualified voting majority, rather than under employment protection legislation that requires unanimous approval from the Council of Ministers. There is fierce debate, especially from Britain, over this procedure.

As some nation states come to fear for European social legislation overriding national policy, so argument is coming to focus upon the concept of 'subsidiarity' within the Community. 'What is best done at the local, regional or national level must not be undertaken at the Community level' (Delors, quoted in Doogan, 1992: 171). The Charter, however, opens up the possibility that some powers related to social policy may be operated at the overall Community level. This arises from a concern that during the process of economic integration there are prospects for 'social dumping' arising 'out of the downward pressure on labour costs and social protection that might evolve from labour market deregulation' (Doogan, 1992: 172). If the Community does not pursue common social protection policies some nations with poor protection will tend to gain an unfair advantage from economic integration, for example the UK, which already has one of the lower measures of de-commodification in Europe (Esping-Anderson, 1990). Thus it is argued within the principle of subsidiarity that the appropriate level for the development of social protection is the Community level. This provides significant opportunity for a major breakthrough in the development of transnational social rights, such as a European safety net for income support (Atkinson, 1992), whatever the initial welfare state forms. Doogan's paper rightly stresses that 'the integration of capital and product markets is of a different nature to the integration of labour markets' (1992: 172). This echoes the argument made in the opening part of this book that labour markets are different from other markets because they involve treating human beings as commodities and human beings resist this where they can. At the present time that resistance takes place at the nation state level and through the diverse social policy instruments of each nation. These national social policy instruments are part of the labour costs of each nation in competition with other nation states. Therefore, unless social integration accompanies economic integration, some nation states will continue to have a competitive advantage over other Community members through their lower social provisions. The UK, in opting out of the Charter, can therefore be seen as wanting both economic integration *and* national economic advantage.

Thus, social integration is an essential part of economic integration and this requires the development of Community-wide social policies. Tension remains between these two forms of integration regarding competition with the world outside the Community. The question remains as to which polices will emerge as the basis for social integration within Europe. How well will European workers be protected from world-wide market pressures to down-bid pay and conditions? Clearly, for the moment, it will be largely in terms of the varying forms of national welfare states described earlier, and to which we return shortly.

Community social policy, however, is already slowly emerging from a different direction. Where tensions exist between Community social policy and that of the member nation states, without it apparently being overtly intended, the European Court of Justice resolves issues of compatibility. Meehan has summarised the position as follows:

> Strictly speaking, Community policy decisions are taken by intergovernmental means at the Council of Ministers but, in practice, a great deal of work in devising Regulations and Directives is carried out by the Commission. And, once agreed upon by the Council of Ministers, Regulations give, and Directives may *give members of national communities rights irrespective of the content of national laws*. Disputes about whether or not national and Community laws are compatible are considered by the European Court of Justice, either at the request of national courts or in non-compliance actions brought against member state governments. (1991: 127; my italics)

Until the Community strengthens its democratic decision-making it seems likely that Europe's social policy will slowly emerge from

Court decisions. As Liebfried (1991b) observes below, progress on social rights gets caught up within the 'democratic deficit' within the Community. We might usually expect the exercise of democratic political rights to lead to the emergence of social rights, but because political rights above the nation state level are still ill-developed within the Community it may be that pressures are emerging for social rights through the exercise of civil rights in the Court. The development of Community social rights through this means may in turn provide the impetus for greater democracy within the European Community. Thus European citizenship may evolve in a quite different sequence from the evolution of citizenship in the UK (Marshall, 1950).

The problems and difficulties of the European Community in developing the social rights of its citizens and in working out, through the principle of 'subsidiarity', what are the most appropriate levels for decision-making should not, however, be regarded with ridicule or disdain. Whether representatives of member states realise it or not they are already engaged in the inevitably long and problematic task of developing an institutionalised form of European citizenship. They are participating in the creation of complex social institutions beyond the nation state. It's not easy – there will be setbacks and difficulties – but if it's not attempted, what is the alternative? National economic rivalry and competition in a world of finite resources! If Europe proves successful it may provide a cross-national model for the development of world citizenship, some day. Liebfried, however, is not so optimistic about development of a European social policy when he observes that

> The founding of a United Europe depends mainly, if not totally, on the 'four freedoms': the free movement of persons, goods, capital and services. Thus 'economic citizenship', which does contain some civil aspects of 'social citizenship' [my 'civil opportunities'], is in the fore. Political as well as social citizenship are presently relatively marginal in the process of European unification. . . . This pattern repeats Anglo-Saxon history. . . . It will not be the unity of an enlightened 'Social Europe', synthesising its traditions of democracy and solidarity, of civil and social right, its traditions of merging the citizen and the worker. (1991b: 31)

Even in a context of rising European unemployment, it is not yet clear whether such pessimism is justified. Membership of the Community is still growing, and this may change the balance of political forces influencing social policy development as shown in the following comparisons between the tax–welfare state traditions of the 'twelve' and the 'sixteen'.

Table 13.1 *Joint tax and welfare state regimes within Europe*

Joint tax and welfare state regimes	The European 'twelve' and 'sixteen'
1 Anglo-American tax, low de-commodification regimes	UK
2 Latin tax, low de-commodification regimes	Ireland
3 Latin tax, medium de-commodification regimes	Italy, (Greece, Portugal)
4 Broad-based tax, medium de-commodification regimes	Germany, France, (Luxemburg, Spain)
5 Broad-based tax, high de-commodification regimes	[Austria,] Belgium, Netherlands
6 Scandinavian tax, medium de-commodification regimes	[Finland]
7 Scandinavian tax, high de-commodification regimes	Denmark, [Sweden, Norway]

Note: Nations in ( ) brackets located by author. Nations in [ ] brackets are the four additional members of the Community.
Source: Developed from Esping-Anderson, 1990, and Peters, 1991

Tax and welfare regimes of the 'twelve' and the 'sixteen'

Liebfried (1991a) has observed how the enlargement of the European Community from six to twelve nations changed it from a relatively homogeneous grouping to a far more heterogeneous grouping. This has possibly made convergence and harmonisation more problematic. However, with the prospect of the twelve soon to become the sixteen through the addition of Austria, Sweden, Norway and Finland the balance of tax and welfare regimes within the European Community will change yet again. Drawing on earlier discussion of tax and welfare regimes, Table 13.1 concentrates on typologies of the 'twelve' and the 'sixteen'. First we should note that Luxemburg, Spain, Greece and Portugal were not included in Esping-Anderson's analysis although they were in Peters, therefore their allocation to a joint tax–welfare cluster is more problematic and is based on the author's judgement. The table suggests seven joint clusters may be identified for the 'twelve' and the 'sixteen'. Focusing first upon the degree of de-commodification, we find of the 'twelve' nations that two are low de-commodification, seven are medium de-commodification, and three high de-commodification nations. A majority are thus medium de-commodification welfare states with a combination of Latin and broad-based tax regimes. When we examine the 'sixteen', however, we find two low de-commodification, eight medium and, now, six high de-commodification nations. The balance of de-commodification has moved more towards the high end, though with no overall majority for any grouping. This perhaps suggests that enlargement to sixteen will, at least, decisively weaken the low de-commodification position of the UK. The UK will appear even more as the 'odd man out' of Europe. On the other hand, problems of rising unemployment may pull some of the high de-commodification nations with broad-based tax regimes towards the medium de-commodification joint group, in which case they would have a majority of the 'sixteen', and so move social policy in a medium de-commodification direction. What seems less likely is that Europe of the 'twelve' or, even less so, of the 'sixteen' will move to a low de-commodification position, even if that were desired by Greece and Portugal. All this assumes that there would be no major shift of nations beyond an adjacent grouping; recent elections in Italy could undermine this assumption. From this analysis we may expect both the 'twelve' and, even more so, the 'sixteen' to resist 'social dumping' by the UK.

Women and the social rights of citizenship

In focusing upon 'workers'' rights the Social Charter is essentially concerned with the rights of those in paid work; thus rights are built around labour market participation. Although women are increasingly participating in the labour market, their participation is often intermittent or part-time. A great deal of their social contribution comes outside the labour market in the form of unpaid work. This is given little recognition by the Charter, which therefore remains a 'workers'' rather than a 'citizens'' charter. A similarly criticism of Esping-Anderson's typology of welfare state regimes has been the absence of gender from his analysis (Langan and Ostner, 1991; Liebfried, 1991b; Taylor-Gooby, 1991; Lewis, 1992). The lives of women are far less *directly* commodified than those of men. The admirable focus on questions of de-commodification in Esping-Anderson's analysis raises particular problems for women. First, their labour market position is more likely to be part-time, irregular, and to be interrupted over their lifecourse because of childbearing and -rearing. Their lifecourse is less commodified. Second, the focus on de-commodification supposes that work is paid work and therefore ignores the unpaid work carried out, largely, by women. In focusing on de-commodification, Esping-Anderson neglects those unpaid activities which contribute to life outside market relationships. As stated in Part One, there is an important social interdependence between men and women due to the role women play in the reproduction of society and in the reproduction of male labour power. This interdependence has been inaccurately redefined as female dependence through the historically dominant role of men in higher-paid employment outside the home. Women then have been defined as being at home rearing children and dependent on the income of men. However, whilst more and more women have been entering the labour market, the unpaid work of women in the home seems to have changed little, and remains undervalued. Welfare states tend to be 'male breadwinner' welfare states.

Women and welfare state regimes

We can build on the criticisms of Esping-Anderson (1990) made by Liebfried (1991b), and of both, made by Langan and Ostner (1991). Liebfried suggests it is more appropriate to identify not three but four welfare state regimes. These are illustrated in Table 13.2. This view is supported by the earlier analysis of tax–welfare regimes. The need for a gender dimension in examining welfare state regimes has been argued by Langan and Ostner. A typology based on their views is also shown in Table 13.2. As Langan and Ostner point out, 'What happens to women in these different regimes is an important indicator of social change. . . . [It is therefore useful to re-examine Liebfried's typology] considering evidence about women's economic and political position under these different regimes' (1991: 134).

We may draw the following conclusions from the comparisons in Table 13.2. As all welfare state regimes, to varying extents, are built around assumptions of labour market participation, they tend to make two broad assumptions. First, that women should be integrated into the labour market (with its class inequalities) as full- or part-time paid workers, and, second, whether they undertake paid work or not, that they should undertake unpaid labour. Unpaid labour is not for men! Arising from the traditional interdependence between welfare states and assumptions concerning the selling of labour power, the other interdependence between paid and unpaid labour, as argued earlier, has been ignored. Therefore a social right

Table 13.2 *Women and welfare state regimes*

Liebfried's typology (1991b)	Langan and Ostner's typology (1991)
Anglo-Saxon: 'residual' welfare states The WS operates as a work-forcing mechanism; selectivity and means-testing makes the WS a compensator of last resort.	*Labour market 'equality' model* [?] WS policies encourage people to stay in the labour market. Formal equality between genders in the marketplace; family is subsumed as dependent on the male.
Latin rim: 'rudimentary' welfare states. There is no right to welfare; stress residualism and forcing entry into the labour market. Religious traditions of welfare. Labour market retains strong agricultural base, a rudimentary household/family or subsistence economy, and a thriving black economy. No full employment policies.	*Mixed women's family support economy* Unregulated employment of women in small firms. Gender-segregated labour market, endorsed by agrarian Catholic culture.
Bismarckian: 'institutional' welfare states Buy-off social problems by subsidising exit from the labour market or by blocking entry. The WS is not primarily an employer but a compensator. Government promises of full employment combined with stable labour markets help to create a fragile universalism.	*Gendered status maintenance model* Dualistic approach; labour market and the family. Money rather than services. Its corporatism supports a traditionally gendered division of work and public duties as well as mutual obligations, or subsidiarity, in families. Maintenance of individuals' former social status.
Scandinavian: 'modern' welfare states Proclaim a universal right to work rather than offering compensatory income transfers. The WS is employer of first resort, particularly women. Subsidised entry into the labour market. 80% of men and women in labour market.	*Universalism of a female social service economy* Women are in principle treated equally as individual wage-earners; individual taxation promotes double-earner households and part-time work. Parental leave. Men work in private industry, women in public services. Women pay service women to enable them to go out to work. Services rather than money.

Source: Developed from Liebfried, 1991b, and Langan and Ostner, 1991

of citizenship that recognises this social interdependence is required if both women and men are to be equal citizens.

From a feminist point of view, Langan and Ostner highlight the assumptions of labour market opportunity that underpin welfare state regimes. For example, in the Scandinavian model, because the

> state has become the major employer, particularly of women. . . . which enables other women to remain in the labour market, [and because] nearly half of all women work part-time, . . . [then] these women must either rely . . . on their partner's income or . . . [have incomes] less than that of the average male worker. . . . It offers equal opportunities, but equal outcomes have never been intended. (Lewis quoted in Langan and Ostner, 1991: 135)

The problem of 'equal opportunities' raises issues of both social class and gender. Men tend to have greater labour market opportunities than women. Unlike most women, they tend to work in the primary labour market and few work part-time. Middle-class men, however, tend to have greater labour market opportunities than working-class men, they tend to work in the primary labour market, have fewer hours of overtime and receive more 'fringe benefits'. Similarly, middle-class women tend to have greater labour market opportunities than working-class women, they too are more likely to work in the primary labour market and are higher paid. On a basis of social class, opportunities within the labour market produce unequal outcomes for both men and women. As *unpaid* workers women are indirectly commodified through dependence on the husband's labour market reward, and as *paid* workers they are either fully or partly directly commodified depending upon whether they work full- or part-time. Whether they are fully, partly or indirectly commodified, their life-chances remain crucially tied to the selling of labour power, their husband's and/or their own. Thus outcomes can never be equal between genders so long as the means to life depends on commodification in the labour market. Neither gender, male nor female, can escape the influence of social class inequalities.

Due to commodification, gender always has a social class dimension but, importantly, social class also has a gender dimension. Class inequalities are gendered due to 'familialisation' (Lister, 1992b: 20). Due to their primary responsibility for unpaid labour in the home, and its variability over the lifecourse, it is extremely difficult for women to compete equally with men in the labour market. Therefore social class will always have a gender dimension. As Langan and Ostner have sharply pointed out,

> Men are commodified, made ready to sell their labour power on the market, by the work done by women in the family. Women, on the other

hand, are de-commodified by their position in the family. . . . It is not possible to examine the position of women in the labour market without considering women's position in the household/family. The private household/family plays a strategic role in a modern capitalist welfare state by providing not only services (Scharpf, 1986), but also a sense of continuity, stability, belonging and mutual obligation. An appreciation of the domestic division of labour and women's pivotal role in the processes of reproduction of modern societies is crucial in understanding the gendered nature of the welfare state and its associated social stratification (Gordon, 1990; Sassoon, 1987). (1991: 131)

Women lose out in these welfare states because they lose out in the labour market, and they lose out in the labour market because they lose out in the domestic division of labour. This is particularly so in the Bismarckian focus on maintaining income status differences in welfare, and even more so in the case of the Anglo-Saxon welfare states' focus upon maintaining labour market incentives.

As argued earlier, by redistributing rewards through social rights, welfare states can contribute to the de-commodification of social relationships. Therefore, we may argue that Esping-Anderson is partly correct in emphasising the de-commodifying nature of welfare states as a key factor in the development of social rights. As there are specific gender differences between paid and unpaid work, however, the focus upon de-commodification of paid work cannot address the situation of those whose work is unpaid (Lewis, 1992). In the same vein, Lister has suggested, 'The dimension of de-commodification needs to be complemented by that of "defamilialisation" if it is to provide a rounded measure of economic independence' (1992b: 20).

A possible answer to these questions of 'de-commodification' and 'defamilialisation' may be found in the debate surrounding proposals for a Basic Income of citizenship (Walter, 1989; Parijs, 1992; Parker 1993). This is the subject of the next chapter.

14

A BASIC INCOME:
AN EMBODIMENT OF SOCIAL
RIGHTS?

Earlier discussion of social policy and social rights identified a number of problems in providing an income adequate for human self-development. Benefits based on means-tested provision or on participation in the labour market were both seen as deficient. Furthermore, both these forms of income raise specific problems for women. Women have a different and more irregular lifecourse engagement with the labour market and there is little direct independent financial recognition of their unpaid work. If social rights are to be citizens' rights rather than workers' rights they must be detached from labour market participation. Proposals for a Basic Income address these problems.

The idea of a Basic Income

Essentially, Basic Income cuts across the social division of welfare embodied in the benefits provided through state and fiscal welfare discussed in Part Four. Arguing in a British context, Parker defines a Basic Income as follows:

> A Basic Income scheme would phase out as many reliefs and allowances against personal income tax and as many existing state-financed cash benefits as practicable; and would replace them with a Basic Income paid automatically to each and every man, woman and child. . . . No national insurance contribution, no earnings rules, no availability for work rules and no cohabitation rules; wives and children treated as equal citizens; benefit as a platform on which all can build without red tape. (1993: 3)

It might thus be called a citizen's income. Financing would come through general, primarily income, taxation. 'Basic Income would be paid for by charging income tax on all (or almost all) other income. . . . The tax rate would depend on the Basic Income amounts, and the phasing out of existing tax reliefs and social security benefits' (Parker, 1993: 6).

As the debate over Basic Income has developed, questions have arisen concerning levels of Basic Income and levels of taxation, phasing in the benefit, and conditionality.

'A Full Basic Income (FBI) is defined as sufficient to cover all basic needs (including housing)' (Parker, 1993: 7). This *might* meet the criteria for the 'optimal development' of human beings, but it *would almost certainly* meet the needs for 'minimal development', as advocated by Doyal and Gough (1991). Furthermore, it might meet the requirements for 'sufficiency' as found in the writings of Daly and Cobb (1990) if 'sustainable development' of the planet's resources is to be achieved. Fromm, too, has advocated a form of 'basic income' that would provide the material base for 'being' rather than 'having' (see Chapter 16).

'Since everyone would receive the Basic Income and virtually everyone would pay tax, the present, invidious distinction between taxpayers and beneficiaries would fade away. [However, and this seems to be the obstacle,] a Full Basic Income (FBI) . . . would require a tax rate on all other income of 70 per cent, and is therefore considered unacceptable' (Parker, 1993: 7). Not surprisingly, it does not seem possible to establish adequate social rights without societal agreement to substantially reduce inequalities of reward. Such agreement may be slow in coming. In the meantime, therefore, advocates of Basic Income have turned to consideration of a Partial Basic Income (PBI). This, however, 'would not be enough to live on, except perhaps for non-householders. Some means-tested benefits would have to be retained for people without paid work or other sources of income' (Parker, 1993: 7). This, we should note, would not be sufficient to provide women without paid work with an adequate income in their own right. Furthermore,

> Neither FBI nor a PBI could be introduced at a stroke – the redistributive effects are too large – for which reason attention has focused on transitional schemes, TBI (Atkinson and Sutherland, 1988; Atkinson, 1989). . . . Such schemes cash out the personal income tax allowance and replace them with them with *very* small Basic Incomes of around £13 for adults and £10 for children in 1991. (Parker, 1993: 8; my italics)

Jordan, too, acknowledges there would be problems of 'transition' to a Basic Income in sudden alterations to established incentives. 'It would be rash to introduce – at stroke – a whole new scheme for flat-rate, universal, non-gender specific, unconditional allowances making some individuals much better off, others much worse off, and shifting the balance of advantage between "work" and "leisure"' (1991: 9). A period of phasing-in and adjustment would be necessary as people accommodated their behaviour to this non-market source of income.

A Basic Income, however, is more than simply a source of non-market income. In the context of the earlier arguments concerning social interdependence, problematic economic growth and pervasive social costs, and gender and class inequalities, it can be seen as addressing a number of complex issues of distributive justice. 'Advocates of a Basic Income have argued that it is *potentially* a device for reconciling economic efficiency with distributive justice under late-twentieth-century economic conditions' (Jordan, 1991: 1). It is argued, in summary form by Jordan, that,

> By giving every adult citizen an unconditional sum, sufficient for basic needs, and irrespective of work or marital status, it would both free up the labour market from the unemployment and poverty traps, allowing *maximum* participation, and give those with low earning power or onerous responsibilities for caring a basic security in a fragmented employment situation. In the longer run it could address inequalities between the work roles and domestic duties of men and women, by redistributing paid and unpaid work. (1991: 1; my italics)

Though it is argued a Basic Income will *increase* incentives to work for many low-paid workers, how are people in general to be motivated to work if they can obtain access to 'sufficient income' as a social right? Labour market participation, either through insurance contributions and/or through the payment of income tax, is the principal source of funding for a social right to a citizen's income. Therefore, if there are no 'conditions for entitlement' to a social right, how will people be motivated to work in the first place to provide the resources to fund the social right? Does this not take us back to the basic dilemma of motivating people to work such that they starve or have a very low level of living if they do not? As Gilder (1982) states, do not the 'poor require the spur of poverty'?

As Jordan has pointed out,

> The remedy increasingly adopted by those who favour a Basic Income, . . . is to introduce an element of conditionality. . . . For example, in the form of a statutory number of paid hours to be worked a year or a life time (Gorz, 1982). A division has emerged within the advocates of a Basic Income between those favouring some conditionality (most German and many French advocates), and those insisting on the centrality of unconditionality to the very notion of a Basic Income (the majority of British, Dutch and Belgian advocates). (1991: 2)

As unemployment and poverty have increased in the 1980s and 1990s, existing 'conditionality' has been tightened up through the developing support for 'workfare' or through conditions to ensure that the unemployed are 'actively seeking work'. It is argued that there is a social obligation or social duty to work. Duties balance rights. Interestingly, it is duties of the low-paid, unskilled workers that are the focus of concern, not the higher-paid, skilled and professional workers (Jordan, 1991). It is a fear that these lower-paid workers would choose not to work at such tasks that occupies centre-stage in the debate over duties and incentives. This is really an argument about maintaining incentives for people to work in jobs of a low-paid, boring, non-self-developing kind. The focus is not on changing the characteristics of the *positions* in the labour market but maintaining incentives for people to *occupy* these positions. Problems of structure can then be presented as problems of individual motivation which in turn have to be maintained by low benefits. In industrial societies where so many people have to sell their labour power as a means to life a Basic Income would, to a degree depending on its level, de-commodify that relationship. Thus, conditionality is essential, at the bottom end of the labour market, to maintaining the power of employers over employees. As Jordan sharply observes, the wider advocates of conditionality within social security systems in general, in terms of ' "targeted" benefit systems, means-tested and with support withdrawn as income rises', are also supporters of 'a fragmented, casualised labour market, free from restrictions such as a minimum wage, with lots of temporary, subcontract and part-time employment and self-employment' (1991: 6). Paradoxically, from the New Right perspective, the needs of individuals and their families take second priority to the needs of markets.

This concern with conditionality, however, can have a different origin. In the welfare state traditions of a number of European nations such as Germany and France, work-based, earnings-related benefits have been at the centre of welfare state development. As Jordan observes, 'earnings related unemployment benefits, [usually] keep better paid workers above the poverty line . . . anxiety over unconditionality is tied in with anxiety over the adequacy of protection. A Basic Income might be better for lone parents and some low-paid workers . . . but not those with higher earnings' (1991: 6). Nations with existing social security systems that reflect differences of class and status within the labour market, such as those with a corporatist tradition (Esping-Anderson, 1990), may therefore see Basic Income as undermining differentials in social security levels. However, the Standard Employment Relationship (SER) that underpins these welfare states is increasingly under pressure with increases in part-time and irregular employment, especially among the growing female element of the workforce (Hinrichs, 1991, on Germany). Thus changes in labour market structure will increasingly threaten the reality of welfare states based upon the SER.

Nevertheless, unlike the case of civil and political rights, concern remains about the 'fairness' of giving people something for nothing as a social right. This question involves issues of values and ethics but also revolves around the assumption that all members of industrial societies can actually sell their labour power and for sufficient reward to finance their human development. Yet, as noted earlier, there is no right to work nor is there a guarantee of adequate pay. Thus, those who live in such a society that cannot deliver that 'promise' for all, yet nevertheless benefit from such opportunities themselves, can be regarded as having some obligation to share what they have with those who do not. In the same way that some people bear the unintended social costs of social change, so others reap the unintended benefits. In the same way that being poor cannot be fully explained in terms of individual effort, so neither can becoming rich and successful. Some are structurally constrained by the very same structures that enable others to be successful, for example changes in spending patterns create demand in new areas even while they destroy jobs in others. Therefore, there is some argument for saying that the successful should share more of their success with the less successful. This argument also addresses Jordan's concern (1991: 13) that a related and more complex argument, in response to the supposed 'free-rider' issue as put forward by Parijs (1991, 1992), will not convince people whose concept of justice involves the 'equalisation of the burdens and benefits of [societal] membership' (Jordan, 1991: 13).

The concept of social interdependence as outlined in the earlier parts of the book provides a powerful rationale for a Basic Income as a means of sharing in industrial societies where people are dependent upon selling their labour power as a means to life, but where this cannot be guaranteed. This is a social structural view of justice rather than the individualistic and often asocial notion of justice that tends to prevail in these debates (Jordan, 1991: 13). Furthermore, the fact that many women for large parts of their lifecourse are not able to sell their labour power, but are none the less engaged in other socially useful and essential activities, provides additional argument that social interdependence is a sound underpinning for Basic Income. Otherwise many women, and for large parts of their lifecourse, will remain dependent upon men, and when in old age that man dies, they will descend into poverty. A Basic Income would not only redistribute between social classes, it would also redistribute from men to women, and over the lifecourse. This was the case with the introduction of Child Benefit in the UK, which is paid to women with dependent children but is, largely, paid for through the taxes of men who at the time have no children (Field, 1988).

Do advocates of Basic Income who also argue for 'conditionality' undermine its potential for de-commodification, which is, for Esping-Anderson, a defining characteristic of a 'social right'? Although it is argued that citizens have duties as well as rights, many female citizens carry out duties without rights to an adequate level of living. What are their duties to contribute to the common weal? In this context Jordan argues for a different form of conditionality, 'that all citizens have an obligation to contribute to the "socially necessary labour" – not necessarily paid employment – of their community' (1991: 16). And isn't this what all women do for most of their lifecourse? More recently Atkinson has argued for a 'participation income' slightly higher than Transitional Basic Income (TBI) whereby conditions may be met by a variety of forms of social participation.

> It would no doubt include: work as an employee or self-employed; absence from work on ground of sickness or injury; inability to work on ground of disability; unemployment, but available for work; engaging in approved forms of education or training; caring for young, elderly or disabled dependants; undertaking approved forms of voluntary work. (1993: 20)

Importantly, the single link with paid work would be broken, our multi-stranded relationships of social interdependence would be recognised. It is because we have come to see contributions to society in money terms that we consistently undervalue and neglect the non-market activities that are an essential part of social interdependence. Hence the inherent individualism of markets and their neglect of externalities that do not have a market. Externalities are an important form of social interdependence little recognised by markets. Environmental economists are increasingly recognising environmental interdependence in treating the world as a total ecological system. Similarly, social interdependence requires we recognise that we live in a social world that is best understood as a total social system. Thus, we tend to agree with Jordan's (1991: 19) criticism of the market individualism of Dworkin's (1990) liberalism. A moral environment is not like an economic environment, people are social beings whose morality comes from 'communal identification and integration' (Jordan, 1991: 19). Individual life projects only make sense and have possibility of realisation because we are social beings who are socially interdependent upon one another, but that social interdependence is not recognised through everyone having the material base from which to develop themselves. Our life projects are socially interdependent. This social interdependence could be recognised through the exercise of democratic political rights that would establish a powerfully social right of citizenship. As is recognised by Jordan,

> This means that citizens have in a sense to be accountable to each other, to define public issues and shared concerns in which they must reach agreements over standards of justice. The burdens and benefits of membership in such a community cannot be equalised, through markets and auctions, by an invisible hand. The political process must be visible, involving shared resources and public standards, in order for citizens to be able to recognise common interests, and organise themselves for the common good. . . . they are required to identify with each other and with their community, and not simply to seek the critical success of their own lives. (1991: 20)

Each must be the defender of the citizenship rights of all. As the creators and re-creators of our social worlds we still have a choice in how we answer the question: what kinds of people do we wish to be?

PART SIX
CITIZENSHIP: UNDERSTANDING AND PERCEPTION

Most discussion of social rights, and this is true of much of this book, is concerned with the material base of citizenship, the provision of income or social services such as health and education. These, however, are to large extent means rather than ends in themselves. A question remains: what are the ends of citizenship? It cannot be simply the increased acquisition of material welfare, for, as argued in Part Two, there are probable limits to ever-increasing material welfare. Though levels of material welfare remain import- ant, and need to be improved for many people, they are, in the main, directed at human development. Human development is concerned with the character of human beings and their relation- ships to one another. This involves matters of understanding and perception. We return again to the question posed by C.Wright Mills (1970) in his discussion of the sociological imagination: what kind of people are we able to be? What kinds of awareness and understanding do we expect of citizens? This question is addressed in Chapter 15 below through a discussion of the sociological imagination as a basis for awareness and understanding. That discussion is then developed further in Chapter 16 through examin- ation of Erich Fromm's (1979) distinction between 'having' and 'being'. In a world where we shall increasingly have to restrain our consumption of material things to limit our impact on the environ- ment, we shall need to concern ourselves with some traditional notions of developing the *inner* human being. There seems con- siderable scope. Thus this remaining discussion of citizenship is concerned with the development of individuals and their relation- ships with one another; of developing their understanding and perception.

15
THE SOCIOLOGICAL IMAGINATION

Put simply and boldly, all citizens should be encouraged to develop a 'sociological imagination'. This is primarily so they may understand that present-day social institutions and social arrangements are socially created and re-created by active human beings. That therefore, in principle, social arrangements may be rearranged; that the ways in which we do things now are not immutable. Citizens must grasp the 'double involvement of individuals and institutions: we create society at the same time as we are created by it' (Giddens, 1982a: 14). The promise of democratic citizenship is the creation of institutional arrangements that enable individuals to develop in the directions they wish. Because individuals cannot escape the influence of institutional arrangements, they must more consciously participate both in their operation *and* in their reconstruction. Without such understanding people will feel trapped within their personal lives. As Mills observed, writing originally in 1959:

> Nowadays men often feel that their private lives are a series of traps. They sense that within their everyday worlds, they cannot overcome their troubles . . . what ordinary men are directly aware of and what they try to do are bounded by the private orbits in which they live; their visions and their power are limited to the close up scenes of job, family, neighbourhood; in other milieux, they move vicariously and remain spectators. (1970: 9)

If people are to escape this feeling of being trapped, they require forms of reasoning that enable them to make links between personal experience and social structure. For many people this is not easy for they do indeed experience life as spectators; where they feel they are subject to vast impersonal forces that they cannot understand, let alone control. Resource depletion and pollution of the environment are obvious examples; less obvious are market operations that may suddenly and unpredictably throw them into unemployment. They remain observers of the political scene rather than conscious actors within it. Mills argued,

> What they need . . . is a quality of mind that will help them to use

information and to develop reason in order to achieve lucid summations of what is going on in the world and of what may be happening within themselves. It is this quality . . . that may be called the sociological imagination. (1970: 11)

T.H. Marshall's (1950) concept of citizenship may be regarded as an excellent example of a 'lucid summation of what is going on the world', or at least in Britain over the previous three hundred years. It provides a framework for understanding ourselves and our relationships to the institutions of society in terms of civil, political and social rights. It is an exercise of the sociological imagination. In Giddens' (1982a) exposition of the sociological imagination he identified three forms of sensitivity indispensable to sociological analysis: historical, anthropological and critical sensitivity. Historical sensitivity is necessary to understand how the present arrangements of society came into being. For though people make themselves, they do not do so in circumstances of their own choosing. We are all born into an ongoing world. Indeed, the world we are initially socialised into comes, at first, to be seen as 'the world'. Its ways of doing things are seen as 'natural' and 'commonsense'. Yet the industrial world that we have created during the past two hundred years is particularly unique in human history. At first the family and neighbourhood, and later the nation, define the world for us. As we enter our teens, however, we become increasingly aware of variations within our nation and of a world beyond our direct experience, and we may come to interpret and question the world into which we were born. In interpreting our own 'national world' an anthropological sensitivity is important to developing an understanding of other cultures and the alternative ways people live their lives. It is important to be able to step back from our taken-for-granted ethnocentric and Eurocentric, industrialised view of the world. This is not easy, for it is deeply imbedded within us.

> The fostering of an historical sense of how recent and how dramatic are the social transformations of the past two centuries is difficult. But it is perhaps even more challenging to break away from the belief, explicit or implicit, that the modes of life which have developed in the West are somehow superior to those of other cultures. (Giddens, 1982a: 22–3)

It increasingly looks as though the materialism at the heart of the world-view we are encouraged to develop in industrialised nations is running into problems of sustainability, and is becoming more problematic as a basis for judging other cultures. An anthropological sensitivity becomes vital if we are to understand the interplay of different cultural forms with the natural environment. 'The valuation of material productivity that is so pronounced in the modern West is itself a specifically anomalous attitude, when compared with other cultures' (Giddens, 1982a: 24). The Western industrialised cultural form has, through military conquest, tended to dominate the globe. It has become *the* measure of progress, yet the limit of its promise to the developing nations is becoming increasingly apparent (Cole and Miles, 1984). Other, less material, measures of progress that are more commonly found in non-industrialised nations require our consideration, such as sufficiency and sharing. Giddens reminds us that 'in most cultures, and for virtually the whole of human history, human beings have lived "in" nature, feeling themselves to be part of it, intermingling aesthetic and religious experience' (1982a: 170). Through the development of historical and anthropological sensitivity we may become aware of the possibility for the world to be arranged differently, if we so wish. It is particularly important to appreciate that sociology is not like a natural science in that 'social processes are governed by unalterable laws. As human beings, we are not condemned to be swept along by forces that have the inevitability of laws of nature' (Giddens, 1982a: 26). Human beings are social creators, they continually invent new social forms, new social arrangements. For example, both markets and welfare states have been socially created. Through the development of a sociological imagination, we may become critically conscious of our ability to continually reconstruct our social worlds. 'As critical theory, sociology does not take the social world as a given, but poses the questions: what types of social change are feasible and desirable, and how should we strive to achieve them?' (Giddens, 1982a: 166). Thus, it is perfectly feasible to argue, through democratic institutions, for the development of a range of social rights that foster human development. The task is to convince others that this is feasible and desirable in a world where we are running up against the 'ecological limits to the utilisation of nature by human industry' (Giddens, 1982a: 171).

As Mills perceived, at present most people 'do not possess the quality of mind essential to grasp the interplay of man and society, of biography and history, of self and world' (1970: 10). 'The sociological imagination enables us to grasp history and biography and the relations between the two in society. That is its task and its promise' (1970: 12). For many people the world is experienced as one in which they are constantly subjected to forces and events that they do not understand. It is difficult for them to relate their personal experiences to the structural organisation of the society in which they live, and appreciate how that structure provides both opportunities and constraints for the choices and decisions they

make. The manner in which structures of opportunity and constraint operate must first be understood before a person can see how
they might be changed. Are the difficulties an individual encounters
in undertaking a 'project' related to some deficiency within the
individual or do they relate to the manner in which opportunities
and constraints are structured for that person? Does the individual
need to change his or her behaviour to accommodate to the
structure, or should the structure be changed either to provide a
new range of opportunities or by removing existing constraints?

In Mills' view, 'Perhaps the most fruitful distinction with which
the sociological imagination works is between the personal troubles
of milieux and the public issues of social structure' (1970: 14). This
classic distinction within sociology is described by Mills in the
following fashion:

> Troubles occur within the character of the individual and within the
> range of his immediate relations with others; they have to do with his self
> and with those limited areas of social life of which he is directly and
> personally aware. Accordingly, the statement and resolution of troubles
> lie within the individual as a biographical entity and within the scope of
> his immediate milieu.
>
> Issues have to do with matters that transcend these local environments
> of the individual and the range of his inner life. They have to do with the
> organisation of many such milieux into the institutions of a historical
> society as a whole, with the ways in which various milieux overlap and
> interpenetrate to form the larger structure of social and historical life.
> (1970: 14)

This distinction is central to debate over political citizenship. The
early emergence of civil rights of citizenship provided opportunity
for members of society to give 'voice' to their concerns, but
depended upon a small propertied élite to respond to those claims.
However, so long as this small élite were the rule-makers, the mass
of society were severely constrained in their ability to change the
structure of opportunity and constraint under which they lived.
What were in many instances 'public issues' were defined by the
élite rule-makers as 'personal troubles' for which they had little
concern. It was a matter for the individual. Such was the case of
poverty in early nineteenth-century Britain. However, once the
mass of society in Britain obtained political rights through extension
of the franchise, they were able to elect and remove rule-makers.
They were thus more able to obtain some social agreement that
certain problems they confronted arose from the structural organisation of society and could be changed. The advent of democratic
government, warts and all, thus opened up possibilities for the
collective reconstructing of social worlds, as it still does today.
Because social worlds are collective social constructs their *conscious*

restructuring is inevitably a collective enterprise, though power to determine events consciously is not equally shared. The development of forms of 'welfare state' and the provisions of social rights by elected governments are examples of the conscious reconstructing of the structure of opportunities and constraints. The development of forms of collective social rights to welfare outside individual market exchange was a significant restructuring of opportunities. Personal troubles were addressed by their recognition as a public issue through the interplay of Marshall's (1950) three elements of citizenship. We should note, however, that what is 'public' and what is 'private', and the relationship between the two, is periodically contested, reflecting changes in the balance of power between social groups. Private unpaid labour in the home is slowly being drawn into the arena of public debate as we come to appreciate the way it reflects the dependency of women on men, and its under-valuation by markets.

Human beings are essentially creative beings, though much of this creativity has become narrowly focused into paid employment, of an often far from creative kind. Fromm considers what he calls the *marketing character* as becoming more dominant in society.

> It is based on experiencing oneself as a commodity, and one's value not as 'use value' but as 'exchange value'. . . . What shapes one's attitude towards oneself is the fact that skill and equipment for performing a given task are not sufficient; one must win in competition with many others in order to have success . . . a person is not concerned with his or her life and happiness, but with becoming saleable. (1979: 146)

In industrial societies where individuals and their families are dependent upon selling their labour power as a commodity, it is incumbent upon society to either provide forms of employment that make human development possible, or provide social rights that allow for the human development of their members. If this is not done, then the ability of many members of the society to develop their 'self' will be adversely affected. 'The powers of reason, of love, of artistic and intellectual creation, all essential powers, grow through the process of being expressed' (Fromm, 1979: 112). So long as what are really public issues remain personal troubles, many people will be unable to express many of their creative powers and thus their human development will be constrained.

HAVING AND BEING

Fromm, in his Introduction to *To Have or to Be?* writes that 'The Great Promise of Unlimited Progress – the promise of domination of nature, of material abundance, of the greatest happiness of the greatest number, and of unimpeded personal freedom – has sustained the hopes and faith of the generations since the beginning of the industrial age' (1979: 11). And though at first socialism and communism aimed at a 'new society and a new man', this changed into an 'ideal of the bourgeois life for all' (1979: 11). Both socialism and communism were reactions to the commodification of social relationships through the development of labour markets whereby human beings as the carriers of labour power are treated as things. Yet, over time it has been our relationship to things which has threatened our relationships to each other as human beings. In the process of having more and more material things we come to treat each other as things. The 'having' mode of existence dominates the 'being' mode. Though having is a means to being, it has taken on a life of its own. Our having of more and more consumer goods, through the increased division of labour, often destroys the being of creative producers who become de-skilled. In 'having' more and more we risk diminishing others' ability to 'be'.

What is having? Fromm argues that it is an external relationship to things which stunts the internal development of the person and his or her relationships to other human beings: 'possession of property fulfils the craving for immortality, and it is for this reason that the having orientation has such strength. If my self is constituted by what I have, then I am immortal, if the things I have are indestructible' (1979: 87). Fromm cites examples from Egyptian mummies to contemporary passing on of property through wills. Though even in the richest industrial nations most people do not have substantial estates to pass on in their wills, they can experience the having orientation through possession of more and more consumer goods. What is the relationship between possession of such goods and the personal development of the self? No doubt a number of these goods ease physical exertion and provide for more leisure time, but does that lead to development of the self? Fromm makes an important distinction between 'existential having' and 'characterological having':

> [Human] existence requires we have, keep, take care of, and use certain things in order to survive. This holds true for our bodies, for food, shelter, clothing and for the tools necessary to produce our needs. This form of having is rooted in human existence. It is a rationally directed impulse in the pursuit of staying alive. In contrast, characterological having is a passionate drive to retain and keep that is not innate, but has developed as the result of the impact of social conditions on the human species as it is biologically given. (1979: 90)

We have socially created and spread characterological having over the past three hundred years through the development of consumer markets. The consumer has replaced the creative producer as the goal of human existence, and in that process having has tended to squeeze out being. The acquisition of goods for reasons of status, as encouraged through advertising and consumerism, and for power over others characterises the having mode. We are called upon less and less to use our creative capacities in developing our 'self' and in re-creating our social world.

What is being? Fromm argues that it relates to internal self-development that takes place through relationships with other human beings. He acknowledges that

> the mode of being is more difficult to define than the mode of having. Having refers to things and things are fixed and describable. Being refers to experience, and human experience is in principle not describable. What is fully describable is our persona – the mask we each wear, the ego we present – for this persona is itself a thing. The living human being cannot be described as a thing . . . the total me, my whole individuality . . . can never be fully understood, not even by empathy, for no two human beings are identical. (1979: 91)

It is only, Fromm suggests, in the mutual relatedness between people that barriers to separateness can be overcome as we 'participate in the dance of life' (1979: 91). Central to 'self'-development are our relationships with other human beings and the institutional arrangements that we and they have created. They may help or hinder the development of the 'self'. Fromm continues, 'The mode of being has as its prerequisites independence, freedom, and the presence of critical reason' (1979: 92). As will have been noted, the centrality of critical reason to human beings was also argued to be a key aspect of the sociological imagination, and this is an important meeting point between acquiring a sociological imagination and the mode of being. The fundamental characteristic of the mode of being is 'being *active*, not in the sense of outward activity, of busyness, but of inner activity, the productive use of our human powers' (1979: 92; my italics). It was argued earlier in Chapter 2 that the commodification of labour power constrained the use of individuals' human productive powers because they were forced to sell these creative powers as a commodity to obtain the means to life. As a consequence many forms of employment do not allow for the expression of a person's creative powers. For Fromm,

> To be active means to give expression to one's faculties, talents, to the wealth of human gifts with which – though in varying degrees – every human being is endowed. It means to renew [constantly develop] oneself, to grow, to flow out, to love, to transcend the prison of one's isolated ego, [to relate to others], to be interested, to give. (1979: 92)

Fromm's notion of 'activity' fits well with the notion of the development of the 'social self' referred to in Chapter 1. He highlights how the notion of 'activity' has changed since prior to the Renaissance. 'Activity in the modern sense . . . makes no distinction between why people are active. It does not matter whether they are interested in their work, like a carpenter or a creative writer, or a scientist or a gardener; or whether they have no inner relation to and satisfaction in what they are doing, like the worker on the assembly line or the postal clerk' (1979: 94). Often, arising out of the need to sell one's labour power as a means to life in industrial societies, we hand over to the buyer of our labour power control of our creative human activity to be used for the employer's purposes but not our own. Human creative activity may thus be used in limited and mechanical ways not requiring the active use and development of human powers of creativity. Such experience by human beings is likely to stunt their 'self'-development such that they take an instrumental attitude to employment, and having takes over from being. They are, in the classic sense, 'alienated from their species being' (Meszaros, 1970). It has become increasingly difficult in complex market societies for the individual to resolve this problem for it properly requires change in the structural organisation of society. It is a public issue rather than a personal trouble. In developing his argument further, Fromm draws a distinction between alienated and non-alienated activity:

> In alienated activity I do not experience myself as the acting subject of my activity; rather, I experience the *outcome* of my activity, . . . as something separated from me and standing above and against me. . . . I have become separated from the result of my activity. . . . In non-alienated activity, I experience *myself* as the *subject* of my activity. Non-alienated activity is a process of giving birth to something, of producing something and remaining related to what I produce. . . . my activity is a manifestation of my powers. . . . I call this non-alienated activity *productive activity*. (1979: 94)

What Fromm calls 'productive activity' refers to the *quality* of the activity; a state of inner activity or what we might call human creativity. He relates this to 'the free conscious activity' as the 'species character of man' as referred to by Marx (Meszaros, 1970). For Marx, labour, as human activity, is life. Thus humans are the active creators of their lives through their creative activity; their labour. They and society grow and develop through human productive activity. We are involved in the 'double hermeneutic' discussed above of humans creating and being created by society. It is this conscious creative activity that is at the heart of 'being' and is an essential part of the sociological imagination. However, as Fromm then argues,

> Only to the extent that we decrease the mode of having, that is of nonbeing – i.e. stop finding security and identity by clinging to what we have . . . by holding on to our ego and our possessions – can the mode of being emerge. 'To be' requires giving up one's egocentricity and selfishness. [But as Fromm recognises,] most people find giving up their having orientation too difficult; any attempt to do so arouses their intense anxiety and feels like giving up all security. . . . What holds them back is the illusion that they . . . would collapse if they were not supported by the things they have. (1979: 93)

It is recognised by Fromm that *both* the having and being orientations to life exist in every human being and that the social structure of society, its values and norms, decides which of the two becomes dominant. The anxiety and insecurity engendered by the danger of losing what one has are absent in the being mode. 'If *I am who I am* and not what I have, nobody can deprive me of or threaten my security or sense of identity. My centre is within myself; my capacity for being and for expressing my essential powers is part of my character structure and depends on me' (1979: 112). In considering the foundations of social character, however, his starting point reaffirms the conceptual point made in our earlier discussion of the sociological imagination, that the 'character structure of the average individual and the socio-economic structure of the society of which they are a part are interdependent' (1979: 133). This view is also shared by Mills (1970) and by most sociologists, and social interdependence as the foundation of citizenship was the subject of discussion in the opening chapters of this book. There is an essential openness in this social interdependence: 'the relation between social character and social structure is never static, since both elements in this relationship are never-ending processes. A change in either factor means a change in *both*' (1979: 133–4; my italics). This thus leaves open the potential for conscious social change by human beings. Fromm observes somewhat pessimistically, however, that

A society whose principles are acquisition, profit and property produces a social character oriented around having, and once the dominant pattern is established, nobody wants to be an outsider, or indeed an outcast; in order to avoid this risk everybody adapts to the majority, . . . the leaders of our society believe that people can be motivated only by the expectation of material advantages, . . . and that they will not react to appeals for solidarity and sacrifice. Hence, except in times of war, these appeals are rarely made, and the chances to observe the possible results of such appeals are lost. (1979: 109)

Following on from the discussion of the probable limits to material growth in Parts Two and Three, it is concluded that in the very near future our leaders will have to make appeals for solidarity and sacrifice. In so doing their chances of convincing people of the fairness of the social and economic changes that will be required will crucially depend upon the kinds of understanding and perception their citizens possess. For as Fromm finally observes,

the human species needs a *frame of orientation* and an *object of devotion* in order to survive. Without a map of our natural and social world – a picture of the world and one's place within it that is structured and has inner cohesion – human beings would be confused and unable to act purposefully and consistently, for there would be no way of orienting oneself, of finding a fixed point that permits one to organise all the impressions that impinge upon each individual. . . . [this] comes from a consensus with those around us. (1979: 137)

There are a variety of levels and degrees of consensus within society. In complex industrial societies such a degree of secular consensus may come from the operations of democratic institutions but it will also require the development of the sociological imagination which encourages tolerance and understanding of conflicting viewpoints. 'But a map,' he continues, 'is not enough as a guide to action; we also need a goal that tells us where to go . . . we need an object of . . . devotion . . . to integrate our energies in one direction' (1979: 138).

Arising from our social interdependence, democratic citizenship should be directed to the social development of all. First, through provision of social rights and, second, through participation in the re-creation of society. The social development of all might provide a secular 'object of devotion', and one with which people from many religions and none might come to agree.

REFERENCES

Abel-Smith, B. and Titmuss, K. (1987) *The Philosophy of Welfare*. London: Allen and Unwin.

Andrews, G. (ed.) (1991) *Citizenship*. London: Lawrence and Wishart.

Arbor, S. and Ginn, J. (1991) *Gender and Late Life*. London: Sage.

Atkinson, A.B. (1989) *Poverty and Social Security*. London: Harvester Wheatsheaf.

Atkinson, A.B. (1992) *Towards a European Social Safety Net?* Discussion Paper WSP/78. STICERD. London: London School of Economics.

Atkinson, A.B. (1993) *Beveridge, the National Minimum, and Its Future in a European Context*. Discussion Paper WSP/85. STICERD. London: London School of Economics.

Atkinson, A.B. and Micklewright, J. (1989) 'Turning the Screws: Benefits for the Unemployed 1979–88', in A. Dilnot and I. Walker (eds), *The Economics of Social Security*. Oxford: Oxford University Press. pp. 4–51.

Atkinson, A.B. and Sutherland, H. (eds) (1988) *Tax Benefit Models*. Occasional Paper No. 10. STICERD. London: London School of Economics.

Baldwin, P. (1990) *The Politics of Social Solidarity*. Cambridge: Cambridge University Press.

Barr, N. and Coulter, F. (1991) 'Social Security: Solution or Problem?', in J. Hills (ed.), *The State of Welfare*. Oxford: Oxford University Press. pp. 274–337.

Bell, D. (1976) *The Cultural Contradictions of Capitalism*. London: Heinemann.

Berger, P. (1987) *The Capitalist Revolution*. Aldershot: Wildwood House.

Berger, P. and Berger, B. (1983) *The War Over the Family*. London: Hutchinson.

Beveridge Report (1942) *Social Insurance and Allied Services*, Cmd 6404. London: HMSO.

Blackburn, C. (1991) *Poverty and Health*. Buckingham: Open University Press.

Blaxter, M. (1990) *Health and Lifestyles*. London: Routledge.

Block, F. (ed.) (1987) *The Mean Season: The Attack on the Welfare State*. New York: Pantheon Books.

Bould, S., Sanborn, B. and Reif, L. (1989) *Eighty-Five Plus: The Oldest Old*. Belmont, CA: Wadsworth.

Bowers, J. (1990) *Economics of the Environment*. Report for the British Association of Nature Conservationists. Telford: British Association of Nature Conservationists.

Brown, C.V. and Jackson, P.M. (1990) *Public Sector Economics*. Oxford: Blackwell.

Brown, J. (1990) *Social Security for Retirement*. York: Joseph Rowntree Trust.

Brown, L.R. (1990) 'The Illusion of Progress', in L.R. Brown (ed.), *State of the World 1990*. London: Unwin Hyman. pp. 3–16.

Brown, L.R., Flavin, C. and Postel, S. (1990) 'Picturing a Sustainable Society', in L.R. Brown (ed.), *State of the World 1990*. London: Unwin Hyman. pp. 173–90.

Brundtland Report (1987) *Our Common Future*. Oxford: Oxford University Press.

Bryson, A. (1989) *Undervalued, Underpaid and Undercut: The Future of Wages Councils*. London: Low Pay Unit.

Butler, S. and Kondratis, A. (1987) *Out of the Poverty Trap: A Conservative Strategy for Welfare Reform*. New York: Free Press.

Central Statistical Office (1992) *Social Trends 22*. London: HMSO.

Charter 88 (1990) *12 leaflets on Charter 88's demands*. London: Charter 88.

Cole, S. and Miles, I. (1984) *Worlds Apart: Technology and North–South Relations in the Global Economy*. Brighton: Wheatsheaf.

Coote, A. (1992) *The Welfare of Citizens*. London: IPPR/Rivers Oram.

Daly, H.E. (1990) 'Sustainable Development: From Concept and Theory to Operational Principles', *Population and Development Review*, Spring: 25–43.

Daly, H.E. and Cobb, J.B. (1990) *For the Common Good*. London: Greenprint.

Davies, B. and Ward, S. (1992) *Women and Personal Pensions*. London: EOC/HMSO.

Davies, N. and Easdale, P. (1994) *The Costs to the British Economy of Work Accidents and Work-Related Ill-Health*. Sudbury: HSE Books.

Deacon, A. and Bradshaw, J. (1983) *Reserved for the Poor*. London: Martin Robertson.

Dearlove, J. and Saunders, P. (1991) *Introduction to British Politics*. 2nd edn. Cambridge: Polity Press.

Department of Employment (1992) *New Earnings Survey 1992*. London: HMSO.

Desai, M. (1986) 'Drawing a Line: On Defining the Poverty Threshold', in P. Golding (ed.), *Excluding the Poor*. London: Child Poverty Action Group. pp. 1–20.

Doogan, K. (1992) 'The Social Charter and the Europeanisation of Employment and Social Policy', *Policy and Politics*, 20 (3): 167–76.

Doyal, L. and Gough, I. (1991) *A Theory of Human Need*. London: Macmillan.

Dworkin, R. (1990) 'Liberal Community', *Berkeley Law Review*, folio.

Elliot, L. and Kelly, R. (1994) 'Tories' £125 a Month Boost to the Rich', *The Guardian*, 9 February.

Esping-Anderson, G. (1990) *The Three Worlds of Welfare Capitalism*. Cambridge: Polity Press.

Ewing, K.D. and Gearty, C.A. (1990) *Freedom Under Thatcher: Civil Liberties in Modern Britain*. Oxford: Clarendon Press.

Falkingham, J. and Johnson, P. (1993a) *A Unified Funded Pension Scheme (UFPS) for Britain*. Discussion Paper WSP/90. STICERD. London: London School of Economics.

Falkingham, J. and Johnson, P. (1993b) 'Reform Could Defuse Pension Timebomb', *The New Review*, No. 22, June/July. London: Low Pay Unit. pp. 6–9.

Field, F. (1987) *Freedom and Wealth in a Socialist Future*. London: Constable.

Field, F. (1988) *What Price a Child? A Historical Review of the Relative Costs of Dependants*. London: Policy Studies Institute.

Flynn, N. (1989) 'The "New Right" and Social Policy', *Policy and Politics*, 17 (2): 97–109.

Forrest, R., Murie, A. and Williams, P. (1990) *Home Ownership*. London: Unwin Hyman.

Friedman, M. (1962) *Capitalism and Freedom*. Chicago: University of Chicago Press.

Friedman, M. and Friedman, R. (1980) *Free to Choose*. London: Penguin.

Fromm, E. (1979) *To Have or to Be?* London: Abacus.

Fryer, D. and Ulah, P. (eds) (1987) *Unemployed People*. Milton Keynes: Open University Press.

Gamble, A. (1988) *The Free Market and the Strong State: The Politics of Thatcherism*. London: Macmillan.

Georgescu-Roegen, N. (1979) 'Energy Analysis and Economic Evaluation', *Southern Economic Journal*, 45(4): 1023–58.

Gibb, K. and Munro, M. (1991) *Housing Finance in the UK*. London: Macmillan.

Giddens, A. (1982a) *Sociology: A Brief, but Critical Introduction*. London: Macmillan.

Giddens, A. (1982b) *Profiles and Critiques in Social Theory*. London: Macmillan.

Gilder, G. (1982) *Wealth and Poverty*. London: Buchan and Enright.

Ginn, J. and Arbor, S. (1991) 'Pension Penalties: Gender and Occupational Pensions'. Paper presented at the Cambridge Social Stratification Research Seminar, 26–7 September, Cambridge.

Glendinning, C. and Millar, J. (eds) (1992) *Women and Poverty in Britain in the 1990s*. Brighton: Wheatsheaf.

Goodin, R.E. and Le Grand, J. (1987) *Not only for the Poor: The Middle Classes and the Welfare State*. London: Allen and Unwin.

Gordon, L. (ed.) (1990) *Women, the State and Welfare*. Madison: University of Wisconsin Press.

Gorz, A. (1982) *Farewell to the Working Class: An Essay on Post-industrial Socialism*. London: Pluto.

Gould, C.C. (1988) *Rethinking Democracy: Freedom and Social Cooperation in Politics, Economy and Society*. Cambridge: Cambridge University Press.

Green, T.H. (1986) *Lectures in the Principles of Political Obligation*. Cambridge: Cambridge University Press.

Greve, J. and Currie, E. (1990) *Homelessness in Britain*. York: Joseph Rowntree Trust.

Groves, D. (1992) 'Occupational Pension Provision and Women's Poverty in Old Age', in C. Glendinning and J. Millar (eds), *Women and Poverty in Britain the 1990s*. Brighton: Wheatsheaf. pp. 193–206.

Handler, J. and Hasenfeld, Y. (1990) *The Moral Construction of Poverty: Welfare Reform in America*. London: Sage.

Hayek, F.A. (1960) *The Constitution of Liberty*. London: Routledge and Kegan Paul.

Heady, C. (1993) 'Optimal Taxation as a Guide to Tax Policy: A Survey', *Fiscal Studies*, 14 (1): 15–41.

Hills, J. (1988) *Changing Tax: How the Tax System Works and How to Change It*. London: Child Poverty Action Group.

Hills, J. (ed.) (1991a) *The State of Welfare*. Oxford: Oxford University Press.

Hills, J. (1991b) *Thirty Nine Steps to Housing Finance Reform*. York: Joseph Rowntree Foundation.

Hills, J. (1993) *The Future of Welfare*. York: Joseph Rowntree Foundation.

Hinrichs, K. (1991) 'Irregular Employment Patterns and the Loose Net of Social Security: Some Findings on the West German Development', in M. Adler, C. Bell, J. Clasen and A. Sinfield (eds), *The Sociology of Social Security*. Edinburgh: Edinburgh University Press. pp. 110–27.

Hirsch, F. (1976) *The Social Limits to Growth*. Cambridge, Mass: Harvard University Press.

IUCN/UNEP/WWF (1991) *World Resources in 1992–93*. Oxford: Oxford University Press.

Johnson, P. and Falkingham, J. (1992) *Ageing and Economic Welfare*. London: Sage.

Jordan, B. (1987) *Rethinking Welfare*. Oxford: Blackwell.

Jordan, B. (1989) *The Common Good: Citizenship, Morality and Self-Interest*. Oxford: Blackwell.

Jordan, B. (1991) 'Efficiency, Justice and the Obligation of Citizenship: The Basic Income Approach'. Paper presented at the Conference on Anglo-German Social Policy, University of Nottingham, 11–13 April.

Kapp, K.W. (1963) *Social Costs of Business Enterprise*. Bombay: Asia Publishing House.

Kapp, K.W. (1969) 'On the Nature and Significance of Social Costs', *Kyklos*, 22: 334–47.

Kiernan, K. and Wicks, M. (1990) *Family Change and Social Policy*. York: Joseph Rowntree Memorial Trust.

King, D.S. (1991) 'Citizenship as Obligation in the United States: Title II of the Family Support Act 1988', in U. Vogel and M. Moran (eds), *Frontiers of Citizenship*. London: Macmillan. pp. 1–31.

King, D.S and Waldron, J. (1988) 'Citizenship, Social Citizenship and the Defence of Welfare Provision', *British Journal of Political Science*, 18: 415–43.

Kleinman, M. and Piachaud, D. (1993) 'European Social Policy: Conceptions and Choices', *Journal of European Social Policy*, 3 (1): 1–19.

Kuhn, T. (1962) *The Structure of Scientific Revolutions*. London: University of Chicago Press.

Land, H. (1989) 'The Construction of Dependency', in M. Bulmer, J. Lewis and D. Piachaud (eds), *Goals of the Welfare State: Past and Future*. London: Unwin Hyman. pp. 141–59.

Langan, M. and Ostner, I. (1991) 'Gender and Welfare: Towards a Comparative Framework', in G. Room (ed.), *Towards a European Welfare State?* Bristol: School of Advanced Urban Studies. pp. 127–50.

Lecomber, R. (1975) *Economic Growth and the Environment*. London: Macmillan.

Lederer, K. (1980) *Human Needs: A Contribution to a Current Debate*. Cambridge: Oelgeschlager, Gunn and Hain.

Levitas, R. (ed.) (1986) *The Ideology of the New Right*. Cambridge: Polity Press.

Lewis, J. (1992) 'Gender and the Development of Welfare State Regime', *Journal of European Social Policy*, 2 (3): 159–73.

Liebfried, S. (1991a) 'Welfare State Europe?'. Paper presented at the Conference on Anglo-German Social Policy, University of Nottingham, 11–13 April.

Liebfried, S. (1991b) 'Towards a European Welfare State? On the Integration Potentials of Poverty Regimes in the EC'. Draft, Centre for Social Policy Research, University of Bremen.

Lister, R. (1989) *The Female Citizen: Eleanor Rathbone Memorial Lecture*. Liverpool: Liverpool University Press.

Lister, R. (1990) 'Women, Economic Dependency and Citizenship', *Journal of Social Policy*, 19 (4): 445–67.

Lister, R. (1992a) *Women's Economic Dependency and Social Security*. Manchester: Equal Opportunities Commission.

Lister, R. (1992b) 'She Has Other Duties – Women, Citizenship and Social Security'. Paper presented at the 50 Years After Beveridge Conference, University of York.

Lister, R. (1993) 'Tracing the Contours of Women's Citizenship', *Policy and Politics*, 21 (1): 3–16.

Loney, M. (ed.) (1987) *The State or the Market?*. London: Sage.

Low Pay Unit (1993) *The New Review*, No. 22, June/July. London: Low Pay Unit.

McCrone, D. (1991) ' "Excessive and Unreasonable": The Politics of the Poll Tax in Scotland', *International Journal of Urban and Regional Research*, 15 (3): 443–52.

MacIntyre, A. (1981) *After Virtue*. London: Duckworth.

Mack, J. and Lansley, S. (1985) *Poor Britain*. London: Allen and Unwin.

McLennan, D., Gibb, K. and More, A. (1991) *Fairer Subsidies, Faster Growth*. York: Joseph Rowntree Trust.

Mann, K. (1992) *The Making of an English 'Underclass'?* Milton Keynes: Open University Press.

Marshall, T.H. (1950) *Citizenship and Social Class*. Cambridge: Cambridge University Press.

Marx, K. (1967) *The Communist Manifesto*. Harmondsworth: Penguin.

Mead, L. (1986) *Beyond Entitlement: The Social Obligations of Citizenship*. New York: Free Press.

Meade, J. (1978) *The Structure and Reform of Direct Taxation: Report*. London: Allen and Unwin.

Meadows, D.H., Meadows, D.L. and Randers, J. (1972) *The Limits to Growth*. New York: Universe Books.

Meadows, D.H., Meadows, D.L. and Randers, J. (1992) *Beyond the Limits*. London: Earthscan.

Meehan, E. (1991) 'European Citizenship and Social Policies', in U. Vogel and M. Moran (eds), *Frontiers of Citizenship*. London: Macmillan. pp. 125–54.

Meszaros, I. (1970) *Marx's Theory of Alienation*. London: Merlin Press.

Miles, I. (1985) *Social Indicators for Human Development*. London: Frances Pinter.

Miller, S.M. (1987) 'The Legacy of Richard Titmuss', in B. Abel-Smith and K. Titmuss (eds), *The Philosophy of Welfare*. London: Allen and Unwin. pp. 1–17.

Mills, C.W. (1970) *The Sociological Imagination*. Harmondsworth: Penguin.

Milne, S. (1994) 'Accidents at Work cost £16 Billion a Year, *The Guardian*, 7 February.

Minford, M. (1991) *The Social Charter and Minimum Wages in Europe: Is Britain the Odd One Out?* London: Low Pay Unit.

Mishra, R. (1984) *The Welfare State in Crisis*. Brighton: Wheatsheaf.

Mitchell, D. (1991) *Income Transfers in Ten Welfare States*. Aldershot: Avebury.

Moorhouse, B. (1973) 'The Political Incorporation of the British Working Class: An Interpretation', *Sociology*, 7 (1): 341–59.

Murray, C. (1984) *Losing Ground: American Social Policy 1950–1980*. New York: Basic Books.

National Audit Office (1990) *The Elderly: Information Requirements for Supporting the Elderly and Implications for the National Insurance Fund*. London: HMSO.

Novak, M. (ed.) (1987) *The New Consensus on Family and Welfare*. Washington, DC: American Enterprise Institute.

Nozick, R. (1974) *Anarchy, State and Utopia*. Oxford: Blackwell.

Nussbaum, M.C. and Sen, A. (1993) *The Quality of Life: A Study*. Oxford: Oxford University Press.

OECD (1988) *The Taxation of Fringe Benefits*. Paris: OECD.

OECD (1990) *The Personal Income Tax Base: A Comparative Survey*. Paris: OECD.

Offe, C. (1982) *Structural Problems of the Capitalist State*. London: Macmillan.

Oppenheim, C. (1993) *Poverty: The Facts*. London: Child Poverty Action Group.

Pahl, J. (1988) 'Earning, Sharing, Spending: Married Couples and their Money', in R. Walker and G. Parker (eds), *Money Matters*. London: Sage. pp. 195–211.

Parijs, P. van (1991) 'Why Surfers Should be Fed', *Philosophy and Public Affairs*, 20 (2): 101–31.

Parijs, P. van (ed.) (1992) *Arguing for Basic Income*. London: Verso.

Parker, H. (ed.) (1993) *Citizen's Income and Women*. London: Citizen's Income. (See also the more extensive discussion in H. Parker (1989) *Instead of the Dole: An Enquiry into Integration of the Tax and Benefit Systems*. London: Routledge.)

Parkin, F. (1972) *Class Inequality and Political Order*. St Albans: Paladin.

Parry, G. (1991) 'Conclusion: Paths to Citizenship', in U. Vogel and M. Moran (eds), *Frontiers of Citizenship*. London: Macmillan. pp. 166–201.

Pearce, D., Markandya, A. and Barbier, E.B. (1989) *Blueprint for a Green Economy*. London: Earthscan.

Perrings, C. (1987) *Economy and Environment: A Theoretical Essay on the Interdependence of Economic and Environmental Systems*. Cambridge: Cambridge University Press.

Peters, G. (1991) *The Politics of Taxation: A Comparative Perspective*. Oxford: Blackwell.

Pierson, C. (1991) *Beyond the Welfare State: The New Political Economy of Welfare*. Cambridge: Polity Press.

Phillipson, C. (1982) *Capitalism and the Construction of Old Age*. London: Macmillan.

Pinker, R. (1971) *Social Theory and Social Policy*. London: Heinemann.

Plant, R. (1992) 'Citizenship, Rights and Welfare', in A. Coote (ed.), *The Welfare of Citizens*. London: IPPR/Rivers Oram. pp. 15–29.

Polanyi, K. (1957) *The Great Transformation*. Boston: Beacon.

Pollard, S. (1992) *The Development of the British Economy 1914–1990*. 4th edn. London: Arnold.

Quick, A. and Wilkinson, R. (1991) *Income and Health*. London: Socialist Health Assocaition.

Quiney, M. (1990) *Sustainable Development and the Economics of the Environment*. Background Paper No. 255. London: House of Commons Library.

Roche, M. (1992) *Rethinking Citizenship*. Cambridge: Polity Press.

Royal Commission on the Distribution of Income and Wealth (1977) *Report No 5*. London: HMSO.

Royal Commission on the Distribution of Income and Wealth (1979) *Report No 7*. London: HMSO.

Sassoon, A.S. (ed.) (1987) *Women and the State: Shifting Boundaries of Public and Private*. London: Hutchinson.

Saunders, P. (1990) *Social Class and Stratification*. London: Routledge.

Scharpf, F.W. (1986) 'Strukturen der Post-Industriellen Gesellschaft oder: Verschwindet die Massenarbeitslosigkeit in der Dienstleistungs- und Informationsökonomie?', *Soziale Welt*, 37 (1): 3–24.

Scott, J. (1992) *Citizenship and Privilege*. Leicester: University of Leicester Press.

Scott, J. (1994) *Power and Wealth: Citizenship, Deprivation and Privilege*. London: Longman.

Sen, A. (1987) *The Standard of Living: The Tanner Lectures 1985*. Cambridge: Cambridge University Press.

Sinfield, A. (1978) 'Analysis in the Social Division of Welfare', *Journal of Social Policy*, 7 (2): 129–56.

Sinfield, A. (1981) *What Unemployment Means*. Oxford: Martin Robertson.
Sinfield, A. and Fraser, M. (1985) *The Real Cost of Unemployment*. BBC North East.
Smail, R., Green, F. and Hadjimatheou, G. (1984) *Unequal Fringes*. London: Low Pay Unit.
Spicker, P. (1991) 'The Principle of Subsidiarity and the Social Policy of the European Community', *Journal of European Social Policy*, 1 (1): 3–14.
Statistics and Economics Office (1992) *Inland Revenue Statistics 1992*. London: HMSO.
Taylor-Gooby, P. (1991) *Social Change, Social Welfare and Social Science*. New York: Harvester.
Thurow, L.C. (1983) *Dangerous Currents: The State of Economics*. Oxford: Oxford University Press.
Titmuss, R.M. (1958) *Essays on the Welfare State*. London: Allen and Unwin.
Titmuss, R.M. (1968) *Commitment to Welfare*. London: Allen and Unwin.
Titmuss, R.M. (1987) 'Equity, Adequacy and Innovation in Social Security', in B. Abel-Smith and K. Titmuss (eds), *The Philosophy of Welfare*. London: Allen and Unwin. pp. 220–31.
Townsend, P. (1979) *Poverty in the United Kingdom*. London: Allen Lane.
Townsend, P. and Davidson, N. (1988) *Inequalities in Health*. Harmondsworth: Penguin.
Turner, B. (1986) *Citizenship and Capitalism*. London: Allen and Unwin.
Twine, F. (1988) *Distribution of Wealth and Income: Patterns and Trends*. Occasional Paper No. 14. Centre for Theology and Public Issues, New College, Edinburgh: University of Edinburgh.
Twine, F. (1992) 'Citizenship: Opportunites, Rights and Routes to Welfare in Old Age', *Journal of Social Policy*, 21 (2): 165–75.
UNDP (1992) *Human Development Report 1992*. Oxford: Oxford University Press.
Vogel, U. and Moran, M. (eds) (1991) *Frontiers of Citizenship*. London: Macmillan.
Walker, A. (ed.) (1982) *The Poverty of Taxation*. London: Child Poverty Action Group.
Walker, A. (1986) 'Pensions and the Production of Poverty in Old Age', in C. Phillipson and A. Walker (eds), *Ageing and Social Policy*. Aldershot: Gower. pp. 184–216.
Walker, A. and Walker, C. (eds) (1987) *The Growing Divide*. London: Child Poverty Action Group.
Walter, T. (1989) *Basic Income: Freedom from Poverty, Freedom from Work*. London: Marion Boyars.
Warr, P. (1985) 'Twelve Questions about Unemployment and Health', in B. Roberts, R. Finnegan and D. Gallie (eds), *New Approaches to Economic Life*. Manchester: Manchester University Press. pp. 302–18.
Weale, A. (1991) 'Citizenship beyond Borders', in U. Vogel and M. Moran (eds), *Frontiers of Citizenship*. London: Macmillan. pp. 155–65.
White, M. (1991) *Against Unemployment*. London: Policy Studies Institute.
Whitehead, C. (1988) *Inequalities in Health*. Harmondsworth: Penguin.
Wilkinson, M. (1986a) 'Tax Expenditures and Public Expenditure in the UK', *Journal of Social Policy*, 17 (1): 23–49.
Wilkinson, R. (1986b) *Class and Health: Research and Longitudinal Data*. London: Tavistock.
Wynn, M. (1970) *Family Policy*. London: Michael Joseph.

INDEX

Abel-Smith, B., 96
access, to welfare 109–11
activity, Fromm's notion of alienated
    and non-alienated, 178–9
Agricultural Wages Board, 117
altruism, 32
Arbor, S., 34, 39, 45
Atkinson, A.B., 108, 154, 164, 168

Baldwin, P., 94
Barr, N., 119
Basic Income, 5, 101, 109, 163–9
    conditionality, 165–6, 168
    and free-rider issue, 167
    Full, 164
    the idea of a, 163–9
    Partial, 164
    Transitional, 164, 168
basic state pension (BSP), flat-rate, 37,
    39–40
being, and having (Fromm), 13, 49, 66,
    75, 78, 164, 170, 176–80
benefits
    'as of right', 95, 96, 100
    contributions-dependent, 95, 100
    earnings-related, 100
    tax-financed, 95
    see also fringe benefits; means-tested
        benefits; sickness benefit;
        unemployment benefit; work-based
        benefits
Beveridge Report (1942), 96, 109,
    110–11
Black Report (1988), 116
Blackburn, C., 35
Blaxter, M., 13
Bould, S., 29, 37
Bowers, J., 61
Bradshaw, J., 96, 97
Bretton-Woods Agreement, 73

Brown, C.V., 98
Brown, J., 38, 39
Brown, L.R., 65, 67, 80, 85, 86
Brundtland Report (1987), 13, 48–9,
    50, 53, 54, 60, 63, 67, 77, 79, 86,
    89–90
Bryson, A., 100, 118
BSP see basic state pension

capital, natural or man-made, 57–8, 60,
    66
capitalism, 33, 44, 103, 107
capitalist labour contract, 21–2
    and democracy, 24–7
centralisation, 137–8
Charter, 88 (1990), 88
Child Benefit, 95, 110, 119, 167–8
childhood, 30–2
choice
    and circumstances, 7–8, 10
    redistribution and democratisation
        of, 23
Churchill, W., 118
citizenship
    crisis of, 86–7
    Marshall's elements of, 13, 24, 35–6,
        44, 91, 104, 175
    social rights of, 102–12
    and structures of income tax, 121–6
    three elements of, 104–7
    understanding and perception,
        170–80
civil opportunity
    or social right to welfare in old age,
        case study, 35–42
    use of term, 36
civil rights, 174
    and crisis of citizenship, 87
class, 161
    and citizenship, 110–11

class *cont.*
  and pensions, 35
  and unemployment, 104
class-coalitions, 106
  and welfare state regimes, 146
Cobb, J.B., 25, 49, 52, 54, 69, 86, 164
Cole, S., 173
collective bargaining, 44
collectivism, authoritarian, 92
commodification, 3, 15–17, 33–4, 178
  gender and class, 161–2
  and unemployment, 107–9
common good, 74–5
communism, 176
compensation, 94, 95, 104
competitive tendering, 88
consensus, 180
Conservatives, 10, 87, 118
constitutional reform, demands for in
  UK, 88
consumerism, 72–3, 78, 176–7
consumption
  interdependence with production,
    72–3
  present versus future, 57–9
contingent rights, 109
contribution rules, 109
corporation tax, 132, 141
corporatism, 166
cost-transfer maximising behaviour,
  70–2
Coulter, F., 119
critical reason, 177
critical theory, 173
Currie, E., 124
customs duties, 136–7

Daly, H.E., 13, 25, 49, 52, 54, 59, 60,
  61, 66, 67, 69, 70, 86, 164
  approach to sustainability, 62–4
Davidson, N., 14, 35, 116
Davies, B., 34, 116
Davies, N., 116
de-commodification, 5, 19, 81, 109,
  162, 168
  in Europe, 154, 157–8
  and social rights, 20–1
  social rights as, 102–4
  tax and welfare state regimes, 149–50
  and unemployment, 107–9
  and welfare state regimes, 145–6

de-familialisation, 5, 162
Deacon, A., 96, 97
Dearlove, J., 86–7
debt repayment, 60–1
decentralisation of decision making,
  86–7
Delors, J., 154
democracy, 174–5
  and the capitalist labour contract,
    24–7
  and choice, 1–2, 4
  emergence of political, 23–4
  in international decision making,
    89–90
  and majority demands, 106
Desai, M., 78
developed nations, 47–8
developing nations, 47
  and redistribution, 60–1
development, use of term, 64
devolution, 86, 87, 137
division of labour, 29–30, 33–4, 107
divorce, 97
Doogan, K., 153–5
Doyal, L., 13, 19, 36, 64, 65, 66, 67,
  101, 164
Durkheim, E., 91
Dworkin, R., 168

earnings
  additions to labour market, 119–20
  average gross weekly (UK 1992),
    114, Table 11.1
  distribution of, 113–21: (UK 1992),
    118–19, Table 11.4
Easdale, P., 116
economic activity
  scale of, 62–3
economic growth, 3–4, 91
  challenged, 47–8
  and inequality, 63–4
  uncoupled from notion of progress,
    73–5
economic restructuring, and
  unemployment in Europe, 151–2,
    153
economic theory, 3
  and market mechanisms, 53–4
economics
  neo-classical, 47–8, 66
  paradigm shift in, 54–5

economy, interdependence with
environment, 46, 74–5
education, access to, 20
educational attainment, 65
'effort bargain', 114
egalitarianism, 92
elderly people
lifecourse interdependence and, 35
right to welfare, 35–42
electoral system (UK), 87
eligibility, rules of, 107, 109–11
Elliot, L., 119
employers, 18–19
and fringe benefits, 132–3
and the poverty trap, 99–100
employment
contract of, 36
full, 82
energy use, 50, 60, 79
environment
protection of, 45
uncertainty about impacts on,
58–9
environmental costs, 55–6, 59, 69–75
environmental economics, 55, 168
environmental interdependence, 3–4,
47–75
with economy, 46, 74–5
'Environmental Perspective to the
Year, 2000' (IUCN/UNEP/WWF),
89
equal opportunities, 100, 161
equity, 75
horizontal, 134
in quality of life, 56–7
of tax burden, 125–6
vertical, 134
Esping-Anderson, G., 94
on class and citizenship, 103, 110–11,
166
on de-commodification, 5, 16, 19,
154, 158–9, 162, 168
on eligibility, 106–7, 109
welfare state regimes, 102, 130, 144,
145–50: linked with Peters' tax
regimes, 147–50
'ethnic cleansing', 105
Europe
committee of the regions, 86

Europe *cont.*
moves towards social rights in,
151–69
European Community
and conflict with national interests,
89
social policy, 151–2
tax harmonisation, 144
working hours directive, 115
see also Social Charter
European Court of Justice, and
national social policy, 155–6
Ewing, K.D., 87
exchange value, 62–4
excise taxes, 132, 136–7
externalities, 2, 33, 69–75, 168

fairness, perceptions of, and tax rates,
122–3, 126–9, 132
Falkingham, J., 34, 39, 42–3, 46n
familialisation, 161–2
family, 30–2
lone-parent, 95, 97
Family Allowance, 110
Family Credit, 98, 99, 119
Family Income Supplement, 98, 99
family size, 52
fashion, changing, 79–80
Field, F., 36, 96, 110, 168
fiscal welfare, 119, 120; *see also* tax
reliefs
Flavin, C., 67
Forrest, R., 143
franchise, 174
female, 31
male, 26
Fraser, M., 34
free-rider issue, and Basic Income, 167
Friedman, M., 93
fringe benefits
cost of in revenue forgone by the
Exchequer, 134–5
tax relief, 124
taxation of, 131–5
Fromm, E., 91
'having' and 'being', 13, 66, 78, 164,
170, 176–80
on the marketing character, 175
To Have or to Be?, 176–80
Fryer, D., 11, 34

GATT (General Agreement on Tariffs and Trade), 73
GDP (gross domestic product), taxation as a proportion of, 129–31
Gearty, C.A., 87
gender
  class dimension, 161
  and means-testing, 100
  and pensions, 35
  relationships of dependency, 2
Georgescu-Roegen, N., 57–8
Germany, federalism, 86
Gibb, K., 124
Giddens, A., 15, 20, 23, 24, 171, 172–3
Gilder, G., 25, 98, 165
Gini coefficient, 138–9
Ginn, J., 34, 39, 45
Glendinning, C., 41
global change, 51–3
GNP (gross national product), 3, 56, 81, 129
  as measure of economic growth, 64, 65–8
  and the mis-measure of progress, 65–8
Goodin, R.E., 110
Gordon, L., 162
Gorz, A., 82, 165
Gough, I., 13, 19, 36, 64, 65, 66, 67, 101, 164
Gould, C.C., 11–13, 19, 86, 105
government
  central funding of sub-national government, 137–8, Table 11.11
  devolved systems of, 137
Green, T.H., 26
Greve, J., 124
Groves, D., 35, 42

Hailsham, Lord, 87
having, and being (Fromm), 13, 49, 66, 75, 78, 164, 170, 176–80
Hayek, F.A., 93
Heady, C., 125–6
health
  and income inequalities, 13–14
  in old age, 35
health services, access to, 20
Hills, J., 38, 93, 122, 125, 126, 143
Hinrichs, K., 166

Hirsch, F., 73, 80
housing, tax treatment of owner-occupied, 143
Housing Benefit, 98, 119, 124, 130
housing policy, 124
human development, 91–2, 170; see also self-development
human development index (HDI), 65, 66
human nature, 9–10

IMF (International Monetary Fund), 73
income
  defining of taxable, 125
  different national concepts of, 128
  distribution of household before and after tax (UK), 120–1, Table 11.5
  gross, 128
  'in kind' see fringe benefits
  'participation', 168
  relative positions, 13–14
  sources of, 113–44
  subject to tax, 128
  taxable, 128
  threshold (UK), 78–9
income indicators, 65
Income Support (UK), means-tested, 37, 38, 95–6
income tax, citizenship and structures of, 121–6
individualism
  market, 92, 168
  of New Right, 1, 7, 10, 78
individuals, and institutions, 171
industrialised nations see developed nations
inflation, policies and unemployment, 108
inheritance, 45
  rules of, 137
institutions, and individuals, 171
interdependence
  across time and space, 45
  between generations, 45
  environmental, 47–75
  environmental and economic, 46, 74–5
  labour markets and, 15–27
  lifecourse, 28–46

interdependence *cont.*
  of self and society, 1, 10–12
  see also social interdependence
international cooperation, 59, 86,
    89–90

Jackson, P.M., 98
Johnson, P., 34, 39, 42–3, 46n
Jordan, B., 164–6, 167, 168–9

Kapp, K.W., 22, 70, 71
Kelly, R., 119
Keynes–Beveridge welfare state, 10, 42
Keynesianism, 73, 111
Kiernan, K., 42
King, D.S., 93–4
Kleinman, M., 151
Kuhn, T., 54

labour, as creative activity, 179
  see also division of labour; work
labour market, 2–3, 103–4, 108–9
  inequalities, and tax and social
    security system, 113–44
  insecurity of, 21–3, 81: and welfare
    state responses, 111
  and interdependence, 15–27
  participation and social rights in
    Europe, 158–9
Labour Party, 21, 26, 88, 103, 110
Land, H., 31, 41
Langan, M., 145, 158, 159–62
Lansley, S., 44, 78
Le Grand, J., 110
Lecomber, R., 66
Lederer, K., 65
legitimacy, moral, 92
leisure time, 82, 98
Lewis, J., 145, 158, 162
Liberals, 21, 26, 88, 103
Liebfried, S., 145, 156, 157, 158,
    159–62
life expectancy, 65
lifecourse interdependence, 12, 28–46
Lister, R., 29, 31, 41, 100, 110, 161,
    162
local government, 43, 87, 88
low-paid workers, 21, 34, 114–16,
    165–6
  social rights of, 42–3

Low Pay Unit (UK), 114

Maastricht Agreement, 118
McCrone, D., 143
MacIntyre, A., 11, 78
Mack, J., 44, 78
McLennan, D., 143
majority, parliamentary, 87
Mann, K., 36, 110
manual workers
  earnings, 114–16
  and pensions, 38, 41
market
  absence of, 61
  and public accountability, 90–1
  relations between rich and poor
    nations, 60–1
  and resource constraints, 60
  self-regulating, 16
market economies, 21, 73, 79
  tension with political democracy,
    103–4
market exchanges, and unintended
    consequences, 70–2
Marshall, T.H., 10, 19, 34, 40, 41, 43,
    87, 94, 106, 108, 156, 172
  elements of citizenship, 13, 24, 35–6,
    44, 91, 104, 175
  on social rights, 102–3
Marx, K., 21, 179
Marxism, 103
materialism, 176–80
Meade, J., 135
Meadows, D.H., 54, 55, 58, 61, 67, 75,
    81
  Beyond the Limits, 49, 50, 50–3
  Limits to Growth, 47–8
  on poverty and unemployment, 82–3
means-tested benefits, 5, 22, 88, 93, 96,
    108
  and gender, 100
  and social exclusion, 97–100
Meehan, E., 155
Meszaros, I., 178, 179
Micklewright, J., 108
Miles, I., 65, 173
Millar, J., 41
Miller, S.M., 97
Mills, C.W., 7, 9, 13, 18, 42, 78, 179
  sociological imagination, 170, 171–5

Milne, S., 116
Minford, M., 118
minimum wage, 25, 100, 118
Mishra, R., 73, 90
Moorhouse, B., 23
moral choice, 18
mortgage interest, tax relief on, 124
motivation, and work, 98–9
Munro, M., 124
Murray, C., 25
Musgrave measure, of progressivity of
    tax systems, 139

nation state, political participation
    beyond and below the, 85–92
National Assistance, 96–7
National Audit Office, 39
National Board for Prices and
    Incomes, 98
National Health Service, 88, 126
National Insurance, 96, 99, 113, 126
    benefits, 95–6
national social policy, and European
    Court of Justice, 155–6
needs
    unmet non-material, 83
    wants and sufficiency, 67–8
New Earnings Survey (UK Department
    of Employment), 114
New Right, 1, 10, 12, 86, 90, 92, 93,
    108, 121, 166
    books on, 6n
    separation between politics and
      economy, 105–6
Nozick, R., 25
Nussbaum, M.C., 64, 65

occupational earnings, by gender (UK
    1992), 116–17, Table 11.3
occupational pension scheme (OPS),
    35, 36, 45, 111, 133
    earnings-related, 37, 38–9, 41
    and tax relief, 123, 124–5
occupational welfare, 110, 119–20; see
    also fringe benefits
OECD, 120, 128, 129, 130, 131, 132,
    133, 134–5
    international income distribution
      comparisons, 138–40
Offe, C., 20
oligopolistic corporations, 106

Oppenheim, C., 34, 97, 108
OPS see occupational pension scheme
Ostner, I., 145, 158, 159–62
Our Common Future see Brundtland
    Report (1987)
over-consumption, 80
overtime, 114–15

Pahl, J., 31
paid work, 5
    sufficiency and the redistribution of,
      80–2
Parijs, P. van, 162, 167
Parker, H., 162, 163, 164
parliamentary democracy, 43, 103
parliamentary sovereignty, 86–7
Parry, G., 10–11
part-time work, 5
    women in Europe, 82
participation, 4, 43–4, 75, 180
    politics of, 76–92
pay, and productivity, 98
Pearce, D., 49, 54–5, 57, 58–9, 60, 64,
    65, 86, 89
pension
    policies (UK), 38, 42
    provision, 35–42
    reform, 42–3
    structure (UK), 37
Perrings, C., 33, 48, 49, 54, 58, 69, 70,
    73, 92
    on interdependence of environment
      and economy, 74–5
personal pension (PP), 37, 38, 39
Peters, G., 5, 122, 124–5, 128, 129,
    135, 145
    typology of tax regimes, 141–4:
      linked with Esping-Anderson's of
      welfare state regimes, 147–50
Phillipson, C., 35
Piachaud, D., 151
Pinker, R., 26
Plant, R., 111
Polanyi, K., 15, 16, 17, 24, 25–6, 102
political economy, 25, 75
political rights, 23–4
    interdependence with social rights,
      43–5
    power in quangos, 87
    and self development, 85

'poll tax' (UK), 143
Pollard, S., 57
pollution
    control, 49, 59
    costs of, 55–6
    international control, 89
    'optimal', 59–60
Poor Laws, 25–6, 94
population
    exponential growth, 51–2
    redistribution to reduce, 60–1
Postel, S., 67
poverty, 60–1, 79, 83, 94
    and level of unemployment benefit,
        108
    and sufficiency, 78–80
    and sustainable development, 89
    UK, 34
    of women in old age, 42
'poverty trap', 98–100
power relations, political and
        economic, 105–6
PP see personal pension
Prime Minister (UK), 87
private, and the public sphere, 174–5
private welfare, 110, 111
privatisation, 66, 90
privilege, 80
production, interdependence with
        consumption, 72–3
productivity, and pay, 98
profitability, and externalities, 72
progress, 2
    belief in, 176
    measures of, 65–8
    uncoupled from economic growth,
        73–5
proportional representation, 88
public, and the private sphere, 174–5
public expenditure
    pensions and, 39–40
    and social rights, 111–12
public services, contracting out, 88

quality of life, 54–5, 56, 64, 65, 75
    measures of, 65
quangos (quasi-autonomous non-
        governmental organisations), 87
Quick, A., 13, 35

Quiney, M., 56, 59, 61

redistribution, 4, 48, 49–50, 56–7,
        74–5
    of freedom of choice, 12
    new politics of, 82–4
    of paid work, and sufficiency, 80–2
    politics of, 76–92
    and sufficiency, 77–84
    to reduce population growth, 60–1
rent rebates, 98
reproduction
    of society, 33–4
    women's role in, 30–2, 159
resource constraints, discounting, 54
resource depletion, 49
    international agreements on, 89
resource distribution, 13–14
resources, and social rights, 111–12
responsibility, social, 86
retirement, 35
    compulsory, 37
    early, 35
revolutions, 15–16, 23
rich, sufficiency and the, 78–80
Royal Commission on the Distribution
        of Income and Wealth, 137

sales tax, 132
Sassoon, A.S., 162
Saunders, P., 72, 86–7
Scharpf, F.W., 162
schools, opting out, 88
Scotland
    devolution, 86, 87, 137
    effects of 'poll tax', 143
Scott, J., 80
self
    and higher education, 81
    selling the, 17–19
    sense of, 3: and stigmatisation, 97
    and society, 9–14
    see also social self
self-development, 4, 11–12, 76, 77
    an adequate income for, 163
    opportunities or rights to, 12–14
    and political participation, 84, 85
    and social relations of love, 32
    and social relationships, 7, 177

Sen, A., 64, 65
sensitivity
    anthropological, 172–3
    critical, 173
    historical, 172
SERPS *see* state earnings-related
    pension scheme
sharing, 83, 100–1, 173
sickness benefit, 109–10
Sinfield, A., 34, 36, 72, 96, 110
Single European Market (SEM), 151–2
Smail, R., 120
social change, 179–80
Social Charter, 5, 21, 118, 153–62
    Action Programme, 153–4
    and the UK, 155
social citizenship, in Europe, 153–62
social constructivism, 174–5
social control, 63, 91–2
social costs, 69–75, 90–1
    of division of labour, 34
    of unemployment, 104
social 'dumping', 154
social exclusion, 11, 36, 78, 105–7
    and means-tested benefits, 97–100
    and social rights, 94, 95–101
    and work–based benefits, 100–1
social expenditure, 129–31
    total taxes and as a percentage of
        GDP, by country, 131, Table
        11.9
social interdependence, 1–3, 168–9,
    179–80
    as a basis for social rights, 7–46
    between generations, 2
    between members of families, 2
social policy, 133
    and social rights, 93–150
social relations of love, 32
social rights, 180
    of citizenship, 102–12
    and crisis of citizenship, 87–8
    and de-commodification, 20–1
    as de-commodification, 102–4
    European, 151–69
    interdependence with political rights,
        43–5
    and resources, 111–12
    and social exclusion, 94, 95–101

social rights *cont.*
    social interdependence as a basis for,
        7–46
    and social policy, 93–150
    to sufficiency, 82–4
    transnational, 154–5
    women and, 158–9
social security, 5, 20
    forms of, 93, 95–101
    and taxation system, 99
social self, 7
    development of the, 9–14
socialism, 176
society, and self, 9–14
sociological imagination, 5–6, 7, 170,
    171–5
sociology, 173
Spain, regional autonomy, 86
Speenhamland System, 25–6
Spicker, P., 86
SPLIT measure, of progressivity of tax
    systems, 140
Standard Employment Relationship
    (SER), 166
state earnings-related pension scheme
    (SERPS), 37–8, 39–41, 130
    contracting out, 38
state intervention, 90–1
    role in protecting the needy, 25–6
state pension scheme, 35, 37, 39–40
state welfare, 119–20; *see also* benefits
stigmatisation, 95, 97
sub-system rationalities, 62, 67–8
subsidiarity, 86, 137, 154, 156
substitutability, 57–9
sufficiency, 75, 173
    needs, wants and, 67–8
    politics of, 76–92
    the poor, the rich and, 78–80
    and redistribution, 77–84
    and the redistribution of paid work,
        80–2
    social rights to, 82–4
Suits measure, of progressivity of tax
    systems, 139
Supplementary Benefit, 96
supranational agencies, 89
sustainability
    Daly's approach to, 62–4
    of the means to life, 50, 51–64
    a systems approach to, 61–4

sustainable development, 3–4
  definition of concept, 53–6
  means of achieving, 54–5
  and poverty, 89
  and sufficiency, 78–9
Sutherland, H., 164

tax, as a percentage of GDP, by
    country, 129–30, Table 11.8
  see also customs duties; excise taxes;
    income tax; VAT
tax allowances, 123
tax avoidance, 132
tax base, size of, 123
tax rates
  aggregate average, by country,
    126–9, Table 11.7
  marginal and average, 126–9
tax regimes, 141–4
  'Anglo-American', 147
  'broad-based', 147
  'Latin', 147
  Peters' typology, 141–4
  'Scandinavian', 147
  and welfare regimes, in European
    Community, 157–8
  and welfare state regimes, 5, 147–50,
    Tables 12.1 and 2
tax reliefs, 123–5
  cost to the Exchequer of main (UK
    1991–2), 123, Table 11.6
  on pensions, 36, 37, 38–9
tax revenues, from direct and indirect
    taxation, 135–6, Table 11.10
tax system
  fairness of, 122–3, 132
  optimal, 125–6
  and social security system, 99
  visibility of, 121, 142–3
taxation
  balance between direct and indirect,
    90, 135–8
  citizenship principles of, 5, 140
  forms of, 113–44
  of fringe benefits, 131–5
  progressive, 125–6, 129, 138–41:
    measures by country, 139, Table
    11.12
  as a proportion of GDP, 129–31
  proportional, 125

taxation cont.
  regressive, 125
  relationship to citizenship, 112,
    113–44
Taylor-Gooby, P., 93, 145, 158
technology
  dependence on, 33–4
  effect on nature, 58
'telos', 78
Thatcher, M., 10, 11, 108, 143
Thurow, L.C., 25, 73
Titmuss, K., 96
Titmuss, R.M., 22, 29–30, 34, 39–40,
    70, 94, 97, 106–7, 110
  social division of welfare, 35, 36–7,
    112, 119
Townsend, P., 11, 14, 19, 35, 36, 78,
    116
transnational corporations, 25, 46
Turner, B., 78
Twine, F., 24, 35, 40, 108, 110

UK
  Constitution, weakness, 87
  poverty, 34
  and Social Charter, 155
  sources of income and forms of
    taxation, 113–44
Ulah, P., 11, 34
underemployment, 37
unemployment, 19, 22, 33–4, 37, 83
  and class, 104
  and de-commodification, 107–9
  in economic growth scenarios,
    69–70
  growth in, 97
  social costs of, 34, 69–73
  technologically produced, 71, 72
  in UK, 81
unemployment benefit
  contributions-dependent, 95, 109
  level and poverty, 108
Unified Funded Pension Scheme
    (UFPS), proposals for UK, 42–3
unions, 44
United Nations Development
    Programme (UNDP), 65, 66
United Nations World Commission on
    Environment and Development,
    49

universalism, flat-rate, 110–11
unpaid work
  and a Basic Income, 167–8
  by women, 5, 31–2
  caring and domestic, 34, 82
  and the Social Charter, 158–9
  and social rights, 42–3
  and welfare state regimes, 159–62
USA, National Accounts, omission of
  natural capital, 66

values, changing, 67–8
VAT, 132, 135

Wages Councils, 117–18
  abolition of, 108
Waldron, J., 93–4
Walker, A., 35, 36, 42, 99, 100
Walker, C., 36
Walter, T., 162
wants
  needs and sufficiency, 67–8
  replaced by needs, 91
  unlimited, 47, 77–8
Ward, S., 34
Warr, P., 11, 34, 35
waste production, 60
Weale, A., 45–6
wealth, distribution in UK, 137
wealth taxes, 137
welfare
  access to, 109–11
  categories of, 36–7
  social division of, 35, 36–7, 110, 112,
    119
  see also fiscal welfare; occupational
    welfare; state welfare; welfare
    provision, as part of the notion of
    citizenship, 93–150
welfare state, 2
  public support for, 93

welfare state regimes, 145–50
  corporatist cluster, 145–6
  liberal cluster, 145, 146
  linked with tax regimes, 147–50,
    Tables 12.1 and 2
  nature of, 5
  social-democratic cluster, 146
  and tax regimes in European
    Community, 157–8
  women and, 159–62, Table 13.2
White, M., 34
Whitehead, C., 14, 35
Wicks, M., 42
Wilkinson, M., 40, 45, 111, 120
Wilkinson, R., 13, 35
women
  Basic Income for, 167–8
  labour market participation, 5, 21:
    and benefits, 31–2, 110
  and pensions, 38, 41–2
  and the reproduction of society,
    30–2
  and social rights of citizenship,
    158–9
  and welfare state regimes, 159–62,
    Table 13.2
  and work-based benefits, 100
work, 33–4
  and motivation, 98–9
  see also labour
work-based benefits, 5, 100–1
workers, rights of in Europe, 153–62
'workfare' programmes, 93, 165
working conditions, 25
working hours, 114–16
  distribution (UK 1992), 115, Table
    11.2
  and Social Charter, 154
World Bank, 73
World Watch Report, 86
Wynn, M., 31